Sarah J. Ablett
Dramatic Disgust

Lettre

Sarah J. Ablett has studied English literature, philosophy, and creative writing at the Universities of Hamburg, Manchester, Heidelberg, and Hildesheim, and completed her doctorate at TU Braunschweig. She has taught literary and cultural studies and was part of the research project »Hyphenated Cultures: Contemporary British-Jewish Theatre« funded by the VolkswagenStiftung.

Sarah J. Ablett
Dramatic Disgust
Aesthetic Theory and Practice from Sophocles to Sarah Kane

[transcript]

This study was submitted as a doctoral thesis in 2017 at the Faculty of Humanities and Studies in Education at the Technische Universität Braunschweig.

Bibliographic information published by the Deutsche Nationalbibliothek
The Deutsche Nationalbibliothek lists this publication in the Deutsche Nationalbibliografie; detailed bibliographic data are available in the Internet at http://dnb.d-nb.de

© 2020 transcript Verlag, Bielefeld

All rights reserved. No part of this book may be reprinted or reproduced or utilized in any form or by any electronic, mechanical, or other means, now known or hereafter invented, including photocopying and recording, or in any information storage or retrieval system, without permission in writing from the publisher.

Cover layout: Maria Arndt, Bielefeld
Cover illustration: Sarah J. Ablett
Printed by Majuskel Medienproduktion GmbH, Wetzlar
Print-ISBN 978-3-8376-5210-9
PDF-ISBN 978-3-8394-5210-3
https://doi.org/10.14361/9783839452103

Printed on permanent acid-free text paper.

Contents

Introduction 9

I.   Greek Tragedy & Pollution 15
The Origin of Tragedy & the Greek God Dionysus 15
Disgust in the Attic Tragedy: *Miasma & Dyschéreia* 16
I.i   Plato's Banishment of the Poets in *The Republic* 25
Spirited Disgust & the Pollution of *Logos* 26
I.ii Aristotle's *Poetics*: *Miasma & Katharsis* 30
Tragedy & Emotions 32
I.iii Summary 36

II. *Ekel* in Eighteenth- & Nineteenth-Century Aesthetic Theory 39
The Senses & Disgust in Aesthetic Theory 40
Horror & Disgust in Eighteenth-Century Tragedy 42
II.i Kant's Aesthetic Ideas: Cognition, Sensation, Disgust 44
Vital Disgust & the *Sublime* 45
Disgust & Consumption 47
Disgust & Civilisation 49
II.ii Nietzsche's *The Birth of Tragedy* 50
Apollonian & Dionysian Forces in Tragedy 50
Science, Tragic Knowledge, & Art 52
II.iii Summary 53

III. The Drama of Existential Disgust & Psychoanalysis 57
Sigmund Freud: Disgust as the Basis of Civilisation 58
Tragic Society & the Death Drive 58
III.i Tragic Existence: Disgust as an Antidote 59
Jean-Paul Sartre: Disgust at Slimy Existence & the Feminine 60
Georges Bataille: *Heterology*: The Science of Excrements 62
III.ii Psychoanalysis: Approaching *Abjection* 65
The Semiotic & the Symbolic 65

Abjection 67
Abjection, *Jouissance*, & Art 69
Purifying *Abjection* through Art 71
III.iii Summary 73

IV. Disgust around the Millennium 75
Sensational Disgust & *Abject* Art: "Sick Stuff" 76
In-Yer-Face Theatre 78
Ekelfernsehen & Viral New Media Content 79
IV.i Contemporary Approaches to Disgust in the Natural & Social Sciences 80
Psychology & Disgust 81
Mirror Neurons, Disgust, & Art 83
Moral Disgust & Socio-Political Hierarchies 84
IV.ii Aesthetic Disgust in the Humanities 86
Disgust in Art as a Matter of Life & Death 87
Disgust & Imagination 88
Art & the Laws of Sympathetic Magic Belief 89
The Aesthetic Effect of Disgust 90
IV.iii Summary 91

V. Theorising Disgust for Drama Analysis 95
Insights from Ancient Disgust 95
Contemporary Disgust in Relation to Distaste & *Abjection* 98
Ekel & Aesthetic Disgust 102
The Aesthetic Effect of Disgust: *Sublime* or *Sublate*? 104
V.i Forms of Dramatic Disgust 105
1. Semantic Fields of Disgust-Elicitation 106
2. Structures & Semiotic Modes of Disgust 113
V.ii Functions & Effects of Dramatic Disgust 116
Mimesis: Bodies on Stage 117
Poiesis: Scene, Atmosphere, Character, Plot 118
Aisthesis: Disgusted Recipients 119
V.iii Summary 124

VI. Case Study: Dramatic Disgust in the Works of Sarah Kane 127
A "nauseating dog's breakfast of a play" 128
VI.i Kane's Early Plays: Manifestations of Disgust in *Blasted, Skin, Phaedra's Love & Cleansed* 130
Blasted: "This disgusting feast of filth" 131
Skin: "English extra sausage" & Bananas 139
Phaedra's Love: "fair is foul, foul is fair" 144
Cleansed: "another bloody amputation" 149

VI.ii Kane's Late Plays: *Abject* Language in *Crave* and *4.48 Psychosis* 152
Crave: "Maggots everywhere" 153
4.48 Psychosis: "we are the abjects" 163
VI.iii Summary 168

Conclusion 173
Outlook 176

Bibliography 177

Acknowledgements 201

Introduction

"I've shat in better places than this" (3) is the opening line of British dramatist Sarah Kane's debut play *Blasted*[1] which premiered at the Royal Court Theatre Upstairs in London in January 1995. As the play progresses, recipients are confronted with a number of gruesome and appalling depictions such as rape, reports of war atrocities, and one man's eyes being sucked out, before the events climax in a nightmarish *mise-en-scène* that can be viewed as a brutal realisation of the main character Ian's initial statement. We witness Ian, raped, blinded, and alone, *"shitting"* (59) in the 'worst place' imaginable, among corpses in a room destroyed by war.

The performance of *Blasted* provoked a media outrage over the highly visceral content and the unusual plot developments of the play, with the overall feeling, as described in critical reviews, being the sentiment of disgust. Jack Tinker of the *Daily Mail* found *Blasted* to be a "disgusting feast of filth" (n.p.) and his colleagues John Gross of the *Sunday Telegraph* and Sheridan Morley of the *Spectator* likewise perceived it as a "gratuitous welter of carnage" (n.p.) and a "sordid little travesty of a play" (n.p.). Critics generally seemed to take their personal disgust reactions as a cue or even proof of the play's supposed deficiency and its author's lack of artistic skill. For them the elicitation of disgust solely disclosed the dramatist's "adolescent desire to shock" the audience (Spencer n.p.; cf. also Curtis n.p., Taylor n.p., Tinker n.p., Hemming n.p., Morley n.p.). In contrast, through Aleks Sierz' coinage of the term 'in-yer-face theatre' in his influential publication *In-Yer-Face Theatre: British Drama Today* (2001), which was aimed at describing and conceptualising the particular properties of the confrontative and highly visceral theatrical works created by young artists like Kane in the last decade of the twentieth century, the shocking effect of taboo-breaking and disgusting aesthetic depictions came to be valued more positively. It arguably led to more favourable evaluations of these dramatists' plays as well as to a plethora of academic articles and books discussing what Sierz describes as a particular phenomenon of the 1990s' *zeitgeist*, which according to him resulted in a "new aesthetic sensibility" ("In-yer-face" n.p.).

---

1 All references to Kane's plays refer to the 2001 Methuen edition of her *Complete Plays*.

While I agree with Sierz that the shocking effect of Kane's and her contemporaries' artistic engagement with appalling topics is a fundamental property of their dramatic work, I find a focus on this effect limiting. Not least because Sierz' definition can in many ways be argued to support critical voices' claim that a 'will to shock' is the main agenda of *in-yer-face* plays. In this study, I instead argue that the lasting effect and popularity of Kane's work especially, is not so much caused by her aesthetic realisation of a particular 1990s' *zeitgeist* that breaks with conventions and taboos to demonstrate dissatisfaction with the political and social establishment of the time, but rather by her ability to aesthetically engage with appalling forms of physical, social, and moral transgression in order to (re)present universal patterns of human conflicts and crises, of suffering, love, abuse, and above all our having to come to terms with the fact of our own incomprehensible mortality. One of the arguments of this study thus is that it is not a "new aesthetic sensibility" that has made the work of Kane (and others) so alluring and thought-provoking, but rather her mastery in having found a modern voice to (re)connect drama to its origin.

Thesis & Aim

My thesis is that aesthetic disgust is a vital ingredient in dramatic works that has animated the genre since its origin in ancient Greece, and is a key component of most classic works of drama because aesthetic engagement with this sensation offers much more potential than to simply shock the audience. Disgust has the ability to tap into some of the most difficult ambiguities and paradoxes we as humans have to face and come to terms with, such as our life being determined by death or our desires being caught up in-between animalistic urges and drives, and social and cultural rules and regulations.

The aim of this study is twofold: a) to delineate relevant stations of aesthetic practice and theory concerned with aesthetic manifestations of disgust in works of drama from the development of the genre in fifth-century BC to the onset of the twenty-first century, and thereby show the intrinsic link between ancient works of drama and contemporary aesthetic practice, and b) to use the historical concepts discussed in the theoretical chapters in order to develop a unique and applicable model of dramatic disgust that sheds light on its forms, functions, and effects and thus not only helps us to understand contemporary aesthetic works that cause feelings of repulsion, but also offers an interpretive key to approach some of the core conflicts encountered in seminal dramatic works throughout history.

Disgust in Drama & Theory

The term 'disgust' only found its way into the English language in the sixteenth century (cf. Menninghaus 4), but disgust-evoking contents have featured prominently in theatrical texts at all times, especially in works of tragedy. From ancient plays like Sophocles' *Philoctetes* (c. 409 BC), where the main character is sent into exile on an uninhabited island because a wound on his foot smells so appalling that its sufferer is perceived as a danger to public order, or Euripides' *Bacchae* (c. 410 BC), which features a mother brutally slaughtering her son and then walking through town parading his head on a stick and imagining the preparation of a festive meal from his remains, through the cannibalistic scenes in Seneca's *Thyestes* (62 AD) or William Shakespeare's Seneca-inspired *Titus Andronicus* (1623), to Kane's *Blasted*, where Ian "shit[s]" on the floor of a bombed hotel room and then rips a baby out of a grave and eats it – repulsive dramatic actions have fascinated and appalled audiences alike. Disgust is indisputably present in a number of canonised dramatic works throughout history. Also, there has been a recent "explosion of research on all aspects of disgust" in the natural sciences (Chapman and Anderson 62). Nonetheless, the sensation has received comparably little attention in literary and theatre studies to this day. To my knowledge only one article exists that directly addresses the particular relation between the dramatic genre and disgust, namely Robert Douglas Fairhurst's "Tragedy and Disgust" in Sarah A. Brown's and Catherine Silverstone's (eds.) *Tragedy in Transition* (58-77).

In the humanities in particular, the long-standing reluctance to treat disgust as an equal counterpart to other aesthetic emotions (e.g. pity and fear) may be partly grounded in the sensation's inherent function to keep contents or objects associated with it at bay (cf. Kolnai 15). Susan Miller argues that scholarly avoidance may be attributed to the contagious nature of disgust, with its "unsociable stink [threatening] to transfer to those who study it" (2). The fear of contagion from substances, actions, or people that are deemed polluted and polluting, can be considered to have played a relevant role in the systematic exclusion of disgust from aesthetic theory. It was first formulated by Plato in *The Republic*, where he urged the banning of the "tragic poets" from an 'ideal' state because of the allegedly contagious (*miaron*) nature of their works and the promotion of irrational emotions, which would pollute (*miaino*) the rational faculties of the recipient's soul (cf. 595a-608c).[2] In the eighteenth century Kant, among others, also declared repulsive contents to be not only unsuitable for the arts, but *per se* antithetical to them in his seminal *Critique of the Power of Judgement* (1790).[3] And despite an endorsement of disgusting contents and forms in early twentieth century, determinedly anti-aesthetic avantgarde movements like existentialism, the theoretical evaluation of disgust as an emotion that

---

[2] All future references to Plato, unless indicated otherwise, refer to the second edition of Allan Bloom's translation of *The Republic* (1991).

[3] All future references to Kant, unless indicated otherwise, refer to the Cambridge edition of *The Critique of the Powers of Judgment* (2002), edited by Paul Guyer and translated by Paul Guyer and Eric Matthews. German quotes are all taken from the Akademie-Ausgabe of Kant's *Gesammelte Schriften*, published by the Preussische Akademie der Wissenschaften (1900ff.).

is too 'base' for the 'fine arts' and thus of little worth for serious scholarly attention can still be observed in a number of contemporary approaches. In *Theatre and Mind* (2013), Bruce McConachie, for example, excludes disgust from his analysis of relevant aesthetic sensations because he conceives of it as a 'prime' emotion, a natural or physiological reflex which, as opposed to 'social' emotions, offers little prospective insight into the complex nature of human minds and conflicts, and their manifestation in works of art (cf. 18f.).

Defining Disgust

McConachie's evaluation of disgust as a simple reflexive response and hence 'non-social' emotion is interesting because it shows how seemingly hard-wired our intuitive grasp of disgust and all things we relate to disgust is. When we experience disgust, it feels like a very natural and instinctive reaction, which more or less automatically leads us to perceive of whatever gave rise to our feeling as naturally disgusting (polluted, foul, defiled, smelly, etc.), too. At first sight, disgust does in fact appear to be an unambiguous emotion, denoting, as its linguistic roots from the French *dégout* (dis-*taste*) suggest, "something that is offensive to the taste [...] readily excited by anything unusual in the appearance, order, or nature of our food" (255), as Charles Darwin defined it in *The Expressions of Emotions in Man and Animals* in 1872. In scientific research following Darwin, disgust has been commonly regarded as a physical reflex of the survival instinct – protecting humans from incorporation of unhealthy substances, such as rotten food, diseases, infection, etc. (cf. Chapman and Anderson 63f.). However, disgust proves to be a much more complex emotion than this straightforward definition suggests. Unlike the biological protective mechanism 'distaste' which scientists generally regard as disgust's evolutionary ancestor (cf. Rozin and Haidt, "Domains of Disgust" 367), disgust has been proven to be a sensation which is neither present in animals nor in young children. This indicates that disgust must be, at least partly, a learned and thus cultural or social emotion (*ibid.*). Furthermore, disgust can be evoked by a broad range of objects and actions, some of which cannot be so readily linked to the survival instinct, such as touching harmless slimy substances, hearing someone belch and burp at the dinner table, or being appalled by foreign rituals and customs (cf. S. Miller 15). And while it is still possible to argue that these different causes of disgust are more abstract derivatives of an instinct to survive (in that they warn against *potentially* health-threatening substances, creatures, and behaviours), the same cannot be said about another common facet of disgust experiences, namely the fascination with, and sometimes even attraction to objects, people, or thoughts that are deemed repulsive.

Overview Chapters

The brief introduction into some historical and recent approaches dealing with the sensation of disgust and its cognates already indicates that there is no straightforward entry into the ubiquitous realm of disgust, more especially in regard to its aesthetic manifestation and function in the dramatic genre. Existing studies on disgust-related phenomena in works of art come from very different academic schools that often do not converge. In order to arrive at a conceptualisation of the dramatic forms, functions, and effects of aesthetic disgust and to show the suitability of using these as a tool for the analysis of drama, I will delineate four relevant stages in the history of dramatic disgust in aesthetic theory and practice in the theoretical part of this study. These can be roughly summarised using the following cognates of disgust, which will determine the structural layout and present the focal point of individual chapters.

(I) *Miasma* and *dyschéreia*: ancient Greek concepts of pollution and breaches of social and cultural codesand their relation to the Greek god Dionysus and the dramatic genre with exemplary analyses of Euripides' *Bacchae* and Sophocles' *Philoctetes* and theoretical focus on Plato's wish to ban the 'tragic poets' in *The Republic* and Aristotle's 'defense' of the tragic genre through the introduction of *katharsis* in his *Poetics*

(II) *Ekel*: German aesthetic approaches from the eighteenth century onwards with a focus on Immanuel Kant's concept of 'aesthetic ideas' and their relation to the *sublime* and *Ekel* in *Critique of the Powers of Judgement* and Friedrich Nietzsche's elaboration on the tragic genre's evolution from a 'Dionysian spirit' and its intrinsic relation to manifestations of existential disgust in *The Birth of Tragedy*

(III) *Abjection*: Post World War I French psychoanalytical and existentialist tradition with a focus on the (anti-)aesthetic practices and theoretical reflections in Georges Bataille's 'Scatology', Jean Paul Sartre's *Nausea* and *Being and Nothingness*, as well Freud's introduction of disgust as the cultural feeling *per se*, and Julia Kristeva's elaboration on *abjection* and its aesthetic representation in *Powers of Horror. An Essay on Abjection*, including its positive effect of producing pleasurable feelings of *jouissance*

(IV) *Disgust*: theoretical and aesthetic approaches to disgust since around the time of the turn to the new millennium with a focus on insights into disgust from the natural sciences, psychology, and sociology, as well as an evaluation of recent general aesthetic approaches to disgust by Winfried Menninghaus in his influential book *Disgust. History and Theory of a Strong Sensation* and Carolyn Korsmeyer's *Savoring Disgust. The Foul and the Fair in Aesthetics*

Chapter V aims to synthesise the insights gained from the historical reflections in the first four chapters in order to develop a unique and applicable theoretical approach for the analysis of disgust in works of drama. This approach will provide a terminology and the hermeneutic tools to determine and evaluate the specific aesthetic properties of dramatic disgust.

In the final chapter (VI), the applicability and suitability of the outlined theoretical approach will be demonstrated in an exemplary analysis of the plays of *in-yer-face* dramatist Kane. The slim *oeuvre* of six plays, which Kane produced between 1995 and 1999, offers a unique possibility for the analysis of the multiple and complex forms and functions the sensation of disgust takes on in theatrical writing, ranging from the depiction of extremely graphical acts of violence and physical mutilation, which will be focused on in the first sub-chapter (VI.i) that is devoted to her early plays: *Blasted* (1995), *Phaedra's Love* (1996), *Skin* (1997), and *Cleansed* (1998), to more abstract engagements with the universal experience of disgust and its relation to our sense of order, our view of ourselves, our evaluation of social and cultural actions and encounters, and our relation to our own mortality, which will be discussed in the second part of the sub-chapter, the analyses of *Crave* (1998) and *4.48 Psychosis* (2000) (VI.ii).

I. Greek Tragedy & Pollution

In fifth-century BC Athens, two significant cultural developments coincided: the evolution of the dramatic genre, including tragedy, and Socrates' introduction of argumentative dialogues as a philosophical method. These events were intrinsically connected, as their shared etymological root in *'theorein'* demonstrates: "the act of seeing or contemplation" forms the base of both 'theatre' and 'theory' (Critchley and Webster 15).

Prominent philosophers of the time esteemed their theoretical mode of 'seeing' and 'contemplation' as much superior to the ways in which in*sights* might be gained from 'contemplating' a theatrical production. In *The Republic*, Plato mentions a long-standing contest (*agon*; 607b) between philosophers and poets[1] and devotes a whole chapter to reasoning why the latter should be banished from an 'ideal' state. His fear was that tragedy would awaken the lowest parts of the soul (*miasmata*; 589e), which he deemed as both polluted and polluting. He proposed that in order to live a 'good' rational life "we shall not be polluted with regard to our psyche" (621c).

Plato's negative assessment of the dramatic genre can be directly linked to the genre's patron, the Greek god Dionysus, who represents much more than a joyful and musical spirit of wine drinking and women loving as he is still commonly portrayed today. Dionysus is also the god of paradoxes and in-betweens: life and death, human and beast, pleasure and pain (cf. Cancik and Schneider 655). In *nuce*, he represents all which defies rational thinking; he is the god of ambiguity and contradictions.

The Origin of Tragedy & the Greek God Dionysus

According to Aristotle, the dramatic genre developed from ritualistic festivals in honour of Dionysus.[2] One founding myth tells the story of how the Dionysian fes-

---

1 'Poetry' (*poiesis*) in this context needs to be understood as fiction in general, with Plato singling out the 'tragic poets' as particularly dangerous (cf. 595b).
2 Aristotle states that drama originates from "the leader of the dithyramb" (1449b) – the dithyramb being a processional hymn to the god. Evidence that it is Dionysus who is meant

tival, established in worship of the god, came into being. It is said to have been initiated when the Athenians failed to receive a statue of Dionysus with the according attitude of worship. Dionysus, "enraged, struck the male sexual organs with an incurable disease" (Sourvinou-Inwood 14f.), which could only be healed by an overt display of honour towards their god, which the Athenians enacted in a ceremonial procession equipped with "manufactured phalluses, penises made of wood and leather" to welcome their god back into the City of Dionysia (ibid.). The myth shows that Dionysus is not only associated with overt and animalistic sexuality, as the representation of phalluses illustrates, but also with the power to inflict disease. Christiane Sourvinou-Inwood maintains that tragedy developed from so-called satyr plays performed at Dionysian festivals (cf. 15).[3] From these ritualistic celebrations for Dionysus developed the satyric drama, which then led to the genesis of tragedies *about* the Greek god and later evolved into an independent genre (cf. Seaford 25). However, the tragic performances were, as Richard Seaford explains, for a long time still followed by a short satyr play – "written by the author of the preceding tragedies", which served as a "reminder of tragedy's humble origins" (25). Paul Gordon argues that "the Dionysian 'goat song' [...] is the ritual marker of humanity's connection to a lower world that it purports to deny" (62). Attic tragedies that developed from the Dionysian plays were still deeply indebted to their patron god and displayed an array of gruesome and repulsive contents like the incest motif in Sophocles' *Oedipus the King* or the appalling wound that leads to the social exclusion of the tragic hero in *Philoctetes*.

Disgust in the Attic Tragedy: *Miasma & Dyschéreia*

Miasma and *dyschéreia* are two of the ancient Greek words that are often used in disgust-eliciting contexts and Attic tragedies offer myriad examples of both concepts being employed for dramatic effect. Both notions are furthermore closely

---

by "the leader of the dithyramb" can be found in Euripides' *Bacchae*, where the Chorus refers to him with the name "Dithrambus" (526). The centrality of Dionysus for form and content of tragedy has only fairly recently become a topic of academic interest and is still highly disputed. For a long time, it was contended that the actions of Attic tragedy were largely unrelated to Dionysus (cf. Cancik and Schneider 655). However, as Richard Seaford (25-38) and others, especially members of the so-called 'Cambridge-ritualists' school, have shown, evidence points in the opposite direction: that tragedy is essentially determined by Dionysus and Dionysian topics, cults, aesthetics and functions (cf. Cancik and Schneider 655).

3   Etymologically, 'tragedy' is derived from '*tragodos*' which refers to the members of a tragic chorus with '*tragos*' meaning 'goat' – the animal that would typically be sacrificed to Dionysus (cf. Sourvinou-Inwood 15). The most generally accepted translation of *tragos* is "singer at the sacrifice of a billy goat," or a "singer for the prize of a billy goat" (Burkert qtd. in *ibid.*).

linked to the Greek god Dionysus, as I will show in the analyses of their presence in Euripides' *Bacchae* and Sophocles' *Philoctetes*, which will follow after brief general definitions of each Greek term.

Miasma

In *Miasma. Pollution and Purification in Early Greek Religion* (1983), Robert Parker draws on the findings of anthropologist Mary Douglas[4] to define the basic sense of the *mia*-words (n. *miasma*, v. *miaino*, adj. *miaros*) as that of "defilement, the impairment of a thing's form or integrity" (3). *Miasma* and its derivatives relate to defilement in two ways: (a) in a medical sense: Hippocrates employs the term to refer to diseases and wounds caused by impurity (cf. Parker 2), and (b) to incidents of ritual transgression or acts of desecration (even if these occur involuntarily; cf. 4). On an abstract level, the term '*miasma*' and its derivates are commonly employed to refer to problems or questions that defy clear rationalisation or categorisation: just like a physical wound 'violates' the integrity of the body, a moral digression, such as incest, violates the given rules of a society and thereby the integrity of its system. Parker finds the vast realm of *miasma*'s meaning best encompassed in the English word 'pollution' (1).

The physio-moral dimension incorporated in the concept of *miasma* can likewise be found in its direct linguistic opposite, the noun *katharmos*, with the verb *kathairo* denoting the physical cleansing of a wound (cf. 4; Gould, "Oedipus" 62), and other variations referring to ritual forms of cleansing, purging or purification. Aristotle's student Theophrastus' description of the "Superstitious Man" in his analysis of *Characters*[5] (c. 319) shows how freely the realms of body and mind overlap with respect to *miasma*: the superstitious man "refuses to step on a gravestone, view a corpse or visit a woman in childbirth[6] [classical cases of *miasma* in Greek antiquity] and says it's the best policy for him not to incur pollution" (109).

As Theophrastus demonstrates in his assessment of the man's behaviour as superstitious, the fear of contagion from one person or realm to another is not so much based on rational reasoning, but rather on some kind of 'magical belief'.

---

4 In her seminal work *Purity and Danger. An Analysis of Concepts of Pollution and Taboo* (1966), Mary Douglas defines filth and dirt as phenomena that upset order. According to her theory, perceived pollutions are incidents where matter falls out of categories and are thus regarded as contaminating the 'purity' of a given system (cf. 44ff.).

5 All future references to Theophrastus refer to the 2003 Cambridge edition of *Characters*, edited and translated by James Diggle. The Loeb version of *Characters* (1993), translated and edited by Jeffrey Rusten et al., will be mentioned directly in case of varying translations.

6 Mireille M. Lee offers a detailed discussion on childbirth "Maternity and Miasma" in *Motherhood and Mothering in Ancient Greece and Rome* (23-42). She describes women's pregnancy as a "liminal period", "a rite of passage" (23).

According to Parker, fifth-century BC Greek society was highly engaged in questions of physical, moral and political purity, and dangers or fears of contamination (cf. 2ff.). *Miasma* was thus associated with regulations that ranged from smaller hygienic rules such as not cutting your nails at a festival to a condemnation of animalistic (i.e. uncivilised) behaviour and prohibitions against coming into contact with corpses (cf. *ibid.*). Deemed as *miaron* were also: a murderer's reputation, dishonesty, injustice before the law, etc. (cf. *ibid.*). Parker argues that the concept of *miasma* is omnipresent in Greek tragedies; a claim that is supported by Fabian Meinel, who finds that in fact all but two of the surviving Greek tragedies address the issue explicitly.[7] According to Meinel's research, only Aeschylus' *Prometheus* and Sophocles' *Philoctetes* fall out of this category (cf. 2), which, however, does not mean that they do not deal with disgust-eliciting issues similar to those caused by *miasma*, as I will show with the example of *Philoctetes* in the later discussion on *dyschéreia*.

Miasma in Euripides' *Bacchae*

The most famous (and only surviving) Dionysian tragedy is Euripides' *Bacchae* (c. 410 BC), with '*Bacchus*' being an alternative name for Dionysus and the '*Bacchae*' denoting the group of his worshipping followers. The play depicts another founding myth concerning the introduction of Dionysus to his town of birth, Thebes, where he arrives from Lydia in Asia, bringing his cult (13f.).

In the *Bacchae*, *miasma* plays a central role and relates to multiple semantic fields that are closely linked to disgust such as: disease, pollution, sexual aberration, contagion, animalistic behaviour, transgression of moral boundaries, and ambiguous states of in-between (animal/human, man/woman, life/death, etc). At the beginning of the play, the Chorus informs us about the historical (i.e. mythological) context of Bacchus' birth. They tell us that he is the child of Semele, princess of Thebes, and the god Zeus. According to their report, Dionysus was born prematurely when his mother was struck by lightning and saved by his father, who sewed him into his thigh and later 'gave birth' to him.

> Zeus received him [...] and concealed him in his thigh, closing it up with golden pins [...]. Then, when fate brought him to term, he gave birth to the god with the horns of a bull and crowned him with garlands of serpents: that is why maenads catch beast-eating snakes and drape their tresses with them. (88-103)

Dionysus' godly/human parentage as well as his birth from a "male womb" (cf. 525-529) illustrate his essentially ambiguous and paradox nature. The gender transgression is reinforced by descriptions of his outer appearance, which is rendered

---

7   Meinel's *Pollution and Crisis in Greek Tragedy* (2015) is to date the only book-length study that discusses the central role of *miasma* in works of ancient Greek tragedy.

as both, highly sexually potent and phallic as well as "effeminate" (352). His animalistic features ("horns of a bull") blur the boundaries between human/animal, which also applies to his companions, the *maenads* (female followers wearing animal skins, eating raw flesh, and allegedly practicing dark forms of sexuality) and the *satyrs* (men often depicted with permanent erections and goat-like features; cf. Cancik and Schneider 654ff.).

Like their leader, the *maenads* and *satyrs* are transgressors of civic norms that defy clear categorical identification and are thus conceived as outsiders of the *polis*. Because of Dionysus' ambiguous characteristics, alongside him being racially discriminated because he was brought up in Asia (i.e. the 'inferior' and 'barbaric' East), the god is perceived as an ultimate 'foreigner', 'stranger' (*xenos*, 1047), 'Other' (cf. Cancik and Schneider 658ff.; Mills 39) by the Greek citizens and met with suspicion and hostility.

Dionysus tells us that his aunts Agave, Ino, and Autonie did not believe him to be the son of Zeus and had slandered his mother's reputation by spreading rumours about her infidel character. As a punishment he turns them and other Theban women to frenzy and drives them to the mountains of Cithaeron to live as *maenads* (cf. 25-42). Dionysus' cousin, Pentheus, who has recently become King of Thebes, is also more than unhappy to hear about "the strange mischief" going on in his city (cf. 215-225). For Pentheus all that is related to the 'foreigner' Dionysus and his ritual practices appears diseased, dangerous, and highly contagious. His fear of physiological contagion becomes most apparent when he aggressively rejects his grandfather Cadmus' attempt to place an ivy crown on his head as a sign of Dionysian worship: "Keep your hands to yourself, don't wipe your folly off on me!" (343-345), he replies.

Pentheus is determined to expel Dionysus, the "symbolical bearer of all the ills and pollutions", from his city and threatens to have him stoned, a penalty that is "usually reserved for the bearer of pollution" as Charles Segal points out in his *Dionysiac Poetics* (42f.). Pentheus maintains that Dionysus "'befouls' (*lymainetai*) the beds of women (352-54)" (Segal, *Dionysiac Poetics* 50), and is "infecting the women with a new disease" (Euripides 352f.). He even believes that should they ever come in contact with the Dionysian drink of wine "in their feasts", it would ultimately lead to "everything about their rites [becoming] diseased" (260-262). His fear with regard to Dionysian defilement is mainly focused on promiscuous and orgiastically aberrant sexual behaviour induced in women (cf. 216-223). A messenger who observed the women hunting in the mountains highlights another Dionysian feature, namely the animalistic and brutal nature of their activities:

> You could have seen one of the women tearing asunder a bellowing fatted calf with her hands, while others tore heifers to pieces. You could have seen their

flanks and cloven hooves hurled this way and that: pieces, drenched with blood, hung dripping from the fir trees. (733-742)

This bleak vision concerning the practice of the Dionysian cult, however, only shows one side of the picture. Both the messenger and the Chorus also report in great detail on the cult's attraction. They describe the lives of the women in the mountains as peaceful, beautiful, awe-striking and even chaste:[8]

> First they let their hair fall to their shoulders, and those whose fastenings had come undone adjusted their fawnskin garments, girdling the dappled skins with snakes that licked their cheeks. New mothers, their babies left behind and their breasts overfull with milk, cradled gazelles or wolf cubs in their arms and gave them to drink from their white milk. [...] All who desired a drink of milk dug with their fingertips in the ground and the white liquid bubbled up. From their ivy-covered thyrsos dripped streams of honey. If you had been there and seen this, you would have approached in prayer the god you now disparage. (695-713)

The women are not only described as caring and loving ("cradled gazelles or wolf cubs in their arms"), but also as highly attractive and arousing, as the use of rich sexually allusive language in this report demonstrates ("snakes that licked their cheeks"; "breasts overfull with milk"; "the white liquid bubbled up"; "dripped streams of honey").

Even Pentheus himself, who consistently expresses aversion to all that Dionysus and his cult represent, displays signs of fascination and even attraction. His enchantment with the god and his worshippers shines through in his account of Bacchus' beauty, in his eagerness to hear about the women from the messenger, and in his fantasies concerning their sexual behaviour (cf. 222-225, 261-262, 354, 486). When Dionysus, in full awareness of Pentheus' (repressed) desires, offers him a sight of the women in action, Pentheus immediately swallows the bait, offering "much gold to do so" (812) – a decision which will ultimately lead to his tragic death. Once Pentheus arrives at the women's dwelling place and climbs up a tree to get a better view of the scene, Dionysus orders his aunts and their female comrades to attack the vicious intruder, whom they fail to recognise as their son, nephew, and king (taking him for a wild animal instead). The news about these deeds is brought to Pentheus' grandfather Cadmus by a messenger, who reports the gruesome events in painstaking detail:

> [Pentheus'] mother was the priestess and began the killing [...]. Taking his right hand in her grip and planting her foot against the poor man's flank, she tore out

---

8   It seems, however, that this peaceful life can only be maintained in the absence of men. As soon as male intruders come to disturb the women, their behaviour turns 'savage' and brutal (cf. 434, 712-713; 769-774).

his arm at the shoulder. [...] Ino was destroying the other side, tearing his flesh, and Autonie and the rest of the bacchic throng attacked him. [...] One of them was carrying an arm, another a foot still in its boots, his flanks were stripped bare, the flesh torn from them, and every woman, hands red with blood, hurled Pentheus' flesh about like a ball. His body lies scattered, some of it under the rough cliffs, other parts in thick-growing woods, no easy thing to look for. (1110-1136)

Not only is the cruel action of ripping apart Pentheus' body and the difficulty of finding the scattered pieces described in vivid detail, but the lurid goriness of the event is heightened even further by the *maenads*' apparent pleasure in the slaughter as they are reported to have played "ball" with the King's blood-dripping remains. Also, the Chorus' evaluation of Agave's involuntary filicide is appallingly cheerful: "A fine endeavour it is to drench one's hand in the blood of a child!" (1163-1164).

But despite the gruesomeness of the event, Dionysus' revenge has not yet come to an end. Agave, who had shamed Dionysus' mother by spreading rumours about her alleged infidelity, has yet to learn her lesson of what it means to be a truly shameful mother. Still taking her butchered son for a wild animal, she proudly parades around her home town, carrying his head on a stick, joyfully suggesting a festive meal to be made from his young flesh, until she comes to her senses and realises her horrendous (*miaron*; 1383) deeds of filicide and threatened cannibalism. If we take Agave, who did not voluntarily join the *maenads*, as a representative of Theban morals, it can be argued that her case displays how the whole discourse on who or what is *miaron* is turned on its head in this tragedy. The ending of the play suggests that it is not so much Dionysus and his cult who are defiled and polluted, but rather the Theban citizens' attitudes and conducts. The Thebans are forced to realise their own dereliction from moral behaviour in the most painful manner: Instead of Pentheus violently destroying Dionysus as the polluting element by "separat[ing] his head from his body" (241); it is Pentheus whose body is torn to pieces for having proven to be an unsuitable and in fact *miaron* leader by not having shown his due worship to the god and by having overestimated his authoritarian powers in leading the city by means of tyranny and threats of violence.[9] He had threatened to shed the women's blood in the mountains: "[W]omen's blood! That's what they deserve, and I shall shed lots of it in the glens of Cithareon!" (796-797), but instead it is his blood which is shed at the women's hands. Pentheus' grandfather Cadmus, who had advised his grandson to "tell a wholesome lie: thus Semele will be thought to have given birth to a god and our whole family will win honor" (330-336), receives his punishment for having acted from false and selfish motives when he joined the

---

9   The prophet Teiresias had warned Pentheus: "[T]hough you think yourself clever and have a ready tongue, there is no intelligence in what you say" (265-271); "don't think that kingly rule is the most powerful force in human life" (309-311); but Pentheus did not listen and instead ordered a violent attack on the prophet for having "taught" Dionysian "madness" (345).

Dionysian worship. Dionysus turns him into the "savage form" of a snake to match his 'sly' nature (cf. 1338, 1357).

Segal states that in the *Bacchae*, Euripides shows how "civilized order [is] cracking apart" (*Dionysiac Poetics* 55) under the corrupt actions of Thebes' citizens in general and the tyrannical attitude of its ruler Pentheus in particular (cf. 215ff, 679f.). Through a reversal of what is deemed *miaron*, in the sense of polluting the *polis*, the play demonstrates that "savage" moral attitudes are much more dangerous to the well-being of a state than people who are perceived as animalistic 'sub-humans' because of their foreign heritage and instinct-driven behaviour.

Dyschéreia

The meaning of the ancient Greek term '*dyschéreia*' is as broad as that of '*miasma*': It ranges from distaste or unpleasantness of food to bad smell, loathing, nausea, and difficult questions (cf. Liddell n.p.). A look into the word's etymology reveals how, like *miasma*, *dyschéreia* relates to physical as well abstract forms of repulsion and their objects: the root '*chér*' means 'hand', but also 'touch' (*ibid.*), which in its negation ('*dys*') can refer to both: (a) physical items that should not be touched and (b) arguments or questions that are "difficult to *handle*" (cf. Liebert 186; my emphasis).[10] *Dyschéreia* can be used to describe reactions to concrete physical items: "annoyance [and/or] disgust caused by things", as well as appalling features, such as "harshness [and] offensiveness" of persons; and abstract problems, such as "troublesome questions" and reactions to these (Liddell n.p.). Associated with *dyschéreia* are thus all objects, activities, persons, and questions one should avoid close contact with (a feature which at least hints at a similar fear of contagion as the fear induced by encounters with *miasma*).

In Theophrastus' work on *Characters* we find a lucid exemplary description of many of *dyschéreia*'s varied meanings and its physio-moral dimensions. Theophrastus describes "The Offensive Man" (*dyschéreia*)[11] as a person who lacks habits of hygiene and displays signs of physical neglect, which are unpleasant for other people. He has black nails, fouling feet, rotten teeth, and suffers from open wounds and diseases, which are exacerbated by his carelessness. He smells like a pigsty, is hairy like a wild animal, and his armpits are infested by lice. His behaviour is also overtly offensive: He blows his nose (with his fingers) while eating, he burps and spits while

---

10 Rana S. Liebert suggests a possible translation as "difficult to stomach" (186; claiming that the etymological root could refer to a now lost word for 'stomach'). She also explains that the Greeks were generally more prone to "attribute [some]thing physical to an ethical stance" (190) than we are today.

11 Rusten et al. translate *dyschéreia* as "squalour" in the Loeb version of the text (cf. 117ff.).

speaking, scratches himself during sacrifice, and does not wash before sexual encounters with his wife. When he does wash, he uses rancid oil to bathe and he wears stained clothes to go to the market (cf. Diggle 119; Rusten et al. 117-121).

Dyschéreia in Sophocles' *Philoctetes*

Sophocles' prize-winning tragedy *Philoctetes*, which centres around the protagonist's wounded foot, its causes, and its consequences, is a play that offers myriad and graphic examples of the use of *dyschéreia* in ancient drama. The main actions of the play take place during the Trojan War, where Philoctetes is sought out by Odysseus and Neoptolemus to persuade him to come back with them to Troy because his skills are needed in combat.

In the opening lines of the play, we learn that Philoctetes had been previously sent into exile on the deserted island of Lemnos because of his diseased foot which was caused by a snakebite as a result of him having accidentally trespassed on sacred grounds. The odious infection of his foot in turn rendered him so repulsive that the authorities of the city sought to have him banished from the city to maintain public order (cf. 1-12; cf. Pentheus' actions and his fate in Euripides' *Bacchae*). At the onset of the play, Philoctetes is thus, like Euripides' Bacchus and his followers, an outsider to the city, inhabiting a liminal space on the borders of civilisation.[12] Only after ten years of social exclusion, when Philoctetes' skills are needed in warfare, does Neoptolemus at the order of Odysseus travel to Lemnos to persuade Philoctetes to join him back to Troy. Odysseus, who had feared Philoctetes to be reluctant to this cause, instructed Neoptolemus to convince the latter by means of lies and deception.

When Neoptolemus and his men arrive on the island they find Philoctetes in an abysmal state. They are appalled, not only by the stench of his still pulsating wound, but also by his animalistic way of life: Philoctetes lives in a cage (16), describes himself as having "turned into something wild" (224-226) and "degraded" (229); he drinks "stained puddle-water" (718), and because of his ill foot sometimes even has to "crawl" (295, 701) to move forward, unable to uphold a 'human' upright walking position (cf. 820-821). Even in his description of the *"savage*-ulcer wound" (270; my emphasis) Philoctetes draws on the semantic field of animality.

In other passages, the loathsome nature of Philoctetes' wound is further stylistically aggravated through detailed references to various bodily fluids and compositional variations relating to food and consumption. Philoctetes' foot is de-

---

[12] Marina B. McCoy points out that the play opens with the Greek word for 'shore', "an appropriate beginning since Philoctetes himself belongs at the periphery, the edge, the space in between belonging to society – to which he naturally as a human being forms a part – and being an island to himself in his isolation on Lemnos" (64).

scribed as: "suppurating with a flesh-*devouring* ulcer" (7), a "*greedy* ulcer" (312; cf. also 795), a "*blood-drunk, hungry* sore" (684; my emphasis). In a near-death state Philoctetes exclaims: "what wretched thing I am. This is the *end*, my son [...] I'm being *eaten* through, my son" (744-745; my emphasis cf. also 1165). He addresses the parasites feeding on his decaying flesh: "This is your chance to *feast*, fix your teeth in vengeance upon my *mottled meat*" (1155; my emphasis). By combining decay and death with food and feasting, Sophocles here achieves the same stomach-turning effect as Euripides did in the scene of Agave expressing her cannibalistic phantasies in the *Bacchae* (cf. 1184-1329). What causes these descriptions to be so emotionally effective is their relation to the ultimate Dionysian paradox, the dichotomous pairing of life and death, which becomes most apparent in Philoctetes' repeated descriptions of himself as "a living corpse" (Sophocles 1018; cf. also 945, 950ff., 1208ff.).

The most thought-provoking aspect of Sophocles' usage of *dyschéreia* in *Philoctetes*, however, does not concern the appalling state of its hero's physical condition, but the moral dimension of self-disgust, which Neoptolemus, who was sent to bring Philoctetes back to Troy, experiences as a result of having let himself be persuaded to do so by means of deceit. Philoctetes' putrid disease thus functions above all as contrasting mirror to unveil what is 'really' revolting, namely: lies, corruption, and deceit. Whereas Winfried Menninghaus and Robert Douglas-Fairhurst in their analyses of *dyschéreia*'s role in *Philoctetes* both suggest that the vivid description of Philoctetes' hideous wound functions above all to test and testify Neoptolemus' noble character in being able to overcome his physical repulsion (cf. Menninghaus 12, Douglas-Fairhurst 6), Emily Allen-Hornblower instead argues that it is the moral dimension of *dyschéreia* expressed in Neoptolemus' feeling of self-disgust that lies at the heart of the play. I agree with Allen-Hornblower's reading as I shall show in a close reading of the scene that marks the reversal from a focus on Philoctetes' physical affliction to Neoptolemus' inner turmoil. The dialogue that discloses this turn takes place after Philoctetes' suffering reaches a climax, during which course he deliriously expresses his trust, gratefulness, and affection towards Neoptolemus, before falling unconscious. When he wakes up, he finds Neoptolemus in a state utter confusion and despair and fears that this may have been caused by his disease. He tries to calm him down by suggesting that "the force of habit will set [him] upright" (i.e. make him 'human') again, but Neoptolemus is not to be consoled since his disgust stems from a different source:

> PHILOCTETES: *It is not disgust [dyschéreia] with my disease that has come upon you and made you give up on the idea of taking me on board as a shipmate, is it?*
> NEOPTOLEMUS: *All is disgust [dyschéreia] when one leaves one's own nature and does what is out of keeping with it!*

> PHILOCTETES: *But you have not been doing or saying anything that is not in keeping with the one who sired you, by helping an honorable man such as I.*
> NEOPTOLEMUS: *I shall be revealed as shameful: that is what has been paining me for a long while now.*
> PHILOCTETES: *Not in your actions, you won't; that's for certain. But your words do worry me. (900-910)*

Neoptolemus' statement that "All is disgust when one leaves one's own nature and does what is out of keeping with it!" can be interpreted in three ways. First, as a reference to the animalistic, inhumane and thus repulsive state Philoctetes has reached because of his wound, which he assumes causes Neoptolemus to be physically disgusted. Second, as a form of self-reproach that Neoptolemus experiences due to stepping out of character (as in cultivated human 'nature') by associating with an animalistic 'sub-human'. And finally, as a form of self-loathing on Neoptolemus' behalf for having 'left his nature' as a good and honest man when he agreed to Odysseus' plan to use lies and deceit to bring Philoctetes to Troy. Whereas the first reading links Neoptolemus' exclamation back to Philoctetes' self-assessment as a base and barely human creature, the second reading marks the transition from disgust at a physically repugnant person to a form of self-loathing caused by engaging with someone disgusting. The second reading is how Philoctetes initially interprets Neoptolemus statement' since it has by now become clear that Neoptolemus' problem is one that does not primarily concern the 'other' (Philoctetes) but himself. It is, however, the third reading that is most crucial for an understanding of this scene, since Neoptolemus' moral self-disgust marks "a key moment in Neoptolemus' evolution, and a turning point in the drama as a whole" (Allen-Hornblower 72).

Similarly to Euripides' *Bacchae* in its negotiation of the polyvalent dimensions of *miasma*, *Philoctetes* too demonstrates by means of inversion that it is not the decaying body or animal-like behaviour that are most repulsive, but 'rotten' moral convictions instead. According to Allen-Hornblower, Sophocles' usage of *dyschéreia* poses fundamental questions of who or what we consider or should consider disgusting, in the sense of being harmful to society: a pressing concern for the citizens of the Greek *polis* at the time, "when conspiracies, lies, and mutual suspicion were threatening the city and the democratic regime's very survival" (85).

I.i Plato's Banishment of the Poets in *The Republic*

In *The Republic*, Plato (c.428-c.348 BC) conceptualises an ideal state mediated in a fictional dialogue between his teacher Socrates and various interlocutors. In Book

X (595a-608c), Socrates discusses the political and social status of poets (cf. also Book II 337b-383c and III 386a-403c). Aiming for a republic that is governed by rational thinking, Socrates condemns the so-called *mimetic* (i.e. representational) arts[13] on grounds of their occupation with forms of representation that he considers to be of low ontological value. For Plato the artistic depictions of characters and actions in works of drama and similar art forms, are mere 'copies' of real-life people and events and reality itself is only a particular manifestation, or 'copy' of metaphysical ideas (596e-602c). From art's purported inferior ontological status, Plato's Socrates deduces various points of ideological and moral critique.

The arguments that will be of main interest for our discussion on aesthetic disgust are Socrates' disapproval of the affective potential of dramatic productions and their effects on recipients, as well as *mimetic* arts' supposed indisposition to provide audiences with 'real' knowledge or understanding. According to Socrates, the strong emotions that can be aroused by engaging with *mimetic* works of art (he uses the specific example of witnessing a theatrical performance) endanger the harmony of the soul (602c-608b). His fear is that audiences may imitate or become 'polluted' by irrational behaviour (*miaron*), which would impair their ability to think rationally: "Between us – and you all won't denounce me to the tragic poets and all the other imitators – all such things seem to maim the thought of those who hear them and do not as a remedy have the knowledge of how they really are" (595b).

Spirited Disgust & the Pollution of *Logos*

Plato's concern regarding the potential of 'tragic poetry' to damage recipients' intellectual faculties is intrinsically linked to the previously discussed concepts of (1) *dyschéreia* and (2) *miasma*, therefore Plato's discussion of these terms shall be presented in some detail in the following sections.

Dyschéreia

In *The Republic*, we find the most important discussion relating to *dyschéreia* in Socrates' conversation with Glaucon on the 'just' state of the soul, which he professes to mirror the functioning principle of an ideal state. Socrates tells the story

---

13 The most common translation of '*mimêsis*' is 'imitation'. Nickolas Pappas, however, points out that "[a]lternatives include 'representation' and 'emulation'" and that the "transliterated Greek word sans diacritical mark [..., the] English 'mimesis' " is most often simply used as a synonym for 'imitation', which does not capture all of the nuances of the original Greek term" (n.p.). As 'representation' offers a broader and potentially creatively more open translation of '*mimesis*', I opt to use this term when talking about the dramatic (=representational) arts, as well as maintaining the anglicised version '*mimetic*' to mark its broader (Greek) meaning.

of a man called Leontius to demonstrate how the soul is composed of three different, potentially conflicting, parts (cf. 435c).

> [He] was going up from the Piraeus [...] when he noticed corpses lying by the public executioner. He *desired to look*, but at the same time he was *disgusted [dyschéreia]* and made himself *turn away*; and for a while he struggled and covered his face. But finally, overpowered by the desire, he opened his eyes wide, ran toward the corpses and said: 'Look, you damned wretches, take your fill of the fair sight.' (439e-440a; my emphasis)

On passing the corpses by the roadside, Leontius experiences strong and contradictory emotional sensations. Like Pentheus in Euripides' *Bacchae*, who, at the same time as being appalled by all that Dionysus represents, is also attracted to him, Leontius simultaneously feels the desire to look at the recently deceased bodies (attraction) as well as an urge to turn away from them (aversion). Socrates concludes from the co-presence of Leontius' conflicting affective responses that the human soul cannot be composed of only two parts, as he had previously assumed: one being rational (*logos*) and the other desiring or appetitive (*ephitumia*);[14] but that there must be a third part at work in the human soul to account for Leontius' paradox reaction, which he calls the 'spirited' part (*thumos*) (439e). He comes to this conclusion because in his view the two contradictory urges (attraction/aversion) can neither both belong to the desirous or appetitive part of the soul ('law of non-contradiction'), nor can one of them be allocated to the rational part since both sensations are highly affectively charged. Socrates thus locates Leontius' desire to look at the corpses in the appetitive part and his aversion in the newly established third, the 'spirited' part of the soul.

Glaucon initially assumes that the 'spirited' part bears similarity to the appetitive part, but Socrates disagrees, claiming that it instead "take[s] up arms on the side of the calculating part" in the "civil war of the soul" (440e).[15] He argues that the spirited part functions as an ally of the rational part with the goal to rule over the desires coming from the lower appetitive part of the soul.[16] The spirited part

---

14   Plato's previous dual structure of the soul was set up as follows: "[W]e claim they are two and different from one another, naming that in the soul with which it reasons the rational and that with which it lusts, hungers, thirsts, and feels the flutter of other appetites, the irrational and appetitive – companion of certain replenishments and pleasures" (439d-e).
15   Glaucon's interpretation is in many ways more intuitively comprehensible. The etymological relation between *thymoeides/thumos* and *epithumetikon/ephitumia* would also point in this direction. For further discussion cf. Liebert (190f.).
16   There is some contradiction in this set-up. Socrates agrees with Glaucon's observation that the spirited part of the soul can already be found in children. He also mentions its presence in animals, which indicates an instinctive nature, rather than a *logos*-informed feature. For further discussion cf. Darren Sheppard (65) and Liebert (186).

of the soul thus aids to protect the just state of the soul (442a) from "injustice, licentiousness, cowardice, lack of learning, and, in sum, vice entire" (444a-b). This dialogue between Socrates and Glaucon demonstrates that Plato views *dyschéreia* as an internalised aversion against what is morally repugnant, which functions as an almost instinctive safeguard against the dangerous appetites of the lower part of the soul. Liebert interprets Plato's *dyschéreia* to denote an "embodied ethical attitude" which "suggests that aversions to wrongdoings are, at least ideally, the product of deep internalization" (182). For Plato these characteristics of *dyschéreia* turn it into a valuable tool for educational training, aimed at the 'cultivation of the rational mind':

> [O]ne who was properly trained [...] would perceive with the greatest acuity the deficiencies of things made or grown without beauty, and so, feeling disgust rightly, he would praise beautiful things and, by taking pleasure in them and receiving them into his soul, he would nourish it by these means and become himself beautiful and good. The ugly, on the other hand, he would rightly blame and hate while still young and yet unable to grasp the reason, but when reason came the man trained in this manner would welcome it most of all, for through their kinship he would already know it. (401d-e)

This passage highlights how Plato conceives of disgust as a kind of acquired moral compass that helps to distinguish between what is 'good' (rational/harmonious), moral, and therefore beautiful, and what ought to be despised as the 'other', the irrational and ugly. It also shows the transference from physical aversion to more abstract concepts of beauty and ugliness, which for Plato mirror concepts of justice and morality. Plato thus conceives of physical health as a manifestation of beauty, and sickness or disease as a manifestation of ugliness, which in turn mirror the just and unjust actions of the soul: "Virtue, then, as it seems, would be a certain health, beauty and good condition of a soul, and vice a sickness, ugliness and weakness" (444c-e). What is most thought-provoking about Plato's evaluation of the sensation of *dyschéreia* is the conclusion he draws and the loophole he leaves regarding further elaboration on the topic. Socrates' discussion with Glaucon on the topic of the spirited part of the soul and *dyschéreia* comes to an end with the former's concession that a complete understanding of the nature of the soul cannot be accomplished by means of logical reasoning via language. He warns: "But know well, Glaucon, that in my opinion, we'll never get a precise grasp of it [the soul] on the basis of procedures such as we're now using in the argument" (435d). Socrates continues with opening up the possibility of "another longer and further road" to reach a conclusion on how to understand the mechanisms of the soul – an offer that is never redeemed.

Miasma

Plato uses the term *miasma* to describe physiological as well as moral forms of pollution. He regards the lowest part of the psyche to be *miaron* "to an extreme degree" (589e), or as Thomas Gould puts it: "entirely without good" ("Oedipus" 65). In an argument that anticipates the Freudian theory of the unconscious, Plato refers to dreams as instances where humans' most *miaron* desires are freely unleashed: "What we wish to recognize is the following: surely some terrible, savage, and lawless form of desire is in every man, even in some of us who seem to be so very measured. And surely this becomes plain in dreams" (571d). Plato's ennumeration of possible dream contents shows us which actions and features he associates with *miasma*:

> [While] the calculating, tame, and ruling part [...] slumbers, [...] the beastly and wild part, gorged with food or drink, is skittish and, pushing sleep away, seeks to go and satisfy its dispositions. You know that in such a state it dares to do everything as though it were released from, and rid of all shame and prudence. And it doesn't shrink from attempting intercourse, as it supposes, with a mother or with anyone else at all – human beings, gods, and beasts; or attempting any foul murder at all, and there is no food from which it abstains. (571b-d)

Many of the actions and characteristics of *miaron* deeds Plato here enumerates are closely related to the god of border transgressions and in-betweens Dionysus and thus unsurprisingly also feature prominently in Attic tragedies of the time. In *Phaedrus* Plato directly mentions the Greek god in relation to the dangers of art, claiming that poetic inspiration is a "form of madness bestowed by the Muses" (in Murray xxviii) which takes a "tender and virgin soul" and "rouses and excites it to Bacchic frenzy" (*ibid*.). For Plato the nature of these kind of base Bacchic frenzies stands in direct opposition to humans' rational faculties and derives from the lowest place in the appetitive part of the soul. Plato thus associates *miasma* with animalistic instinct-driven behaviour: "savage", "beastly", and "wild", actions that defy all rules of etiquette and social order ("rid of all shame and prudence") and transgress the most sacred taboos of human societies: incest, intercourse with "gods, and beasts", as well as murders of the worst kind like patricide or filicide (Gould "Oedipus" 65; cf. also Liebert 190). By placing *miasma* in the appetitive part of the soul Plato furthermore directly connects the notion to manifestations and modes of excessive and improper food consumption: "gorged with food and drink", "there is no food from which it abstains", which could even include cannibalism (cf. Liebert 190; Gould "Oedipus" 65). Plato's usage of the term *miasma*, with meanings ranging from improper food to immoral behaviour, highlights the physio-moral nature of the sensation which also becomes apparent in his 'somatic' rendering of tragedy's supposed aesthetic effect. He describes this effect in terms of excessive food consumption such as "filling", "stuffing", and "satisfying" the lowest part of the psyche (606a; cf. also 576c).

For Plato the tragic hero of Sophocles' *Oedipus the King* is a prime example of a *miaron* character, since he brings the plague to his town, sleeps with his mother, and kills his father (regardless of the fact that Oedipus unknowingly commits these crimes). Plato's assumption is that any kind of contact with *miasma*, even in the form of artistic representation like the performance of the *Oedipus* play, is highly dangerous and contagious. As Gould puts it: "anyone who allowed himself to get sympathetically excited by this crime was risking that most dangerous *miasmata*, the surrender to the part of his psyche that is just as *miaros* as Oedipus" ("Oedipus" 66). In his fear of *miasma*'s contagious nature Plato goes so far as to claim that an infection with *miasma* lasts even into afterlife (cf. 621c).

I.ii   Aristotle's *Poetics*: *Miasma* & *Katharsis*

For Aristotle, like Plato, *miasma* is central to his reflection on the dramatic genre, and like his teacher he discusses the concept in relation to the specific characteristics of the *mimetic* arts. In his *Poetics* Aristotle agrees with his teacher's assumption concerning the 'infectious' nature of the theatre, meaning that dramatic works can have a strong emotional impact on their recipients. But for him this kind of emotional affliction does not pollute (*miaino*) the soul, but can instead induce a cleansing of undesirable emotional states, a *katharsis* (1449b).

Even though Aristotle never directly refers to his teacher, the *Poetics* is generally regarded as a defence of the *mimetic* arts against Plato's critique. Thomas Gould points out that there are only five occurrences of the word *miasma* in Aristotle's entire *oeuvre*, of which three can be found in the *Poetics* (cf. "Oedipus" 65). He sees this as an indication for Aristotle directly reacting to Plato's accusations against *mimetic* arts' supposed *miaron* nature with an attempt to answer "the question why we should enjoy [tragedy]" (*ibid.*) and what can be gained from engagement with this form of art through his concept of *katharsis*. By introducing the notion of *katharsis*, Aristotle offers an effective antidote to Plato's contention that dramatic works are ultimately of a *miaron* and thus potentially *logos*-harming nature. He points to the valuable lessons that can be learned from encounters with the *mimetic* arts as well as to the pleasure provided from gaining knowledge in this way.[17] Together these arguments present a possible solution to the so-called 'para-

---

17   For Aristotle, *mimesis* and learning are intrinsically linked, since, in his view, children first learn through *mimesis* by imitating grown-ups' behaviour and actions. He thus believes that engagement with the *mimetic* arts encourages our natural desire for knowledge and learning (cf. 1448b).

dox of aversion' – the question of why and how we can derive pleasure from artistic presentation of objects and actions which we would avoid contact with in real life (cf. Korsmeyer 44).

Aristotle's argumentation on why pleasure can be derived from tragic forms of art is grounded on the premise that humans take pleasure in learning. He claims that when "a destructive or painful action, such as death on the stage, bodily agony, wounds, and the like" (1452b) is encountered in forms of artistic presentation, pleasure results from the fact that we learn something about the specific nature of the items or actions on display. Additionally, he claims that we delight in acknowledging the particular craftsmanship the creator employed in producing the work of art (1448b). According to Aristotle these positive experiences outbalance the negative emotions that real-life encounters with objects such as "contemptible insects or dead bodies" could provoke:

> [W]e delight in contemplating the most accurately made images of the very things that are painful for us to see, such as the forms of the most contemptible insects and of dead bodies. What is responsible even for this is that understanding [*manthanein*] is most pleasant [*hediston*] not only for philosophers but in a similar way for everyone else, though they share in it to a short extent. They delight in seeing images for this reason: because understanding and reasoning of what each thing is results when they contemplate them, for instance "that's who this is," since if one happens not to have seen him before, the image will not produce pleasure as an imitation, but only on account of its workmanship or coloring or for some other such reason. (1448b)

The solution Aristotle offers to the 'paradox of aversion' is that repulsive depictions are not so much pleasant for perception (*aisthesis*), but rather for our intellect with regard to (a) acknowledgement of skilful craftsmanship (*poiesis*, *techne*),[18] and (b) enhanced understanding (*manthanein*) of the nature of things on display. What this quote nevertheless illustrates is that Aristotle's solution to the 'paradox of aversion', as well as his view on the function of art is, like his teacher Plato's, to a large degree *logos*-based.

While Plato dismisses the *mimetic* arts because he maintains that dramatists have no real knowledge about the contents they depict and are thus 'bad' teachers, Aristotle argues that it is a different kind of knowledge that dramatic works convey. Against Plato's accusation that the *mimetic* arts do no more than depict 'lies' about the world, Aristotle counters that the events displayed by tragedy are not, and are in fact not meant to be, 'copies' of particular real-life events, but are instead representative of "universal" principles of actions (cf. 1451b). He compares the artist's task

---

18　For further elaboration on the idea of art as a product of special craftsmanship (*techne*) cf., for example, Jonathan Lear (322) or Karel Thein (218).

to that of the historian, claiming that unlike the latter, dramatists do not "speak [...] of things that have happened but of the sort of things that might happen and possibilities that come from what is likely or necessary" (1451a). Tragedy's capability to represent "things that are universal" makes it a highly relevant genre for enhancing human understanding in Aristotle's point of view. He esteems tragedy as "more philosophical (*philosophoteron*) and more serious (*spoudaioteron*)" than other academic disciplines like history, which can only gain insight from "things that are particular" (1451b). This argument is Aristotle's strongest point against his teacher's condemnation of the 'tragic poets' on the basis of them allegedly presenting copies of copies of particular actions of which they do not have the required 'expert knowledge' (cf. Plato 597a-602a). The case Aristotle makes for *mimetic* art's superiority over other academic disciplines in its potential to depict universal human conflicts is also a crucial element of the aesthetic discourse that was to follow the ancient Greek reflections on art. Aristotle's standpoint highlights the unique aesthetic, social and educational values that engagement with *mimetic* works of art are able to offer: insight into human conduct and motivation, as well as a simulated 'training' of the emotional states involved in basic human conflicts.

Tragedy & Emotions

Overall, Aristotle's view on emotions is not as exclusive as that of his teacher Plato: for Aristotle all emotions are essential components of human development. In his *Rhetoric* he postulates that "emotions are those things through which, by undergoing change, people come to differ in their judgments" (in Eden 48). For Aristotle emotions are also integral to the lessons to be learned from encounters with art. Out of the different literary genres existent at his time, Aristotle selects tragedy as the highest form of art with regard to the desired strong emotional impact on its recipients. He argues that tragedy presents the events in greater unity and compression than other genres (e.g. the epic) and is therefore more intense. Because of drama's representation of direct speech, it is, according to Aristotle, also more vivid (*enarges*) than other genres (*Poetics* 1461a-1462b).

Aristotle singles out the sensations of pity (*eleos*) and fear (*phobos*) as those affectionate states that are fitting to the genre and suited to offer insight to the essential nature of human existence. He suggests that the evocation of pity and fear through tragedy not only enhances intellectual understanding (*manathanein*, 1448b), but that these particular emotional states are furthermore capable of inducing a *katharsis*, a cleansing of these undesirable negative feelings from the recipients' souls (cf.

1449b). What Aristotle seems to mean by *katharsis* in this context[19] is that an experience of pity and fear within the realm of the theatre can free audience members from being highly affected by these emotions when confronted with tragic events in real life. In a nutshell one could say that audiences become acquainted with unpleasant feelings like pity and fear and are thereby strengthened and equipped for future events where the same feeling could be evoked; or to put it in modern terms: recipients of tragic plays receive a simulated crisis-training, teaching them to control their emotions, while at the same time offering a safe space to 'let go' of negative feelings which they may be harbouring in their souls.

By introducing the term '*katharsis*' to the theoretical reflections on the dramatic genre, Aristotle in many ways manages to turn the tables in the discussion about the polluting nature of tragedy by suggesting that the activation of *katharsis* offers a direct cure for *miaron* infection (cf. Gould, "Oedipus" 66f.). The experience of *katharsis* through the evocation of pity and fear can be viewed as a remedy against the sensually oversaturating 'dangers' that Plato saw in the reception of the *mimetic* arts; a kind of 'vomitive' which alleviates audiences from the 'filling' and 'stuffing' effects of *miaron* aesthetic representations.

It is important to note that in his discussion of the potential of tragedy, Aristotle distinctly addresses the generic advantages of the dramatic text and not the theatrical performance or spectacle as responsible for inducing the desired emotional effect on its recipients. Aristotle markedly dismisses overtly spectacular stagings of dramatic plays, claiming that tragedy's emotional effectiveness lies primarily in the content and not in its staging. Thus he states that "it is possible for what is frightening and pitiable to arise out of the spectacle, but it is also possible for it to arise from the very organization of actions, and it is exactly that which takes precedence and is the mark of a better poet" (1453b). Aristotle sharply distinguishes between

---

19   Penelope Murray points to the fact that Aristotle nowhere offers a detailed definition of *katharsis*. According to Murray, the closest to an explanation of the term can be found in *Politics*, where Aristotle discusses the use of music: "The emotions which violently affect some minds exist in all, but in different degrees, for example pity and fear, and 'enthusiasms' too, for some people are subject to this disturbance. We can see the effect of sacred music on such people when they make use of melodies that arouse the mind to frenzy, and are restored to health and attain, as it were, healing and catharsis. The same effect will necessarily be experienced in the case of those prone to pity or fear, or any other emotion, in the proportion appropriate to each individual; all experience a catharsis and pleasurable relief" (1342a4-15 in Murray xxxiii). Murray proposes that this means that *katharsis* is brought about by dint of being immersed in emotions, which are unpleasurable at first, in order to eventually feel pleasure from their relief: "Aristotle here observes that people who are morbidly prone to 'enthusiasm" (that is, ecstatic frenzy of the kind associated with the orgiastic religious cults like that of Dionysus), can be relieved from their symptoms by the same kind of music as that which induces their frenzy. In other words, catharsis is a kind of homeopathic therapy that can be used in the treatment of neurotics" (xxxiii).

shocking spectacular effects caused by performative means and the emotional impact that results from the plot structure. For him the "grotesque [*to teratodes*]"[20] or monstrous effects of the spectacle do in fact "present not something frightening [*to phoberon*]", and thus have "nothing in common with tragedy" (1453b). And while he attests that the monstrous spectacle can indeed be a source of pleasure, he regards this kind of pleasure as unsuitable to the genre, arguing that it is not "the sort of pleasure appropriate to [tragedy]" (1453b).

It is difficult to decipher which pleasures and emotional effects would in fact be considered to be 'appropriate' by Aristotle. Whereas the above-cited passage from the *Poetics* seems to indicate that Aristotle condemns the utilisation of shocking effects as something too base for the noble genre of tragedy, his comparison of playwrights' writing style is not so clearly dismissive of shock-enhancing tactics. Aristotle's elaboration on the different versions of *Philoctetes* by Aeschylus and Euripides demonstrates a clear support of the latter's more visceral and 'shocking' phrasing:

> For example, the same iambic line was made by Aeschylus and Euripides with only one word replaced, a foreign one in place of the customary prevalent one, and while one appears beautiful, the other is of a dime-a-dozen sort. For Aeschylus in his *Philoctetes* made the line "The cancer that eats the flesh of my foot" but the other poet, in place of "eats" substituted "feasts on." (1458b)

The content-wise already repulsive depiction of a crawling animal feeding on Philoctetes' opened wound is further enhanced by Euripides' substitution of the neutral term "eat[ing]" with "feast[ing] on" (*ibid.*). The nauseating combination of one creature feeding on the other's decaying body parts, which already incorporates the disgust-evoking dichotomous pairing of life and death, is heightened by the rich associative potential of the word "feast on" in this context. The cancer "feasting on" the rotting wound implies not only the excessiveness of the action, but also links one creature's suffering to the other's festive joy, and what is more: all power relations and hierarchical structures seem to have been turned around in this description. Instead of man feeding on animals, the animal here feeds on the man, and whereas the cancer is attributed with typical human characteristics of feasting, Philoctetes has become reduced to a waste-product, a part of a parasite's 'dinner'.

---

20 We can assume a relation between *teratodes* and disgust here, because not only does Aristotle associate the monstrous with some kind of pleasure, but also because, like *dyschéreia* and *miasma*, the term is related to forms of taboos, crossings of social and sacred norms and borders. It is variously described as: "religious shock", "spectacular violence", "sensation", "strangeness", etc. (cf. Gould's *The Ancient Quarrel between Poetry and Philosophy*; Bernd Seidensticker's and Vöhler's "Gewalt und Ästhetik"; Eric Caspo's and William J. Slater's *The Context of Ancient Drama*).

Aristotle's reasoning of why he prefers Euripides' style of writing over Aeschylus' not only demonstrates his acknowledgement of the affective power of poetic language, but also restates his contention that mastery in craftsmanship can turn the representation of something appalling into a product of beauty (thereby contributing to solving the paradox of aversion). Yet the emotions evoked by the image of a cancer feasting on Philoctetes' foot are not likely to be the sensations of pity and fear, but more probably feelings of horror and disgust. Paradoxically, this aesthetic effect seems to be out of line with the affective impact Aristotle esteems 'appropriate' for the tragic genre.

In his description of the different fates that can befall tragic heroes, Aristotle distinctly places the evocation of repulsion in opposition to pity and fear: "it is clear first that decent men ought not to be shown changing from good to bad fortune (since this is neither frightening nor pitiable but repellent [*miaron*])" (1452b). Aristotle's differentiation of the aesthetic effects to be induced by 'proper' works of tragedy illustrates that despite his promotion of audiences' emotional involvement with tragic plays and his favouring of visceral stylistic devices (*poiesis*), from close up he seems to be just as dismissive of *miaron*, illogical and thus disgust-eliciting dramatic effects (*aisthesis*) as Plato. This becomes evident in Aristotle's further line of argumentation, where he tries to rebut Plato's contention that Sophocles' Oedipus is a throughly *miaron* character (cf. 1453a). His argument runs as follows: Had a character like Oedipus intentionally and in full knowledge performed incest and patricide, both intention and action would have "something repellent [*miaron*] about it and [would not be] tragic, since there is no suffering" (1543b, *phatos tragikon*). But because the character acts in ignorance "and once having acted make[s] the discovery, [...] there is nothing repellent (*miaron*) connected with it, and the discovery is awe-striking" (1454a; cf. also 1453b for a more detailed discussion of Sophocles' *Oedipus the King*).[21] Aristotle thus posits the desirable "awe-striking" effect[22] in direct opposition to a *miaron* effect. The latter is construed as an unambiguous reaction to witnessing evidently and intentionally 'bad' (i.e. illogical, unnatural) forms of behaviour. In order to account for a tragic (i.e. the hero needs to do something wrong, if he is to suffer) but logical and non-*miaron* chain of events in plays such as *Oedipus the King*, Aristotle then introduces the notion of *hamartia* (imperfection; 1453a) in the character to justify his 'tragic' (but non-*miaron*) deeds.

---

21 What is interesting is that Aristotle here argues that the best tragic plot would be one where the protagonist has no 'bad' intention, and, after realisation (*anagnorisis*), does not perform the deed (1454a). This scenario, however, is not reconcilable with Aristotle's previously mentioned preference for an unhappy ending. Gould regards this contradiction as yet another indication that Aristotle's ultimate aim was to keep tragedy as "free of *miaria* as a story of such violation could be" ("Oedipus" 62; my emphasis).

22 This effect is conceptualised as the so-called '*sublime*' in later theoretical approaches, which will be discussed in the ensuing chapter (cf. II; cf. also IV and V).

According to this approach, the fault (*hamartia*) thus lies in Oedipus not knowing whom he was sleeping with and who he was killing and not in his actions, which are tragic but nevertheless logical consequences of his former ignorance.

The problem that arises from this 'solution' is not only that if Oedipus were to remain a decent man, his downfall would not induce the desired emotions of pity and fear, but would need to be considered as *miaron* instead (according to Aristotle's own argument; cf. 1543b), but also that this scenario would make the whole *manoeuvre* of introducing *katharsis* as *miasma*'s counterpart and remedy somehow obsolete since there would be nothing left to the tragic plot that would be in any need of cleansing.

I.iii Summary

The preceding overview on the genesis of the dramatic genre from the cult of the Greek god Dionysus, its close link to the two disgust-related notions of *dyschéreia* and *miasma*, their presence in Attic drama, and Plato's and Aristotle's reflections on the topic show that the sensation of disgust already played an eminent role in artistic and theoretical approaches of the Greek *polis*. The ancient Greek concepts of *dyschéreia* and *miasma* cover a broad range of what we would today refer to as disgust or disgusting. Both are related to bad smells, categories of food and improper ways of eating; diseases and wounds linked to impurity and lack of hygiene, animalistic behaviour and features, and disregard or transgression of social and especially sacred rules. Their abstract manifestations furthermore both denote instances of, or reactions to, situations of logical paradoxes that cannot be solved by means of rational reasoning. In terms of family resemblance *dyschéreia* and *miasma* thus share a large amount of defining features; but the concept of *dyschéreia* seems to be slightly broader than the physio-moral dimensions of *miasma*, in that it does not necessarily contain the idea of pollution, filth, or dirt.[23] *Dyschéreia* can theoretically be caused by any kind of contradiction to what is logical.

However, despite similar domains of application for *miasma* and *dyschéreia*, there is one crucial difference (at least in Plato's theory): Whereas *miasma* is construed exclusively in negative terms as something utterly base, low, and part of humans' instinct-driven appetitive part of the soul, *dyschéreia* is conceptualised as a sensation that can also take on an important protective and thus positive role in society. According to Plato, the feeling of *dyschéreia* can work as a kind of embodied

---

23   Even though this seems to be *dyschéreia*'s main domain of application (cf. Theophrastus). Also, the linguistic root of the word (*dys*=not, *chér*=hand/touch) points to a close relation to the notion of *miasma*, since the washing of hands played an important role in ancient Greek rituals of cleansing (cf. Parker 289ff).

moral compass. Plato comes to this conclusion through his important observation that things which cause repulsion can also have an alluring or attracting effect. Since, in his view, these two simultaneous yet contradictory affective impulses can be neither regarded as products of *logos*, nor both be expressions of the appetitive part of the soul (law of non-contradiction), he establishes a tripartite structure of the soul and places the feeling of repulsion (*dyschéreia*) in the space in-between humans' natural drives (appetitive part of the soul) and their rational faculties (*logos*). This theoretical construction in many ways anticipates the Freudian understanding of disgust as a cultural emotion that keeps animalistic drives at bay (cf. III), as well as contemporary scientific research into the field of disgust, which finds that disgust developed "biologically *and* culturally" (Rozin and Haidt, "Domains of Disgust" 1; my emphasis; cf. IV.i).

Because of the emotion's protective properties, Plato advocated a sensitisation of *dyschéreia* as part of his educational programme to reinforce students' ability to distinguish between items that are "good" and "beautiful" and those that are disagreeable, "ugly", and "other" (401d-e). Theoretically, Plato could have transferred his insights regarding the educational merits of a disgust-training to the *mimetic* arts and argued that representations of appalling actions and persons could be used as a basis for teaching students to internalise the ability to discriminate between 'good' and 'bad' actions in characters. But Plato discusses the *mimetic* arts exclusively negatively in terms of *miasma*. He draws on the semantic field of excessive consumption to describe tragedy as "filling" and "stuffing" the lowest part of the psyche (606a). Plato's observation that tragedies commonly depict *miaron* characters and actions seems accurate. This becomes evident in the discussion of some exemplary ancient tragedies, where many of the examples Plato lists as cases of *miasma* feature prominently (e.g. incest, animalistic behaviour, excess). Since Plato believed the depiction of *miaron* persons and actions to be highly contagious and able to render infected recipients *miaron* themselves even into afterlife (cf. 621c), his banning of the tragic poets from an ideal state follows only naturally.

Plato's student Aristotle goes a long way to defend the emotional impact of tragic plays against Plato's accusation of their *logos*-polluting nature by introducing *miasma*'s linguistic opposite *katharsis* into the debate. He welcomes recipients' emotional 'infection', because in his understanding of the *mimetic* arts, tragedy basically functions as a medium for universal crisis-simulation which not only provides recipients with the material for training their emotional responses, but also with a safe space to 'let go' of negative feelings in a *cathartic* process. As useful as Aristotle's move of turning the tables in the debate about the ratio-affective effects of tragedy on recipients appears at first sight, at second sight, his theoretical approach turns out to be just as *logos*-based as his teacher Plato's and therefore incapable of incorporating anything that relates to *miasma* or *dyschéreia*, since these concepts essentially denote ambiguous states. Jonathan Lear argues that Aristotle's distinction between what is pitiable and frightening, and what is repellent (*miaron*), does in fact help us to understand what we today generally refer to as disgust or disgusting. He claims: "Disgust is something we feel in response to what we take to be a total absence of rationality" (329).

In summary, both Plato and Aristotle agree that *miaron* contents and effects need to be excluded from the dramatic genre, because they conceive of these as unexplainable by means of rational reasoning. But whereas Plato, who fears recipients' contagion with *mimetic miasma*, at least acknowledges *miaron* contents to be part of the psyche as well as of artistic practices, Aristotle tries to eliminate the irrationality that *miasma* encapsulates from existence within 'good people' and the 'noble' genre of tragedy altogether. Aristotle's 'defence of tragedy' against Plato's views of the *mimetic* arts' *miaron* nature here thus comes to bite its own tail, since once tragedy has been purged from anything *miaron*, the whole manoeuvre of introducing *katharsis* as *miasma*'s counterpart and remedy becomes obsolete; there would be simply nothing left in need of any such cleansing.

A *miasma*-free version of tragedy is also very far from reflecting the reality in fifth-century BC Greece, where *miaron* elements and ideas are employed ubiquitously by dramatists at the time (cf. Parker 13). As the brief discussions of *miasma* and *dyschéreia* in Euripdides' *Bacchae* and Sophocles' *Philoctetes* demonstrated, even the slightest glance at ancient drama shows that the kind of "rationalizing filters" (Sourvinou-Inwood 18) that Plato and Aristotle would like to see applied to the *mimetic* arts are ill-suited to do justice to the tragic genre. This is not surprising, since tragedy in fifth-century BC Greece was still deeply indebted to the god of illogical mess, Dionysus. In this way, Dionysus seems to serve as a much better patron to the dramatic genre than its 'theoretical' father Aristotle. If we were for instance to imagine the actions of the stock character of a classical tragedy, King Oedipus, how he learns that it was his father he killed and his mother he had sexual intercourse with: how likely would it be that our emotional response would be dominated by feelings of pity and fear? Would we not much more likely feel strongly disgusted?

II. *Ekel* in Eighteenth- & Nineteenth-Century Aesthetic Theory

Aristotle's *Poetics* and the aesthetic function of disgust came to play an important role in the artistic practice and theoretical approaches to the dramatic genre in the wake of the Enlightenment across Europe in the eighteenth and nineteenth century.[1] Especially Germany saw a flourishing of theoretical approaches to art as well as a rise in artistic productions occupied with the evocation of disgust.[2] In a revival 'hype' of the Greek classics, artists and scholars increasingly turned their interest to the connection between emotions and cognition in the reception of artworks, which eventually led to Alexander Gottlieb Baumgarten's establishment of 'aesthetics' as an independent academic discipline, aimed at finding rational explanations and rules for humans' sensual engagement with art works (cf. *Aesthetica*).

The sensation of disgust as a particularly visceral emotion became not only the aesthetic feature *par excellence* to feed a "growing hunger for strong sensations" that resulted from Western society for the first time in history experiencing the "burden of information and [...a] chaotic flood of stimuli" (Menninghaus 9).[3] It also

---

1   Winfried Menninghaus and others have researched this era in some detail. For a more thorough discussion of different theories concerned with the role of disgust in eighteenth-century aesthetic theory, cf. the titles listed by Menninghaus such as Herbert Dieckman's "Das Abscheuliche und Schreckliche in der Kunsttheorie des 18. Jahrhunderts", Jacques Derrida's "Economimesis", or Till Kuhnle's "Der Ernst des Ekels" (406).
2   Menninghaus claims that neither the French nor the English achieved a similar depth in systematically examining the role of disgust in aesthetic theories as the Germans (cf. 26). It needs to be pointed out though that research into, for example, British Romanticism, especially regarding the emergence of Gothic literature (e.g. Matthew G. Lewis' *The Monk*, 1796), would surely add to the understanding of aesthetic disgust, and has indeed received attention from psychoanalytically-oriented literary approaches that focus on the disgust-related notions of the *abject* and the *grotesque*. Cf., for example, Kelly Hurley's "Abject and Grotesque" in *The Routledge Companion to Gothic* (137-146).
3   For Menninghaus the "disgusting figures as an extreme subspecies of a modern aesthetics of the 'shocking'" which he views as a product of German Romanticism (9). For a detailed discussion cf. his chapter on "Disgusting Souls, Disgusting Times, and the Art of the Disgusting: The 'Romantic' Ubiquity of the Once-Tabood" (128ff.).

came to play a dominant role in major theoretical aesthetic approaches after Baumgarten's first attempt to systematically categorise the interrelation between feeling and thinking involved in humans' engagement with works of art. Two of the most famous German philosophers who reflected on the role of disgust in works of art were Immanuel Kant and Friedrich Nietzsche – who in many ways represent diametrically opposed theoretical approaches. Whereas Kant placed *Ekel* as antipodal to what he considered to be an aesthetic product, Nietzsche allocated a central role to the sensation, not only in his aesthetical reflections, but also in his works on epistemological, ethical, and existential affairs. Both approaches will be scrutinised after a brief and contextualising overview of the general sentiments and intellectual developments of the time.

The Senses & Disgust in Aesthetic Theory

As mentioned above, the establishment of aesthetics as an independent discipline is generally credited to Baumgarten, who was the first to develop a theory of art that focuses on the senses as being able to provide a form of knowledge that is analogous to the knowledge attained by rational thinking in his *Aesthetica* (1750-1758) and earlier writings. Baumgarten's theory differs from Plato's and Aristotle's, who both evaluated art first and foremost with regard to its impact on the rational faculties. Baumgarten instead postulates that through the senses, art can enable particular sensitive epistemological insights ("unteres Erkentnißvermögen", *Metaphysica* §§519-533), which allow for their own idiosyncratic form of judgement determined by what he calls 'taste' (*Geschmack*; cf. §§607-609). According to Baumgarten, taste enables us to gain a specific kind of knowledge that is emotionally induced (cf. §451).

One could assume that disgust, as an emotion that is strongly connected to both body and mind (as Plato already convincingly demonstrated in his discussion on *dyschéreia*; cf. I.i), would be of prime interest in an evaluation of the relation between cognition and emotions in works of art. But this is not the case in eighteenth-century aesthetic approaches, or rather: it is, but mainly in a negatively defining way. Whereas Plato and Aristotle excluded *miaron* contents from the arts because of their supposed *logos*-polluting impact, the focus in eighteenth-century theoretical evaluation shifts to the newly conceptualised notions of beauty and pleasure as defining features of art to which all that relates to *Ekel* is construed as the ultimate 'other'. Most of the major aesthetic approaches after Baumgarten, led by prominent figures such as Johann Gottfried von Herder, Gotthold Ephraim Lessing, Moses Mendelssohn, and Johann Adolf Schlegel, wanted to see *Ekel* excluded from what they conceived of as beautiful or fine arts (cf. Menninghaus 38).[4] In these theories, the two related arguments that were generally brought forward against the presence of *Ekel* in aesthetic products are the following:

First, *Ekel* is too 'base' for the fine arts. Mendelssohn, for example, claims that things that cause disgust can only be experienced by "the darkest of all senses, such as taste, smell, and touch" (in Menninghaus 38). Mendelssohn here establishes a hierarchy of the senses, with the 'low senses' (taste, smell, touch) being subordinate to the 'high senses', or as he calls them, the "more lucid senses" of seeing and hearing (cf. *ibid*.). Like Plato, who perceived the lowest part of the appetitive part of the soul as *miaron* "to an extreme degree" (589e, cf. I.i), Mendelssohn relates disgust to the darkest of all senses. And similarly to Plato's banishment of the tragic poets from an ideal state because of their engagement with dangerous *miaron* content, Mendelssohn contends that a sensation as dark, low, and base as disgust could by its nature not even be allowed to play "the slightest role in fine arts" and should thus be "unconditionally excluded" from the aesthetic realm (in Menninghaus 38). This argument to some degree resonates with Aristotle's dismissal of monstrous and spectacular stagings of tragic works, which he considered to be too base and thus inappropriate for the highly esteemed tragic genre (cf. 1453b, I.ii).

The second related argument brought forward against *Ekel*'s presence in works of art was that the sensation is too real to cause aesthetic pleasure. This argument is concerned with affective force ascribed to the feeling of *Ekel*. Mendelssohn claims that the mere idea (*blosse Vorstellung*) of something disgusting was sufficient to produce 'real' physical revulsion: "when lively enough, the mere idea of disgusting objects can, in itself and for itself, prompt revulsion – and indeed, notably, without the soul needing to imagine [*vorstellen*] the objects as real" (in Menninghaus 38).[5] Lessing renders Mendelssohn's thoughts on the topic at length in his seminal essay on *Laokoon. Über die Grenzen der Mahlerey und Poesie* (1766):

---

4   It must be noted here that the exclusion of disgust from aesthetic theories not only prevails in Germany, but is present in most European aesthetic theories of the time. Korsmeyer mentions for example the British philosopher Edmund Burke, who differentiates between terror and disgust when he says that "[t]hings which are terrible are always great; but when things possess disagreeable qualities, or such as have indeed some degree of danger, but of a danger easily overcome, they are merely odious, as toads and spiders" (46). In his writing on tragedy, David Hume likewise draws the line at disgust when he admits contents that arouse sorrow, terror, and anxiety, but speaks out against the depiction of "mingled brains and gore" on stage (in Korsmeyer 46).

5   According to Menninghaus, Schlegel was the first to formulate this argument in a footnote to his translation of Charles Batteux' *Les beaux arts réduits à un même principe* (1751), where he states that it is "disgust alone" that "is excluded from those unpleasant sensations whose nature can be altered through imitation" (34).

[Mendelssohn says that representations of fear,] of melancholy, terror, compassion, etc., can arouse our dislike only insofar as we believe the evil to be real. Hence, these feelings can be transformed into pleasant ones by recalling that it is an artificial illusion. But whether or not we believe the object to be real, the disagreeable sensation of disgust results, by virtue of the law of our imagination, from the mere mental image. Is the fact that the artistic imitation is ever so recognizable sufficient to reconcile the offended sensibilities? Our dislike did not arise from the supposition that the evil was real, but from the mere mental image of it, which is indeed real. Feelings of disgust are therefore always real and never imitations. (English transl. in Korsmeyer 47)

As this passage demonstrates, Mendelssohn singles out disgust as the one negative emotion that in contrast to other sensations such as terror, fear, and sadness cannot be transformed into the positive feeling of aesthetic pleasure. The premise of this argument is in accordance with Aristotle's idea of a simulated training of affections in which, in order to cause aesthetic pleasure, the perceived content of the artwork needs to be perceived as not being real. Disgust, according to Mendelssohn, breaks through these *mimetic* borders, as it is "always real" (in Menninghaus 38). In a majority of theoretical treatises on art at the time, *Ekel* was henceforth rejected on the basis of its alleged inaptness to overcome the paradox of aversion and conceptualised as being diametrically opposed to beauty and art.

Horror & Disgust in Eighteenth-Century Tragedy

The dramatist and drama theorist Gotthold Ephraim Lessing, like most of his contemporaries, disapproved of the depiction of *Ekel* in works of art. In his reasoning he goes even further than Aristotle, who had acknowledged that artistic craftsmanship and gain of intellectual insight could theoretically turn otherwise unpleasant objects into a source of pleasure when encountered in works of art (cf. 1448b), when he questions whether *anything* 'ugly' could be rendered pleasurable in artistic representation at all (cf. Korsmeyer 48).

Despite Lessing's strong theoretical opposition to the aesthetic representation of *Ekel* and anything that could be considered ugly, we find him elsewhere defending the appalling depictions found in, for example, Sophocles' *Philoctetes*. Lessing argues that the particular literary form of drama permits to show what would be considered too disgusting if presented by other, more visual aesthetic forms such as painting (cf. Korsmeyer 48). This argument is not convincing since drama as a form of art that is generally intended for performance on stage is even more vivid and visceral than aesthetic representations in paintings or other forms of the visual arts. Also, Lessing's own tragedies are far from eschewing descriptions that could cause recipients to recoil in disgust. In his *Miss Sara Sampson* (1755), for example, the main character Sara describes her phantasies of torturing her child in order to take revenge on a former lover in most stomach-turning detail:

> I will rearrange, distort and eradicate every feature that she has from you. With eager hand I will separate limb from limb, artery from artery, nerve from nerve, and will not cease to cut and burn even the smallest of these when she will have been reduced to no more than an insensitive carrion. (English transl. in Richter 441f.)

Like Pentheus' mother in Euripides' *Bacchae* or Sophocles' mother-figure in *Medea*, Lessing's Sara exhibits phantasies of the most abhorred nature: in her wish to kill the child that reminds her of the former union to its father, she does not rest at envisioning its simple extermination by death, but imagines the complete destruction of its human features in a dismantling of limbs and nerves and ensuing burning of even the smallest remains. These descriptions of a slaughtering filicide by far exceed the evocation of the Aristotelean tragic sensations of pity and fear. They include a number of social taboos, which are generally deemed disgusting: filicide, a mother wishing harm and destruction of her child instead of offering care and protection, the dismantling of the human body, and dehumanisation (slaughter like an animal, reduction to an inanimate object).

Lessing's friend Mendelssohn harshly criticised Lessing for his employment of these revolting depictions. Lessing answered to the criticism by introducing the term 'horror' (*Schrecken*) into the debate and thereby justifies his choice of content and wording in *Miss Sara Sampson*. He sidelines Mendelssohn's accusation by evading a direct discussion of disgust, and instead promoting the aesthetic effectiveness of 'horror', which he regards to have a potentially strong psycho-physical impact on the audience. Lessing claims that the evocation of horror, like fear (*phobos*), does in fact stand in the service of evoking the recipients' sympathy (*eleos*, pity, *Mitleid*), which he regards as tragedy's ultimate aim.[6]

---

6 Lessing claims that the emotions of *phobos* to be aroused by tragedy (cf. Aristotle 1449b) had commonly been mistranslated as '*Schrecken*' (*terreur*, terror) instead of fear (*Furcht*). He furthermore prioritises the evocation of *Mitleid* (sympathy/empathy/*eleos*) over the sensation of *Furcht* (fear), which he argues to merely stand in the service of the former. In line with Enlightenment ideals of his time, Lessing believes theatre's main function to be the education of its audience, to train it in *eleos* (empathy/sympathy): "The most sympathizing person is the best person, most disposed to all social virtues, to all manner of generosity" (in Richter 442).

II.i Kant's Aesthetic Ideas: Cognition, Sensation, Disgust

Like his ancient predecessors, Kant famously advocated the high value of the rational faculties and ferociously excluded the sensation of disgust from his aesthetic theory. In doing so, however, he ironically also laid down a detailed theoretical basis for the aesthetic interplay of cognition and affect which helped the development of a conceptualisation of an aesthetics of disgust in theories to come.

In Book I of his *The Critique of the Powers of Judgement* (1790),[7] the "Critique of the Powers of Aesthetic Judgement", Kant, like Baumgarten, acknowledges the necessity and value of the senses to unite with the cognitive faculties in order to produce a judgement of taste. He discusses the specific sensations that can be aroused by encounters with works of art and the way in which they can be converted into a principled system of cognitive universal judgement.

> Now the judgment of taste [...] determines the object [...] only through sensation. The animation of both faculties (the imagination and the understanding) to an activity that is indeterminate but yet, through the stimulus of the given representation, in unison, namely that which belongs to a cognition in general, is the sensation whose universal communicability is postulated by the judgment of taste. (§9)

In Kant's approach, 'taste' characterises the judgment's specific form of synthesis between feeling and knowing. For him, an aesthetic judgement is the result of the "free play of our mental powers" (*ibid.*) whereby an 'aesthetic idea' is construed which can be viewed as a counterpart to rational ideas.[8] As in Baumgarten's theory, for Kant, it is the senses/sensitivity (*Sinnlichkeit*) that allow for an understanding of works of art by means of being 'affected' by them.[9] Kant argues that an

---

7   All future references to Kant, unless indicated otherwise, refer to the Cambridge edition of *The Critique of the Powers of Judgment* (2002), edited by Paul Guyer and translated by Paul Guyer and Eric Matthews. German quotes are all taken from the Akademie-Ausgabe of Kant's *Gesammelte Schriften*, published by the Preussische Akademie der Wissenschaften (1900ff.).

8   Michel Chaouli convincingly argues that the relation between aesthetic and rational ideas is more complex than this comparison suggests. He points out that, according to previous writings of Kant, the possibility of an aesthetic idea is actually impossible, as 'ideas' are thought to be concepts "whose objects simply cannot be encountered in experience (*Lectures on Logic* 92)". Chaouli thus argues that aesthetic ideas should be taken as an "afterthought that occasions a rethinking of the beforethoughts" ("Surfeit in Thinking" 55ff.).

9   Kant already expressed his thoughts on sensual insights in the first of his three critiques (*The Critique of Pure Reason*). In the first paragraph of *Kritik der reinen Vernunft* (1781), which deals with transcendental aesthetics, he writes: "Die Fähigkeit (Receptivität), Vorstellungen durch die Art, wie wir von Gegenständen afficirt werden, zu bekommen, heißt Sinnlichkeit. Vermittelst der Sinnlichkeit also werden uns Gegenstände gegeben, und sie allein liefert uns Anschauungen; durch den Verstand aber werden sie gedacht, und von ihm entspringen Begrif-

aesthetic idea "stimulates so much thinking that it can never be grasped in a determinate concept [...] and sets the faculty of intellectual ideas (reason) into motion" (§49). An 'aesthetic idea' is thus construed as a particular sensual ability of gaining knowledge (*productives Erkenntnißvermögen, ibid.*). This aspect of Kant's theoretical approach is crucial because it allows us to think of aesthetic apprehension as a form of knowledge that surpasses articulation in plain language (i.e. *Erkenntniß* by means of logical thinking and linguistic expression).

Vital Disgust & the *Sublime*

Like his predecessors, Kant reflects on the 'paradox of aversion' in his discussion on how to judge artistic objects. He claims that "[b]eautiful art displays its excellence precisely by describing beautifully things that in nature would be ugly or displeasing. The furies, diseases, devastation of war, and the like can, as harmful things, be very beautifully described", and indeed cause pleasure (§48). This argument is reminiscent of Aristotle's statement that what is experienced as unpleasant in real-life encounters can cause pleasure in its artistic representation because of the excellency of craftsmanship on display (cf. 1448b). However, despite Kant's mentioning of (potentially disgusting) diseases as a possible source of aesthetic pleasure, disgust is explicitly excluded from his list of emotions capable of inducing 'aesthetic ideas'. Following the line of argumentation brought forward by Schlegel and Mendelssohn, Kant too contends that *Ekel* is the only "kind of ugliness that cannot be represented in a way adequate to nature without destroying all aesthetic satisfaction, hence beauty in art" (§48). Since in "this strange sensation [...] the object is represented as if it were imposing the enjoyment which we are nevertheless forcibly resisting", any representation of disgust "is no longer distinguished in our sensation [...] from the nature of the object itself, and it then becomes impossible for the former to be taken as beautiful" (§48). Kant defines *Ekel* as ultimate ugliness, a 'pure' opposition to beauty: "[N]othing is so much set against the beautiful as disgust" (*ibid.*).[10] For Kant too, *Ekel* thus needs to be expelled from the aesthetic realm

---

fe" (§1). For a more detailed discussion on Kant's 'aesthetic ideas' cf. also Anne Pollak (30ff.) or Cinzia Ferrini (140ff.).

10 This is an almost literal quote from Lessing's *Laocoon. An Essay on the Limits of Painting and Poetry* (cf. Menninghaus 103). For further discussion cf. Serena Feloj's "Is there a Negative Judgment of Taste? Disgust as the Real Ugliness in Kant's Aesthetics", where she offers a detailed discussion on the relation between beauty, the ugly, and the role of disgust in Kant's theory on aesthetic judgments (175 ff.).

on the basis of its transgression of *mimetic* borders. He calls it a "vital sensation",[11] which produces something 'real' and thereby presents, as Sianne Ngai phrases it, an "endpoint of mimetic art" (348).

In his chapter on the "Analytic of the Sublime" in Book II of the *Critique of the Power of Judgement*, Kant follows the aesthetic tradition of his time by differentiating between notions of the 'beautiful' (which causes 'simple' pleasure) and the so-called '*sublime*', which is used to describe the aesthetic experience of 'negative pleasures' (cf. paradox of aversion, I.i).[12] The term '*sublime*' is adopted from the scientific realm of chemistry, where it is used to describe the state of a substance when it passes directly from solid to gas (without the intermediate liquid state), to denote the pleasurable feeling ("vaporous", "boundless", and "expansive") that can be evoked by aesthetic manifestations of fear (Korsmeyer 132). Kant distinguishes between the aesthetic pleasures invoked by the beautiful and the *sublime* as follows:

> [The beautiful...] directly brings with it a feeling of the promotion of life [...], while [... the feeling of the sublime] is a pleasure that arises only indirectly, being generated, namely, by the feeling of a momentary *inhibition of vital powers* and the immediately following and all the more powerful outpouring of them; hence as an emotion it seems to be not play but something serious in the activity of the imagination. Hence [...], since the mind is not merely *attracted* by the object, but is also always reciprocally *repelled* by it, the satisfaction in the sublime does not so much contain positive pleasure as it does admiration or respect, i.e., it deserves to be called negative pleasure. (§23; my emphasis)

Kant characterises the *sublime* experience as a process where "vital powers" are first inhibited and then poured out. Kant describes the experience of contradictory feelings, of being simultaneously "attracted by the object" and "repelled by it" (*ibid.*) in a similar manner to Plato in his Leontius-narration (cf. I.i). However, Kant in no way relates these insights on the aesthetic effect of the *sublime*, which so closely resembles common experiences of confrontation with repulsive objects, to the sensation of disgust (just like Plato never transferred his reflections on *dyschéreia* to his estimation of *miasma* in works of art; cf. I.i).

Kant's 'variational' definitions of the 'beautiful' further complicate the attempt to give a consistent overview of his thoughts on disgust in relation to the *sublime*. Focusing on the *Critique of the Power of Judgement* alone, one feels compelled to simply

---

11   Kant discusses *Ekel* as a "vital sensation" in *Anthropology from a Pragmatic Point of View* (qtd. in Menninghaus 1). For further discussion on the meaning of vital sensations cf. Menninghaus (111f.).

12   The notion of the '*sublime*' is central to literary criticism of eighteenth-century Europe. The idea is credited to the ancient writer Longinus, whose text *On the Sublime* was discovered in the Renaissance and translated in 1674 (cf. Murray xliv). Cf., for example, Burke's *A Philosophical Enquiry into the Origin of Our Ideas of the Sublime and Beautiful* (1757).

'fill in the gap' and include the sensation of disgust within the realm of the *sublime*. This, however, becomes logically impossible if we take into account one of Kant's earlier differentiations between the beautiful and the *sublime* where he stated that the *sublime* "swells the heart and makes the attention fixed and tense [...], it exhausts", while the beautiful "lets the soul melt in soft sensation [...and] puts the feeling into a gentler emotion, which, however, where it goes too far, transcends into weariness, surfeit and disgust" (*Observations on the Feeling of the Beautiful and the Sublime* 79). If we take both of Kant's texts into account, disgust can be neither understood as part of the *sublime*, nor as oppositional to the beautiful, as it is actually defined as the latter's overdose.

Disgust & Consumption

Kant follows Baumgarten in focusing on the notion of taste (*Geschmack*) in his evaluation of art, whereby aesthetic effects became more closely intertwined with the semantic field of nourishment and consumption than they had been in ancient approaches (cf. I). Matters of food and consumption in the sense of being an emblem of refined taste featured prominently in the newly established academic discipline of aesthetics. 'Good' taste became a determinant of what was to be considered as beautiful and consumable, whereas 'bad' taste and 'distasteful' were construed as indicators of the ugly and associated with the reflex to vomit. A refined taste, one that is able to accurately distinguish between the beautiful and the ugly, was perceived as a sign of learning and cultivation and as a distinguishing marker from instinct driven animalistic appetites.[13]

In his *Anthropology from a Pragmatic Point of View* (1798), Kant directly links disgust to *Genuss* (consumption/pleasure) stating that *Ekel* "press[es] us to consume" (qtd. in Menninghaus 104). He thereby not only connects disgust to the semantic field of food and consumption, but also demonstrates that he acknowledges the attractive or alluring effect that revolting items elicit. Menninghaus claims that Kant was the first to incorporate the alluring or attractive (appetitive) aspect of disgust in his theoretical reflections, but this is not quite accurate, since already Plato discussed this ambiguity in his Leontius narration (cf. I.i). In view of the importance Menninghaus accords to Kant with regard to his conceptualisation of the alluring component of disgust reactions, it comes as a surprise that he does not

---

13 As already mentioned in the context of Mendelssohn's dismissal of disgust as a base and low sensation, we find in eighteenth-century theories of aesthetics and taste a clear categorical separation of the senses into those that were considered low (smell, taste, touch) and those that were seen as valuable because they were thought to enable epistemological insights (seeing and hearing; cf. Menninghaus 31).

address this two-sidedness when he discusses Kant's reflections on the relation between disgust and consumption. In his reading of Kant's usage of the German word '*Genuss*' (which, as Menninghaus' English translator notes, "ordinarily conveys a dual meaning of 'enjoyment' [...] and gustatory 'consumption'", 419), Menninghaus defines it as being used by Kant exclusively in the second sense as "[signifying] inner intake alone and precisely not enjoyment" (105). This interpretation may be in accordance with Menninghaus' understanding of Kantian disgust's "incompatibility with pleasure" (*ibid*.), but it falls short of accounting for Kant's argument that disgust, on the one hand, provokes an impulse "to free oneself of food through the shortest way out of the esophagus (to vomit)", thus an aversive reaction, but, on the other hand, also causes "mental pleasure" (qtd. in Menninghaus 106). Without stating it explicitly, Kant here seems to either indicate that the successful riddance of something appalling causes pleasure in the Aristotelean sense of a *katharsis* or that *Ekel* itself is able to induce pleasure.

This pleasure, however, needs to be differentiated from the kinds of pleasure we experience when engaging with works of art, since Kant earlier distinctly excluded *Ekel* from the aesthetic sensations. It is possible that Kant perceived the pleasure gained from *Ekel* as a kind of 'base' pleasure unsuitable for the more refined realms of human culture such as art; which would again mirror Aristotle's contention that for example the pleasures attained through monstrous spectacular staging need to be considered as inappropriate for the tragic genre (cf.I.ii).

Nevertheless Kant, like his ancient predecessors, repeatedly emphasises disgust's psychosomatic dimension by drawing on imagery from the semantic field of food consumption and surfeit when talking about matters of the mind:

> There is also, however, an intellectual consumption consisting in the communication of thought. But when such consumption is pressed upon us, even though it is not wholesome as nourishment for the intellect, the mind finds it repugnant. [...] Thus the natural instinct to get rid of such nourishment is by analogy called disgust (qtd. in Menninghaus 114).

What this passage once again demonstrates, is how freely the sensation of disgust is able to move between body and mind, thought and feeling, between physical nausea caused by overconsumption and feeling intellectual repulsion at abstract entities or problems. All of these phenomena are, for Kant, intrinsically linked to concepts of beauty and ugliness, with disgust presenting an overdose, or oversaturation of what is being consumed.

Disgust & Civilisation

Like Plato, Kant advocates a disgust-training in the education of the young and thereby notably identifies the crucial role disgust plays in the process of civilisation. Menninghaus thus argues that some time before the sociologist Norbert Elias[14] or psychoanalyst Sigmund Freud pointed to the importance of the sensation for establishing and keeping up the social order of so-called 'civilised' cultures, Kant already conceived of disgust as a "supreme cultural sign" (Menninghaus 108). In "Reflexionen zur Anthropologie", Kant connects disgust to dirt and a need for hygiene and cleanliness, arguing that:

> We [...] find that disgust at filth is only present in cultivated nations; the uncultivated nation has no qualms about filth. Cleanliness demonstrates the greatest human cultivation [*Bildung*], since it is the least natural human quality, causing much exertion and hardship. (qtd. in *ibid*.)

As a cultivator of human behaviour, Kant, like Plato before him, placed the sensitisation of disgust at the top of his list of educational goals to be attained (cf. *ibid*.). As Menninghaus points out, Kant maintains that unlike other strong emotions, such as hate, disgust does not invite for aggression, but is nevertheless able to "maintain decisive moral border-demarcations", which makes "the dark, sensory basis of *Ekel* serviceable for 'higher' goals" (*ibid*. 109). In the *Metaphysics of Morals*, Kant argues that, "[in] an aesthetics of morals [...], the feelings that accompany the constraining power of the moral law (e.g., disgust, horror, etc., which make moral aversion sensible) make its efficacy felt, in order to get the better of merely sensible incitements" (qtd. in *ibid*. 354). This position closely resonates with Plato's 'spirited part of the soul' and the function of disgust therein. Like Plato, Kant sees in disgust a possible agent to support and sharpen moral judgments by adding an emotive 'edge' or drive to rational assessments. But like Plato, Kant also failed to transfer his insights into disgust to his theoretical reflection on art.

---

14 Elias' *Über den Prozeß der Zivilisation* (1939) is commonly regarded as the first formal analysis and theory of civilisation.

II.ii Nietzsche's *The Birth of Tragedy*

'Wretched, ephemeral race, children of chance and tribulation, why do you force me to tell you the very thing which it would be most profitable for you *not* to hear? The very best thing is utterly beyond your reach: not to have been born, not to *be*, to be *nothing*. However, the second best thing for you is: to die soon.' (Nietzsche, *The Birth of Tragedy* 23; original emphasis)[15]

In *The Birth of Tragedy*, Nietzsche draws on Aristotle's *Poetics* (1449b) to argue for a genesis of tragedy from the essence of the Dionysian cult (20f.). In this provoking and often polemic early work, Nietzsche raises a number of eminent questions concerning art in general and tragedy in particular, as well as their relation to forms of social life and human nature. In his reflections, *Ekel* plays an important role through its function of subverting the foundations of occidental thinking from ancient times to Nietzsche's days. For Nietzsche, the aim of tragedy is nothing less than to enable insight into the tragic dimension of existence itself: that we are a "[w]retched ephemeral race, children of chance and tribulation" (23). According to Nietzsche, this insight comes at the price of causing disgust, but, as he furthermore points out, tragedy produced in the 'Dionysian spirit' can also console us with the tragic truth of our existence.

Apollonian & Dionysian Forces in Tragedy

The impact of Dionysus and his role in the genesis of the dramatic arts has already been pointed out in the previous chapter (cf. I). In his *The Birth of Tragedy*, Nietzsche introduces Dionysus' counterpart Apollo and locates the specific manifestation of Attic tragedy in the interplay between these two contradictory forces (cf. 76). The Greek god of sculpture, Apollo, embodies "the drive toward distinction, discreteness and individuality, toward the drawing and respecting of boundaries and limits; he teaches an ethic of moderation and self-control" (Geuss xi). Apollo is also associated with images and dreams, and is thus an emblem of appearances (*Schein*) and prophecies, of keeping order and procuring sense and meaning. Nietzsche describes the god as follows:

> He is the 'luminous one' through and through; at his deepest root he is a god of the sun and light who reveals himself in brilliance. 'Beauty' is his element, eternal youth his companion. But the lovely semblance of the world of dreams is his realm too; the higher truth, the perfection of these dream-states in contrast to the

---

15 All future references to Nietzsche, unless indicated otherwise, refer to the Cambridge edition of *The Birth of Tragedy* (2007), edited and translated by Raymond Geuss and Ronald Speirs.

only partially intelligible reality of the daylight world, raise him to the status of a prophetic god, but equally certainly to that of an artistic god. (120)

In Nietzsche's theoretical set-up, Apollo is not only the "artistic god", but functions in his reign over "lovely semblances" also as a kind of cover-up of reality. Nietzsche regards the Apollonian principle as a life coping device that is helping us to deal with difficult situations by means of (self-)deception in the name of a "higher truth". What Nietzsche refers to as "higher truth" is our ability to construct 'reality' and 'meaning' in a way that is comfortable for us. In summary, Apollo, the god of a "higher truth", deceives and cheats in order to present an intelligible world-view that helps humans to maintain mental stability.

Apollo's counterpart Dionysus, on the other hand, embodies the "drive towards the transgression of limits, the dissolution of boundaries, the destruction of individuality, and excess" (Geuss xi). In Nietzsche's theory, Dionysus is construed as the destroyer of the "usual barriers and limits of existence", leading to ecstasy and oblivion and insight into "the true essence of things" (40) – reality beneath the Apollonian appearances. According to Nietzsche, these insights into the "the true essence of things" result in a feeling of disgust at life and everyday reality.

For Nietzsche the seemingly contradictory artistic drives of the Dionysian and the Apollonian come together at "the high point of Hellenic culture" (121), the Attic tragedy. Like Aristotle, Nietzsche regards tragedy as the highest form of art, since it allows the spectator to experience the full spectrum of the human condition (cf. 28). The inherent duality between the representable Apollonian (form, concept, logic) and the unrepresentable Dionysian (unintelligible reality) also mirrors aspects of Kant's conceptualisation of 'aesthetic ideas'. But in contrast to his predecessors, Nietzsche decisively foregrounds the affective Dionysian component at work in aesthetic productions and experiences. He argues:

> We shall have gained much for the science of aesthetics when we have come to realize, not just through logical insight but also with the certainty of something directly apprehended (*Anschauung*), that the continuous evolution of art is bound up with the duality of the *Apolline* and the *Dionysiac*. (14; original emphasis)

By focusing and elaborating on the non-cognitive aspect of art, Nietzsche takes Kant's conceptualisation of ratio-affective aesthetic ideas one step further, and also discusses the physiological component of artistic apprehension. Josephine Machon points to the specific psycho-somatic nature of aesthetic appreciation in Nietzsche's theoretical set-up. She claims that art in a Nietzschean sense is to "(re)invigorate mind as body, where one 'hears with one's muscles, one even reads with one's muscles" (29).

Science, Tragic Knowledge, & Art

Nietzsche very much condemns post-Socratic Western philosophy's focus on the *logos*.[16] He maintains that Plato's aim to grasp the essence of things and existence by means of logical reasoning (science) is delusional (cf. 73). According to Nietzsche, *logos*-based science does little more than "make existence *appear* comprehensible and thus justified" (*ibid.*; my emphasis). He deems scientific practice as particularly problematic with regard to questions concerning death and human mortality. Nietzsche is convinced that neither reason nor knowledge can resolve the dilemma of coming to terms with mortality, wherefore science would ultimately run into a *cul-de-sac* and continue only in form of 'myth', "the necessary consequence, indeed intention, of science" (*ibid.*).[17]

For Nietzsche, only art is able to deal with humans' apprehension of death (i.e. the only true knowledge) appropriately: "[T]ragic knowledge, which, simply to be endured, needs art for protection and as medicine" (75). Repeatedly Nietzsche refers to this form of tragic knowledge as the wisdom of Silenus (*satyr* and teacher of Dionysus). According to Nietzsche's approach, the apprehension of death conveyed by the Dionysian principle not only constitutes humans' essentially tragic disposition, but also lies at the heart of the tragic genre. Nietzsche compares the person who has gained insight, the "Dionysiac man", to Shakespeare's Hamlet:

> [Both] have acquired knowledge and they find action repulsive, for their actions can do nothing to change the eternal essence of things; they regard it as laughable or shameful that they should be expected to set to rights a world so out of joint. Knowledge kills action; action requires one to be shrouded in a veil of illusion – this is the lesson of Hamlet, not that cheap wisdom about Jack the Dreamer who does not get around to acting because he reflects too much [...]. No, it is not reflection, it is true knowledge, insight into the terrible truth, which outweighs every motive for action [...]. Now no solace has any effect there is a longing for a world beyond death, beyond the gods themselves; existence is denied, along with its treacherous reflection in the gods or in some immortal Beyond. Once truth has

---

16   For Nietzsche, the image of the dying Socrates has become an emblem of Western enlightened society, because, as he polemically claims, Socrates was "the first man who was capable, not just of living by the instinct of science, but also, and this is much more, of dying by it" (73).

17   According to Nietzsche, the establishment of scientific myths caused the destruction of original myths (myths in their classical sense; e.g. stories of the gods), which helped mankind to deal with its tragic existence, offering a "mythical home, a mythical maternal womb" (109). Consequently, Nietzsche holds the scientific principle responsible for all ills of 'modern culture'. He predicts, however, that the scientific principle (reigning during his lifetime – Positivism) is "hurrying unstoppably to its limits, where the optimism hidden in the essence of logic will founder and break up" (75) and man will inevitably see "how logic curls up around itself at these limits and finally bites [...] its own tail" (*ibid.*).

been seen, the consciousness of it prompts man to see only what is terrible or absurd in existence wherever he looks; now he [...] grasps the wisdom of the wood-god Silenus: he feels revulsion. (40)

In this vivid description of Hamlet's encounter with "the innermost core of things" we learn how Hamlet gains insight into the "eternal essence of things", a "terrible truth", which nevertheless equips him with "true knowledge" (ibid.). This kind of 'truth' is not to be mistaken for the intelligible form of a 'higher truth' that Apollo embodies. In this passage, Nietzsche de-masks and mocks the Apollonian 'truth' as a kind of "cheap wisdom of Jack the Dreamer" (ibid.). The "terrible truth" Nietzsche here dramatically conveys is humans' knowledge of inescapable death, Silenus' wisdom: that the best would have been not to have been born and thus brought into the state of having to live with the knowledge of life ending in death, which makes all worldly activities ultimately futile; or at least to be able to die soon to shorten the period of death-inflected life. According to Nietzsche, the knowledge that life only has one goal, which is death, constitutes humans' essentially tragic disposition, and the feeling that results from the apprehension of this fact is ultimate and utmost *Ekel*, disgust at existence, life *per se*. The only remedy for this kind of existential repulsion, for Nietzsche, is art. He conceives of tragedy not only as a conveyer of the "terrible truth", but also as a 'saviour':

> Here, at this moment of supreme danger for the will, art approaches as a saving sorceress [*Zauberin*] with the power to heal. Art alone can re-direct those repulsive thoughts about the terrible or absurd nature of existence into representations with which man can live; these representations are the *sublime*, whereby the terrible is tamed by artistic means, and the comical, whereby disgust at absurdity is discharged by artistic means. (40; my emphasis)

In this passage, Nietzsche offers a concept of the *sublime* that is similar to Kant's, with the exception that he decisively advocates the representation of revolting content.

II.iii Summary

In the wake of an increased interest in classical Greek literature and philosophy, eighteenth- and nineteenth-century Germany proved highly productive in the establishment of an independent discipline of aesthetics, which more than the ancient Greeks focused on the sensual experience of humans' engagement with works of art. Yet, whereas the Aristotelean sensations of pity and fear were widely discussed and their evocation through works of drama strongly supported, *Ekel* once again came to be assigned a negative position in a majority of aesthetic treatises of the time.

Kant followed the trend of his time in emphasising the ways in which the senses engage with cognition in our perception of artworks. He refers to the insights gained from these experiences as 'aesthetic ideas', which he evaluates positively in their ability to "set [...] the faculty of intellectual ideas (reason) into motion" and "stimulate [...] so much thinking that [they] can never be grasped in a determinate concept" (§49). Kant refers to the pleasures we experience when encountering things in art that would in real life be the cause of negative feelings (fear, etc.) as *sublime*. But, despite his mention of (disgusting) diseases as a possible source of this kind of aesthetic pleasure, he explicitly excludes representations of *Ekel* from being able to induce it. Kant's contention is that disgust is too 'vital' to qualify as an aesthetic sensation able to induce pleasure, because whether disgusting things are encountered in real life or in the form of artistic representation, the negative feelings that are evoked are always *real* (cf. §48). This ability of disgust to transgress *mimetic* boundaries led Kant to place *Ekel* as oppositional to the aesthetic realm *per se*. Despite the clear devaluation of *Ekel* as a potentially meaningful and useful tool in artistic productions, Kant, like Plato before him, nevertheless highly valued the sensation's educational potential in the cultivation of human behaviour. He argues that *Ekel* could be seen as a sensual reaction to the trespassing of moral laws, which would then strengthen the cognitive evaluation of such incidents. This claim closely resonates with how Plato conceived of the so-called spirited part of the soul and the function of disgust therein. Like Plato, Kant saw in disgust a possible agent to support and sharpen moral judgments by adding an emotive 'edge' (or drive) to rational assessments. But like Plato, Kant also failed to transfer these insights into his theoretical reflections on the value of our engagement with works of art. Nevertheless, Kant's elaboration on sensual engagement with aesthetic products and his understanding of the *sublime* effects of art offer a productive model to explain the interaction of emotions and cognition at work in our perception of art, which is particularly potent for an integration of the sensation of disgust. More than any other emotion, disgust can be argued to fit Kant's description of a ratio-affective state where "the mind is not merely attracted by the object, but is also always reciprocally repelled by it" (§23), which in his view initiates the aesthetic experience of *sublime* pleasure.

Even Nietzsche, who had much to say against Kant's metaphysical idealism, acknowledges the latter's contribution to the philosophical field of epistemology: "the healthy bit of sensualism that he took over into his theory of knowledge" (*Dawn* 4). In *The Birth of Tragedy*, Nietzsche brings this "healthy bit of sensualism" to centre stage in his argument for an ideal form of tragedy that is modelled on the Attic tragedy of ancient Greece. For Nietzsche this ideal form of art is accomplished when the contradictory forces of the Apollonian (form, concept, logic) and the Dionysian (chaos, in-between, transgression) come together, since only a representation of both can mirror the full spectrum of the human condition and thus enable recipients to gain insight into the "true essence of things" (40). The collaboration of a rational Apollonian force and a more instinctive and ambiguous Dionysian drive bears some resemblance to Kant's conceptualisation of 'aesthetic ideas'. But whereas Kant appears to value the 'aesthetic idea' especially for its ability to induce further processes of rational thinking, Nietzsche instead contends that this kind of aesthetic experience induces a "certainty of something directly apprehended" (14). For Nietzsche, this apprehended certainty, "the true essence of things" (40), always addresses our most basic human conflict: Silenus' wisdom – the knowledge about our inevitable mortality. In Nietzsche's approach, apprehension of this fact is intrinsically linked to the emotional effect of *Ekel*.

Tragedy, in Nietzsche's point of view, essentially engages with metaphysical *Ekel* in two ways, first as cause and then as remedy: It provokes existential disgust by confronting us with our inherently ambiguous condition through the interplay of Apollonian and Dionysian forces, but then it is also the only kind of "medicine" available to console us with this "tragic knowledge" (75). According to Nietzsche, only art is able to "re-direct those repulsive thoughts about the terrible or absurd nature of existence into representations with which man can live" (40) and turn them into something *sublime*. When Nietzsche states that through the *sublime* "disgust at absurdity is discharged by artistic means" (40), it becomes clear that he not only, like Kant, conceives of the *sublime* as the provider of some kind of aesthetic pleasure, but that he also understands it to enable the possibility of an emotional *katharsis* in the Aristotelean sense.

III. The Drama of Existential Disgust & Psychoanalysis

> [A]s in true theater, without makeup or masks, refuse and corpses *show me* what I permanently thrust aside in order to live. These body fluids, this defilement, this shit are what life withstands, hardly and with difficulty, on the part of death. There, I am at the border of my condition as a living being. (Kristeva, *Powers of Horror* 3; original emphasis)[1]

In the first half of the twentieth century, psychoanalysis and existential philosophy were two prominent disciplines occupied with what Nietzsche had termed the 'Silenian wisdom': the knowledge of life's finiteness and the futility of actions – the tragic core of human existence. In an often determined anti-aesthetic approach, philosophy and art addressed this tragic core, allowing much closer contact to, not to say indulgence in, the sensation of disgust. Famous artists and intellectuals were seeking to create what Menninghaus terms an "affirmative aesthetic of the repellent" (343). This became especially apparent in the existentialist theories and avant-garde writings of Jean-Paul Sartre and Georges Bataille, as well as in the newly developed discipline of psychoanalysis by Sigmund Freud and his successors Jacques Lacan and Julia Kristeva. Because Freud's writings had a major impact on all of the above-named artists and scholars, a brief overview of his most important observations on the topic of disgust will be given at the beginning of this chapter. The ensuing sub-chapters will take a more detailed look at the "structure of feeling" (Williams 128) of the Interwar period in Europe and its aesthetic manifestation in relation to disgust in leading existentialists' works of the time, as well as the psychoanalytical developments that accompanied, reacted to and reflected on these changes, most importantly Kristeva's conceptualisation of the disgust-related notion of *abjection*.

---

[1] All future references to Kristeva, unless otherwise indicated, refer to Leon S. Roudiez' translation: *Powers of Horror. Essay on Abjection* (1982).

Sigmund Freud: Disgust as the Basis of Civilisation

In psychoanalytical theory, disgust plays an eminent role. Freud, like Kant and Nietzsche, locates disgust at the basis of human civilisation and identifies it as the "source of morality" (in Menninghaus 185). Freud construes disgust as a social mechanism which functions to suppress *libidinal* (i.e. animalistic/natural) drives in order to distinguish humans from their animalistic ancestry. For him, disgust (alongside the related sensation of shame) is the cultural feeling *par excellence*, which allowed for the establishment of culture in opposition to the natural world. He came to this conclusion through the observation that neither animals nor young children seemed to experience disgust (cf. *Unbehagen* 65). By arguing that disgust marks the point of separation between nature and culture, Freud challenged the scientific trend of his time, which generally followed Charles Darwin's contention that disgust was one of six basic instinctive emotions, a thesis laid out in Darwin's seminal work *The Expressions of Emotions in Man and Animals* (1872).

Freud argues that disgust developed as a result of humans' unique upright walking position, which brought about a significant change in the functions of the senses. He claims that because of the further distance to the ground, olfactory stimuli, especially sexual ones, were replaced by visual ones. According to Freud, from then on, orientation via smell and all things related to it (sexuality, excrements, etc.) became associated with animalistic and thus 'lower desires' that needed to be repressed into the unconscious to allow for humans' 'cultivated' behaviour and lifestyle (cf. *Unbehagen* 64f.). What makes Freud's theoretical groundwork on the topic of disgust important for this study is the fact that he explicitly addresses the sensation's unique relation to desire and attraction (*libido*; cf. Menninghaus 190). Freud's approach bears some resemblance to Plato's reflection on the simultaneous attraction (placed in the appetitive/desirous part of the soul) and aversion experienced by Leontius at the sight of recently deceased bodies (*dyschéreia*; cf. I.i). The connection Freud draws between *libido* and disgust helps us to understand the sensation's inherent two-sidedness.

Tragic Society & the Death Drive

For Freud the human condition, as one that is inherently torn between natural and cultural demands, is ultimately 'tragic'. He maintains that the constant repression of animalistic/natural drives can lead to serious psychological illnesses. In *Civilisation and its Discontents* (1930), he argues that the multitude of cultural restrictions imposed by the society of his time was the cause for a rising number of perversions and neuroses among his contemporaries (passim).

According to Freud, the main object of repression is death, which he viewed as being linked to humans' desires and drives. In *Beyond the Pleasure Principle* (1920), he developed the idea of a so-called 'death-drive' (*Thanatos*) as an oppositional force to the life-affirming pleasure principle (*Eros*). There he argues that death was not only the logical consequence of life, but also reminiscent of its origin: "[E]verything living dies from causes within itself, and returns to the inorganic, [wherefore] we can only say '*The goal of all life is death*', and, casting back, '*The inanimate was there before the animate*'" (V.7; original emphasis). For Freud the death-drive is thus a return to an original state prior to forms of individuation. In *Civilization and its Discontents*, he confidently came to the conclusion that: "The meaning of evolution of civilization is no longer obscure to us. It must present the struggle between Eros and Death, between the instinct of life and the instinct of destruction, as it works itself out in the human species" (73). This struggle for civilization commonly manifests itself in the feeling of disgust, which, according to Freud, connects humans simultaneously to their natural drives and to their sentiments as 'cultured' members of the society they live in.

III.i Tragic Existence: Disgust as an Antidote

The Interwar period of the early twentieth century saw an unprecedented explosion of radical forms of European art, many of which dealt with repulsive contents such as excrements, decay, and aberrant forms of sexuality. These new forms of art bore witness to a time of profound change in society's 'structure of feeling' and found expression in a multitude of avant-garde movements, such as Existentialism, Surrealism, Dadaism, and Expressionism, which were to a large degree influenced by Freud's psychoanalytical findings.

According to the cultural theorist Sylvère Lotringer, this transformation of the European mindset not only resulted from the devastating experience of the First World War, but also from the immense "leap of technology", which catapulted "rural, pre-industrial society" into the "full-fledged madness of a modernity" (n.p.). During the First World War, Europe's citizens for the first time experienced the impersonal 'mass destruction' of more than 17 million people by mechanical weapons. Many came out of the war "shell shocked", which led to a general numbing down and loss of affection across society (*ibid*.). For Lotringer this unprecedented insensitivity not only explains the immediate rise of political fascism, the "brown plague" (*ibid*.), but also the emergence of radical and sensational agendas in the arts, predominantly aimed at making people 'feel' and thereby offering an effective antidote to the rising extremist movements of the time. He argues that for most of the avant-garde artists, the goal was to re-unite body and mind, and to liberate suppressed feelings (cf. *ibid*.). In order to accomplish this task, artists of the time aimed to reach beneath the surface of 'scientific truths' and otherwise 'cultured' forms of existence, down to the most base and repulsive core of what it means to be human. In the following sections, I will briefly introduce two prominent theoretical and aesthetic approaches of the time that discuss the function of art with regard to repulsive contents and effects.

Jean-Paul Sartre: Disgust at Slimy Existence & the Feminine

In *Being and Nothingness. An Essay on Phenomenological Ontology* (1943),[2] Sartre explores the tragic conflict of humans as being situated in-between the demands of nature and culture by comparing this state to the qualities of the viscous (*visqueux*). Sartre thus approaches disgust-reactions towards existence through an extended metaphor of slime. In a nutshell his claim is that, just like slime, the existential condition clings to humans, but can never be completely brought under control. Camille Paglia aptly points to the similarity between Sartre's notion of the viscous and Nietzsche's understanding of the Dionysian spirit when she describes Sartre's slime as "Dionysus' swamp" (93).

According to Sartre, existence disgusts us because it cannot be grasped. Like slime it is formless and "ambiguous" (607), which resembles the difficult relation we as humans experience between our nature (=In-itself) and our consciousness (=For-itself).[3] For Sartre disgust is a natural reaction to humans' essential conflict with existence. It can be evoked by a wide range of actions and objects which in one way or another relate to this conflict: "A handshake, a smile, a thought, a feeling can be slimy", as well as, "oysters" and "raw eggs" (604ff.), "snails leeches, fungus, and molluscs; bogholes and quicksand; liars, weaklings, and deceivers – everything 'base'" (Heinämaa 157). Similar to Nietzsche's conception of the Dionysian principle, Sartre argues that in the in-between of the slimy, all distinctions between nature and culture, the physical and the psychological, are being transcended (cf. 611f.).

Sartre furthermore connects the experiences of slimy encounters with power relations and to some specific qualities that he attributes to the different genders.[4] He compares the inherent ambiguity of slime and sliminess to female attributes

---

2   All further references to Sartre, unless otherwise indicated, refer to Hazel E. Barnes' translation of *Being and Nothingness* (2001).

3   The notions of the 'In-itself' (=the thing itself, materiality, nature, pure being, objects in the world) and the 'For-itself' (=ego, imaginary, human consciousness) are central in Sartre's existentialism. Cf. the second chapter of *Being and Nothingness* (73-220) for an elaboration of these terms.

4   An approach which has gained Sartre much critique, especially from feminist scholars. The most famous critique appeared in 1973 in an article called "Holes and Slime: Sexism in Sartre's Psychoanalysis" by Margery Collins and Christine Pierce.

and qualities: "It is a soft, yielding action, a moist and feminine sucking" (609). In opposition to these 'soft' female qualities (="between two states [solid and liquid]", 607), Sartre places the qualities of the "reassuring inertia of the solid" (609), which he associates with power, possession, and freedom: "If an object which I hold in my hands is solid, I can let go when I please; its inertia symbolizes for me my total power; I give it its foundation, but it does not furnish any foundation for me" (608). Slime, on the other hand, "gives us at first the impression that it is a being which can be possessed [...], but] at the very moment when I believe that I possess it, behold by a curious reversal, it possesses me" (608). The 'classical' power relations between male (solid) and female (soft, 'slimy') are here reversed; the female only gives the impression of being controllable. Sartre vividly describes how he perceives the seductive power of 'feminine slime':

> [I]t draws me to it as the bottom of a precipice might draw me. There is something like a tactile fascination in the slimy. I am no longer the master in arresting the process of appropriation. It continues. In one sense it is like the supreme docility of the possessed, the fidelity of a dog who *gives himself* even when one does not want him any longer (609; original emphasis).

The 'swallowing up' of the subject by slime, which in Sartre's theory not only represents the feminine, but also our essentially tragic human condition, is here described as, on the one hand, threatening in its taking over control and agency, but, on the other hand, also experienced as attractive ("it draws me to it") and fascinating, which, once acknowledged, leads to some kind of consolation with one's powerless state ("give in", "docility").

These descriptions once again illustrate the paradox and inherently ambiguous affective reactions commonly experienced towards repulsive objects and actions, the simultaneous attraction and aversion. What is threatening or compromising about the 'feminine slime' and thus met with aversion in Sartre's approach is its relatedness to the pure nature or materiality (the In-itself), which compromises consciousness (the For-itself) once it has taken over control.[5] But, the feminine in Sartre's theory does not only represent the limits of thoughts and concepts of self (For-itself) and thereby the limits of humans' rational faculties with regard to addressing the most essential questions of existence. The feminine also incorporates a life-affirming component, an "appeal to being" (613). In its 'appeal to being' (=life), slime and the feminine are attractive and connect humans to their essential nature, their own sliminess.

---

5   Sartre goes so far as to claim that slimy substances are in fact the "sickly sweet feminine revenge" of the In-itself (610).

> A sugary sliminess is the ideal of the slimy; it symbolizes the sugary death of the For-itself (like that of the wasp which sinks into the jam and drowns in it). But at the same time the slimy is myself, by the very fact that I outline an appropriation of the slimy substance. That sucking of the slimy which I feel on my hands outlines a kind of continuity of the slimy substance in myself. (609)

Sartre's vivid rendering of a "sugary sliminess", a "sugary death" illustrates how slime brings us into contact with the contingency of being, humans' nature and material existence, or, in Sartre's words, the facticity of the In-itself. The In-Itself is just as essentially part of the human constitution as the constant effort to consciously gain control over it by means of the For-itself. According to Sartre's approach, slime and the feminine show us *what we are*. Sartre describes the insight gained from 'slimy' experiences as a "non-positional apprehension of a contingency which [one] is, as a pure apprehension of self as a factual existence" (343).

For Sartre, like Nietzsche before him, the existential fact of contingency can best be expressed, as well as overcome, or at least endured, by means of art. In his seminal existentialist novel *Nausea*, Sartre describes the soothing effect that Jazz music has on the nauseated protagonist Antoine Roquentin, who finds some form of almost magical consolation with existence through it.

> The Negress sings. Can you justify your existence then? Just a little? I feel extraordinarily intimidated. It isn't because I have much hope. But I am like a man completely frozen after a trek through the snow and who suddenly comes into a warm room. (143)

Jazz is here construed, like Nietzsche's Attic tragedy, as a form of art that offers not only consolation, but also a kind of understanding that is beyond representation in rational terms (cf. also Kant's 'aesthetic idea', II.i). Roquentin tells us how he at first feels "completely frozen" – a death-like state that is induced and then overcome by art, offering warmth and a 'home' for the self in contact with its essence.

Georges Bataille: *Heterology*: The Science of Excrements

Like his contemporary Sartre, Georges Bataille – *enfant terrible* of his time[6] – argues that there is "nothing [...] more important for us than that we recognize that we are bound and sworn to that which horrifies us most, that which provokes our most intense disgust" ("Attraction and Repulsion II" 114); a statement that clearly marks his debt to Nietzsche and Freud (cf. II.ii, III). Bataille, however, not only adopts

---

6   Bataille was in his times probably best known for his explicit erotic fiction. Today, however, he is also generally regarded as one of the driving forces of early Poststructuralism (cf. Grauer 2).

his predecessors' theoretical propositions regarding the significance of disgust for cultural development, he also radically implements these ideas in his own aesthetic reflections and productions.[7]

Following Nietzsche in the denunciation of *logos*-based philosophical approaches since Socrates, Bataille suggests an alternative theoretical model which he refers to as *'heterology'*: the "science of what is completely other", "the science of excrement" (i.e. *"Scatology"*; cf. "Value of de Sade" 102).[8] Bataille employs the category of the *'heterogeneous'* to account for phenomena in society that are treated as *'foreign'* (e.g. the *"foreign body"* – *"daz ganz Anderes* [sic]" 94). According to Bataille, foreign elements are all linked to the human impulse of excretion, which he relates to actions and substances such as: faeces, sex, menstrual blood, decomposing bodies, and death (cf. 94).

In opposition to the *heterogeneous*, Bataille places the category of *homogeneity*: the human impulse of appropriation, which is in its "elementary form [...] oral consumption, considered as communion (participation, identification, or assimilation)" (95). Compared to the *heterogeneous*, the *homogeneous* is relatively static and linked to conventions and social rules. Similar to the 'scientific principle' as well as the Apollonian force introduced by Nietzsche, Bataille argues that the *homogeneous* impulse for appropriation results in "replacing *a priori* inconceivable objects with classified series of conceptions or ideas" with the goal to establish "the *homogeneity* of the world" (96). Condemning the shallow and 'false' truths of the *homogeneous*, Bataille calls out for a radical turning point in the application of philosophy, where the *heterogeneous* is to take lead. His "Heterological Theory of Knowledge" is therefore worth quoting at length:

> When one says that heterology scientifically considers questions of heterogeneity, one does not mean that heterology is, in the usual sense of such a formula, the science of the heterogeneous. The heterogeneous is even resolutely placed outside the reach of scientific knowledge, which by definition is only applicable to homogeneous elements. Above all, heterology is opposed to any homogeneous representation of the world, in other words to any philosophical system. The goal of such representations is always the deprivation of our universe's sources of excitation and the development of a servile human species, fit only for the fabrication, rational consumption, and conservation of products. But the intellectual process automatically limits itself by producing of its own accord its own waste products,

---

7   Cf. for example Bataille's works *Histoire de l'oeil* (1928), *L'Anus solaire* (1931), or *Les larmes d'Éros* (1961), which were translated into English only much later.
8   Bataille suggests that "the term agiology would perhaps be more precise, but one would have to catch the double meaning of agio (analogous to the double meaning of sacer), soiled as well as holy" (102).

thus liberating in a disordered way the heterogeneous excremental element. Heterology is restricted to taking up again, consciously and resolutely, this terminal process, which up until now has been seen as the abortion and the shame of human thought.

In that way it [heterology] leads to the complete reversal of the philosophical process, which ceases to be the instrument of appropriation, and now serves excretion; it introduces the demand for the violent gratifications implied by social life. (97; original emphasis)

Like Nietzsche before him, Bataille postulates an approach to theoretical reflection that is able to respond to those moments in life when "the effort at rational comprehension ends in contradiction" (99). And like the former, Bataille sees a great potential for epistemological insight from the experience of disgust in art. Similar to Nietzsche's conceptualisation of the Dionysian as a counterpart of the Apollonian and Sartre's notion of slime, Bataille introduces the notion of *'informe'* (i.e. formless) as a philosophical and artistic mode that counters idealistic and thus *homogeneous* aesthetic forms. In an entry for the 'critical dictionary' of the surrealist journal *Documents* (1929-30), he defines *informe* as "a term that serves to bring things down in the world, generally requiring that each thing have its form. What it designates has no rights in any sense and gets itself squashed everywhere, like a spider or an earthworm" ("Formless" in *Visions of Excess* 31).[9]

Through the *informe* paradox and ambiguous contents can be realised. The *informe* is thus a mode that enables the aesthetic representation of "that which horrifies us most, that which provokes our most intense disgust" ("Attraction and Repulsion II" 114). In "The Inner Experience", Bataille explains how through the realisation of the *informe* art can function as a "middle term" between the rationally comprehensible and the unrepresentable: "it conceals the known with the unknown" (112). As in Nietzsche's concept of the Dionysian, for Bataille the binary relation between life and death, as well as a consolation with this ambiguity, lies at the heart of such aesthetic representations: "[T]hrough [poetry] I escaped the world of discourse which had become the natural world for me; with poetry I entered a kind of grave where the infinity of the possible was born from the death of the logical

---

9   The whole entry reads: "A dictionary begins when it no longer gives the meaning of words, but their tasks. Thus formless is not only an adjective having a given meaning, but a term that serves to bring things down in the world, generally requiring that each thing have its form. What it designates has no rights in any sense and gets itself squashed everywhere, like a spider or an earthworm. In fact, for academic men to be happy, the universe would have to take shape. All of philosophy has no other goal: it is a matter of giving a frock coat to what is, a mathematical frock coat. On the other hand, affirming that the universe resembles nothing and is only formless amounts to saying that the universe is something like a spider or spit" ("Formless" in *Visions of Excess* 31).

world" (111). The 'grave of the logical world' entered via poetry not only entails death, but also offers the comfort or hope of a birth of "the infinity of the possible" (ibid.).

III.ii Psychoanalysis: Approaching *Abjection*

> There looms, within abjection, one of those violent, obscure revolts of being, directed against a threat that seems to emanate from an exorbitant outside or inside, hurled beyond the scope of the possible, the tolerable, the thinkable. It lies there, quite near, but it cannot be assimilated. It beseeches, worries, and fascinates desire, which, nevertheless, does not let itself be seduced. Apprehensive, desire turns aside; disgusted, it rejects. (Kristeva, *Powers of Horror* 1)

Julia Kristeva states that she borrows the term *abjection* from Bataille who defines it as "the inability to assume with sufficient strength the imperative act of excluding abject things" (qtd. in *ibid.* 56). Whereas Bataille does not elaborate on the term in much detail, Kristeva's notion of *abjection* – "a vortex of summons and repulsion" (1) – most convincingly highlights the eminent role of disgust in the development of the human subject as well as in its aesthetic manifestations. It is therefore worthwhile to represent her theoretical approach in some detail. In *Revolution in Poetic Language* (1974),[10] Kristeva presents a theory of language that is at the same time a theory of subjectivity. In order to understand her concept of the disgust-related notion of *abjection*, it is instructive to first take a look at her conceptualisation of the psychosocial subject formation within the orders of the so-called 'semiotic' and the 'symbolic' realms of existence.[11]

The Semiotic & the Symbolic

For Kristeva the semiotic and the symbolic are two intertwined modalities of the signifying process. She traces the term 'semiotic' back to its Greek source (*semeion*), defining it as a "distinctive mark, [...] trace, figuration" (*Revolution* 25), and employs it to describe a primordial site of communication. In the semiotic, the infant that has not yet joined the world of linguistic communication is closest to the pure materiality of existence. It is, however, not without articulation. Kristeva claims

---

10   All future references to Kristeva's *Revolution in Poetic Language* (1985) refer to Margaret Waller's translation.
11   Extracts of an earlier version of the ensuing summarising passages on Kristeva's theory of *abjection* were also used as background information for articles on *abjection* and religious imagery in Sarah Kane's *Blasted* and on the role of disgust in Samuel Beckett's novel *Molloy* (cf. Ablett, "Genesis" 251-53; "Molloy" 89-92).

that the subject's cries and laughter, sound and touch are semiotic forms of its "drives and their articulations" (43). The semiotic can be viewed as a "psychosomatic modality of the signifying process" (96):

> [Q]uantities of energy move through the body of the subject who is not yet constituted as such and, in the course of its development, they are arranged according to the various constraints imposed on this body – by family and social structure. In this way the drives, which are energy charges as well as 'psychical' marks, articulate what we call a *chora*: a nonexpressive totality formed by the drives and their stases in motility. (25)

The modes of articulation of the semiotic (*chora*) are pre-verbal and thereby by definition a-symbolic. Noelle McAfee describes the semiotic as the "extraverbal way in which bodily energy and affects make their way into language" (17). According to Kristeva, the semiotic can, for example, be found in: intonation, music, dance, or other forms of non-linguistic articulation, such as poetic language. Kelly Oliver explains that these "rhythms and tones do not *represent* bodily drives; rather bodily drives are *discharged* through rhythms and tones. [... The] semiotic element is 'translinguistic' or 'nonlinguistic'" ("Crisis of Meaning" 38; original emphasis)[12].

The symbolic, on the other hand, represents the linguistic realm of producing meaning (Kristeva, *Revolution* 24). For Kristeva the symbolic order encompasses "messages or objects that are transmitted in a social contract of communication" (38). Kristeva argues that the symbolic and the semiotic modes of articulation are always manifest in a dialectic relationship, which means that the semiotic stage is not simply left behind once the subject enters the symbolic. Oliver explicates the meaning of this dialectic interaction as follows: "The interdependence of the symbolic and semiotic elements of signification guarantees a relationship between language and life, signification and experience, and between body (*soma*) and soul (*psyche*)" ("Crisis of Meaning" 38; cf. also *Portable Kristeva* xvi). The different combinations of the semiotic and symbolic modes of expression designate the various types of discourse we find. Kristeva distinguishes between *genotext* and *phenotext* (cf. *Revolution* 86ff.). A scientific discourse will aim at close adherence to the symbolic order (*phenotext*), whereas a poetic discourse will be closer to the emotive function of language (*genotext*).[13]

---

12 For further elaboration on the semiotic cf. also Stacey Keltner (22f.) or McAfee (21f.).
13 Josephine Machon discusses these two forms of text in some detail (cf. 72f.).

Abjection

In *Powers of Horror. An Essay on Abjection*, Kristeva extends her theoretical groundwork on the process of signification and its interrelation to subject formation by introducing the notion of the '*abject*'.[14] She defines *abjection* as "a vortex of summons and repulsion" (1), which, she argues, induces the infant's separation from its mother and its entry into the stage of language. Kristeva maintains that the experience of *abjection* is necessary for the child to develop borders in order to gain a sense of self, to experience itself as different from its surroundings and the m/other. She locates the emergence of subjectivity within the intrinsically connected orders of the pre-verbal stage and the symbolic stage of psychosexual development and gives special attention to the experience which the 'subject in process' (cf. *Polylogue* 55-106) undergoes during this stage of separation. Kristeva asks for the infant's motivation to initiate the traumatic experience of separation from the mother and comes to the conclusion that this can only be caused by (while at the same time leading to) an ambiguous experience of rejection which she comes to call '*abjection*'. She poetically describes the confrontation with *abjection* as encountering

> a 'something' that I do not recognize as a thing. A weight of meaninglessness, about which there is nothing insignificant, and which crushes me. On the edge of non-existence and hallucination, of a reality that, if I acknowledge it, annihilates me. There, abject and abjection are my safeguards. The primers of my culture. (2)

According to Kristeva's approach, *abjection* is first experienced physically at the pre-verbal semiotic stage – "'something'" that is "not recognize[d] as a thing" (*ibid.*). The child rejects or *abjects* that which is other from itself because it is experienced as a threat: "The abject has only one quality of the object – that of being opposed to *I*" (1). For Kristeva *abjection* is by implication furthermore the experience of a lack of something (that which is not I) and "[a]ll abjection is in fact recognition of the *want* on which any being, meaning, language, or desire is founded" (5). The subject's attempts to repress the threat of *abjection*, which it recognises as a lack, initiates its wants and desires and results in its setting up of an *Ersatz* (=substitute) for what it experiences as lacking. This is accomplished by symbolic means (i.e. language), which provide a world of meaning and order. Thereby, in Kristeva's approach, *abjection*, just like disgust in Freud's theory, can be understood as the "primer of [...] culture" (2; cf. III).

According to Kristeva's theory, *abjection* is an experience inherent to the human condition throughout life, as it is not left behind with the successful entry into the

---

14 The English and French words derive from the Latin *abicere* (to cast away) and *abiectum* (outcast) (cf. Menninghaus 365).

symbolic order. *Abjection* remains as a memory of the body in the state of separation. Like the child that is threatened by the separation from its mother's body, the subject that experiences traumatic states of ambiguity is haunted by these states of in-betweenness through *abjection*. According to Kristeva, "food loathing is perhaps the most elementary and most archaic form of abjection" (2), which she illustrates with the famous example of loathing the skin that commonly forms on top of milk: the skin, being neither part of, nor clearly different from the milk, bringing up embodied memories of one's separation from the mother (cf. *ibid.*). For Kristeva, food loathing and the associated act of vomiting are early manifestations of *abjection*, which are connected to humans' first act of rejection, the *abjection* of the mother, the object of "primal repression" (12f.). This first act of rejection allows us to become who we are, but it also always threatens the fragile concept we establish of ourselves: "[D]uring that course in which 'I' become, I give birth to myself amid the violence of sobs, of vomit" (3). Physiologically, phenomena of in-betweenness such as vomiting are all related to the bodily orifices. Body fluids, wounds, excrements, etc., which are simultaneously part of the inside and the outside of the body, thus equally give rise to *abjection*:

> [W]hat goes out of the body, out of its pores and openings, points to the infinitude of the body proper and gives rise to abjection. Faecal matter signifies [...] what never ceases to separate from a body in a state of permanent loss in order to become *autonomous, distinct* from the mixtures, alterations, and decay that run through it. (108; original emphasis)

However, as the quoted passage already indicates ("in order to become autonomous, distinct from the mixtures"), *abjection* is not limited to physiological states in Kristeva's theory. Because *abjection* is intrinsically linked to the child's entry into the symbolic order, on a more abstract level, anything that "disturbs identity, system, order" (4) is able to cause repulsion. Kristeva gives the example of "the traitor, the liar, the criminal with a good conscience, the shameless rapist, the killer who claims he is a savior" (4) to illustrate this point. Similar to the way Nietzsche views the tragic essence of life as lying in Silenus' wisdom, Kristeva argues that death, or more specifically "death infecting life" (4), manifests the essence of *abjection*.[15]

---

15 Kristeva distinguishes between the knowledge or meaning of death (as parts of the symbolical order) and the (traumatic) experience of being confronted with the materiality of (our) death: "A wound with blood and pus, or the sickly, acrid smell of sweat, of decay, does not signify death. In the presence of signified death – a flat encephalograph, for instance – I would understand, react, or accept. No, [...] refuse and corpses show me what I permanently thrust aside in order to live. [...]. There, I am at the border of my condition as a living being" (3).

In Kristeva's theory on *abjection* we also find the idea already expressed by Kant and Freud (and to a lesser degree by Plato): that disgust represents a marker of distinction of what is considered culturally adequate. Kristeva too maintains that *abjection* is not only that which terrifies us, but also represents the other side of what is generally regarded as cultural achievement (2).[16] Because of the need to repress that which is experienced as *abject*, the *abject* motivates us to set up taboos in the symbolic order of societies. For Christian-influenced Western society, the Bible can be seen as the most prominent example of a symbolic order that serves the function of regulating and restricting the 'chaotic' emotions and drives (of the semiotic).[17] Kristeva thus states that the *abject* can be regarded as the "other facet of religious, moral, and ideological codes on which rest the sleep of individuals and the breathing spells of societies" (209).

Abjection, Jouissance, & Art

As mentioned above, *abjection* is both a threat to the subject and expressive of the subject's needs and the development of desires. *Abjection* is ultimately governed by ambiguity, as it not only causes revulsion, but also a specific kind of pleasure which Kristeva calls *jouissance* (='unspeakable bliss').[18] With the notion of *jouissance*, Kristeva re-establishes and further develops the intricate link Freud had already made between *libido* and disgust. For Kristeva *jouissance* is a special type of pleasure: "One does not know it, one does not desire it, one joys in it [*on en jouit*]. Violently and painfully" (9). This 'pleasurable' component of *abjection* explains why the subject should be motivated to enter the original process of separation from its mother in the first place. She argues that in later life the pleasure of *jouissance* is realised in 'joyful' transgressions of the law or other forms of embracement of the in-between and the ambiguous (9). In Kristeva's approach, *jouissance* also describes the kind of pleasure that can be drawn from engagement with aesthetic representations

---

16   For further elaboration cf. Megan Becker-Leckrone (151f.).
17   Kristeva, in following Douglas' examination of Christian rules in *Purity and Danger*, finds that these are especially prevalent in Leviticus (111ff.). In the Bible, taboos such as incest, murder, certain foods, and others are transferred to the realm of 'sin' for a categorical restoration of order.
18   The term is omnipresent in French theory of the mid-twentieth century. Therefore, it is hard to discern who introduced the notion. Kristeva's supervisor and mentor Roland Barthes employs the term for his literary theory laid out in *The Pleasure of the Text* (1973). In this work he distinguishes it from *plaisir*, which he defines as "linked to cultural enjoyment" in the sense that it results from a text that does not threaten the identity of the reader, whereas *jouissance* challenges the reader's identity by fracturing the structures on which her certainties rest. For Kristeva's elaborations on the notion of *jouissance* regarding literary texts cf. *Revolution* (68f., 79f., 103f.,146, 157, 164).

of *abjection*. By confronting *abjection* through art, we are brought in contact with our human essence as determined by "death-infecting life" (4), a realisation that can help us come to terms with this condition and can even give rise to bliss. In this regard, Kristeva's notion of *jouissance* closely resembles some of the Dionysian features in Nietzsche's theory (cf. I.ii).

Kristeva's main source for the analysis of artistic manifestations of *abjection* is modern literature.[19] Her prime example of *abject* literature, which she attends to in most detail, is Louis-Ferdinand Céline's *Journey to the End of the Night* (1934).[20] Céline's novel deals with the horrifying experiences of WWI and life in the Interwar period. It not only depicts gruesome and disgusting contents (such as decaying and wounded bodies), but also presents a unique literary style, which Kristeva refers to as *abject* writing: a style of writing that mirrors the unbearable horrors it depicts, which defy articulation in plain language. *Abject* writing is also highly affectively charged: "Excitement and disgust, joy and repulsion – the reader deciphers them very fast on these lines pitted with blank spaces where emotion does not allow itself to be dolled up in flowery sentences" (204). Kristeva uses the psychopathological term 'perversion'[21] to describe content and form of *abject* writing: "The writer, fascinated by the abject, imagines its logic, projects himself into it, introjects it, and as a consequence perverts language – style and content" (16). This perversion of style and content, which Kristeva also refers to as a form of "corruption" (*ibid.*), occurs on different levels and can manifest itself in various forms. She gives the example of Céline's *Journey to the End of the Night*, which, she claims, mirrors the "crying-out theme [...] of suffering horror" (141) on the level of content in a style of writing that is characterised by a "recasting of syntax and vocabulary – the violence of poetry, and silence" (*ibid.*). Kristeva contends that when the "narrated identity" becomes unbearable, "the narrative is what is challenged first. If it continues nevertheless, its make-up changes; its linearity is shattered, it proceeds in flashes, enigmas, short cuts, incompletion, tangles, and cuts" (14).

---

19 Modernist writers Kristeva mentions include: Fyodor Dostoyevsky, Marcel Proust, James Joyce, Antonin Artaud, Jorge Luis Borges, Comte de Lautreamont, Franz Kafka, Stéphane Mallarmé, and Georges Bataille.

20 Kristeva's section on Céline's literature is frequently neglected in analyses of her work. It does, however, offer an insightful understanding of the possible functions and poetics of artworks dealing with *abjection*. Rina Arya is the first to attend to Kristeva's analysis of Céline in detail (cf. passim). Cf. also my article on "Approaching Abjection in Sarah Kane's *Blasted*", which draws on the *abject* writing style of Céline to analyse Kane's play (63-71).

21 Kristeva identifies *abjection* with perversion, which by implication also makes second-order *abjection*, as it appears in art, perverse: "The abject is perverse because it neither gives up nor assumes a prohibition, a rule, or a law; but turns them aside, misleads, corrupts; uses them, takes advantage of them, the better to deny them. It kills in the name of life – a progressive despot; it lives at the behest of death – an operator in genetic experimentations" (15).

Kristeva's elaboration on James Joyce's oral and musical writing style further demonstrates how the poetic manifestation of the *abject* functions as a medium of reconnection of author and recipient with the semiotic realm of signification: "The abject lies beyond the themes, and for Joyce generally, in *the way one speaks*; it is verbal communication, it is the Word that discloses the abject" (23; my emphasis).

Purifying *Abjection* through Art

Kristeva adapts Aristotle's notion of *katharsis* for her theoretical reflection on the role of art with relation to *abjection*. She advocates the representation of the *abject* in a homeotherapeutic sense, describing it as "an impure process that protects from the abject only by dint of being immersed in it" (29). For her, *katharsis* here has the power of immunisation, which once again mirrors Nietzsche's proposition to confront disgust in order to overcome it. She argues that by purifying the *abject*, art fulfils a function similar to that which religion originally occupied: "The various means of *purifying* the abject – the various catharses – make up the history of religions, [... and] end up with that catharsis par excellence called art" (17; original emphasis):

> Through the mimesis of passions – ranging from enthusiasm to suffering – in 'language with pleasurable accessories,' [...] the soul reaches orgy and purity at the same time. What is involved is a purification of body and soul by means of a heterogeneous and complex circuit, going from 'bile' to 'fire,' from 'manly warmth' to the 'enthusiasm' of the 'mind.' Rhythm and song hence arouse the impure, the other of mind, the passionate-corporeal-sexual-virile, but they harmonize it, arrange it differently than the wise man's knowledge does. (28f.)

Kristeva privileges art over religion in its function to purify the *abject*, because she claims art to be better able to respond to the needs of contemporary Western societies, which she argues to be in a state of crisis – one that is "deeper than anything since the beginning of our era, the beginning of Christianity" because of a loss of set values and beliefs (in Morgan and Morris 27). She regards modern artists' writings as "masterful sublimations of those crises of subjectivity" (in Meisel 131). For Kristeva the breakdown of symbolic systems (such as Christianity) resembles states of pathological psychosis. She maintains that art is able to confront *abjection* by "descend[ing] into the foundations of the symbolic construct" and "retracing the fragile limits of the speaking being, closest to its dawn" (*Powers of Horror* 18). Thereby, she argues, art offers a form of sublimation, which can defer the eruption of psychosis in real life (cf. Kristeva in Morgan and Morris 27).[22] Kristeva's understanding of sublimation here goes hand in hand with the Aristotelean notion of *katharsis*, with sublimation describing the (positive) effect that immersion with an aesthetically mediated dose of that which is generally rejected (the *abject*) has for the balance of the soul/our psychological health of artists and recipients. By giving a form to those horrors of human existence that symbolical systems (religious belief, science, etc.) increasingly fail to convincingly contain, control, and make sense of, *abject* art allows a release of the negative feelings we experience as a result of our tragic condition (in-between life and death). In her description of different reactions of people confronted with *abject* art, Kristeva furthermore points to the possibility for recipients to experience a sense of communion:

> As for the public, they can react in two ways. There are those who repress this state of crisis, who refuse to acknowledge it, in which case they either don't come or find the works disgusting, stupid, insipid, insignificant [...]. Others may be looking for a form of catharsis. When they look at these objects, their ugliness and their strangeness, they see their own regression, their own abjection, and at that moment what occurs is a veritable state of communion. (23)

For Kristeva *abject* art thus not only allows for integration of the *abject* in everyday life and a release or *katharsis* of the negative emotions related to it, it can also give people the feeling of not being alone with their essential conflicts. When Kristeva talks about the possibility of experiencing a "state of communion", she not only refers to the relation between artist and recipients, but also to the relations among visitors at the venue (and essentially between all people, since all people have to come to terms with *abjection*).

The aesthetic experience of *abjection* is thus closely linked to Nietzsche's understanding of a Dionysian communion in its originary ritualistic function. Like Nietzsche, who had credited art with the "power to heal" in *The Birth of Tragedy* (40), Kristeva argues that works of *abject* art enable a kind of 'remedy for life'. Kristeva's notion of sublimation is also very similar to Nietzsche's understanding of the *sublime*, which he uses to describe works of art dealing with the "repulsive thoughts about the terrible or absurd nature of existence" where "disgust at absurdity is discharged by artistic means" (40). Both argue that through artistic manifestations of the *abject*, the revolting truth about human nature can be experienced and therefore

---

22 In an interview with Stuart Morgan, Kristeva argues that the state of psychosis, "close [...] to that of borderline patients on an unstable frontier between the inside and the outside" is an increasingly common symptom, as "[t]he frontiers between sign and body, inside and outside, self and other are threatened" (27) in contemporary society. For further elaboration cf. Kristeva's *New Maladies of the Soul* (1995).

better endured. Art is thus able to replace classical mythological structures and rituals, as well as more modern systems and orders (e.g. religious belief, science, etc.), and bring about a *katharsis*, a confrontation that offers a form of healing through immersion, as well as the consoling feeling of communion among recipients.

III.iii Summary

The effects of technological progress and the first World War resulted in an unprecedented change in European societies' 'structure of feeling' and led to radical new forms of aesthetic practice and theory. Society in the early twentieth century was not only confronted with the lack of certainty regarding Christian beliefs due to scientific progress (Darwin, Freud, etc.), but also witnessed the mechanical destruction of vast areas of lands and their populations. Considering the dramatic exposure to life's uncertainties and brutalities, artists' and scholars' departure from idealistic philosophical theories à la Kant and turn to approaches that focused on the 'darker sides' of existence like those of Nietzsche or Freud does not come as a surprise.

Dissatisfied with the results of a *logos*-based world and 'Apollonian-surface-existence' that had ceased to offer meaning, avant-garde artists like Bataille and Sartre sought to reconnect philosophical thinking and art with the 'real' life, to embrace the Silenian wisdom that life is finite and human action futile. Aiming to liberate and confront suppressed instincts and desires and thereby offer an antidote to the eruption of these drives in forms of political extremism, they promoted an "affirmative aesthetic of the repellent" (Menninghaus 343; Lotringer n.p.). Avant-garde artists and intellectuals of the time acknowledged and explicitly addressed the destructive component of human existence, which Nietzsche had already reflected in *The Birth of Tragedy* and Freud had elaborated on with his notion of the 'death-drive'.

In decoding humanity's death-born condition, Kristeva finds much material in the aesthetic productions and reflections of early twentieth-century modernist writers. With her notion of *abjection*, she offers a useful approach to analyse the effects of disgust-inflected works of art. According to her approach, *abject* works of art offer insight by means of affecting recipients directly on a sensual level; they present a synthesis of cognition and feeling, an 'aesthetic idea' in the Kantian sense, which grasps the unrepresentable – "stimulat[ing] so much thinking that it can never be grasped in a determinate concept [....,] set[ting] the faculty of intellectual ideas (reason) into motion" (Kant §49). But, while Kant goes a long way to explain why disgust should be excluded from the aesthetic realm for being too powerfully 'vital' and 'real', Kristeva, like Nietzsche, Freud, Sartre, and Bataille, convincingly argues the opposite, namely that the reality of *abjection* brings us in touch with the essence of our being, precisely *because of* its capacity to break the illusionary or imaginary veil of *mimesis*. Nietzsche's conceptualisation of the Dionysian and Apollonian drives at work in the Attic tragedy can in many ways be regarded as a precursor of Kristeva's conceptualisation of a semiotic and a symbolic order connected by *abjection* and expressed by art. And like Nietzsche, who perceived of art as functioning like a sublime sorceress (*Zauberin*) that can help humans to overcome their disgust at existence, Kristeva claims that *abject* works of art function as "masterful sublimations" (in Meisel 131), which provide consolation and communion among their recipients. As this chapter has shown, Kristeva's contribution to aesthetic theory is highly relevant for a number of reasons:

- By introducing the notion of *abjection*, which bears much resemblance to Nietzsche's conceptualisation of the Dionysian principle, Kristeva offers a more theoretical and general term as well as a more elaborated framework for an analysis of aesthetic disgust.
- She brings the material, maternal, non-linguistic order of the semiotic to the fore (against classical psychoanalytic and post-structuralist theories that focus almost exclusively on the paternal symbolic). Thereby she presents another terminology for the investigation of the ratio-affective nature of not only feelings of revulsion in general, but also of our aesthetic perception, which offers a theoretical framework that incorporates both Kant's notion of 'aesthetic ideas' and Nietzsche's concept of the Dionysian spirit.
- By conceptualising the peculiar form of attraction (i.e. *jouissance*) that appalling objects, persons, and actions can elicit, Kristeva not only acknowledges the ambivalent pleasure and fascination with disgust (in real life as well as in art), but also introduces an applicable term that encompasses the ambiguity pertaining to the sort of pleasure that can be attained from experiences of abjection.
- Kristeva offers an explanation for art's cathartic function that combines Aristotle's understanding of *katharsis* with Nietzsche's notion of the Dionysian principle and the sublime effect of art. Thereby she reconnects the dramatic genre to its origin in ritual practices and states of communion and construes art as a possible 'coping-strategy' for modern and contemporary crises.

IV. Disgust around the Millennium

Towards the turn of the new millennium aesthetic disgust peaked across the Western art scenes and increasingly began to enter the realms of popular culture. Hal Foster describes the aesthetic agenda of the avant-gardes at the end of the twentieth century as a *Return to the Real* (1996), a bursting through the superficial layers of commodities and forms of signification that had come to be experienced as hollow and meaningless (cf. 127f.). This stipulated agenda resembles the aims of the early twentieth-century avant-gardes in their reaction to the loss of affection in societies of their time. A notable difference, however, is that this time, the emotional numbness in society was not caused by a 'shell shock' following the atrocities of war (cf. III), but by an overflow of information, content, and meaning, including vast media coverage of, for example, the Bosnian War or the Rwandan Civil War and the associated genocides, which was omnipresent, yet largely experienced as distant, through ever-increasing forms of global media.[1]

Through the evocation of disgust and other highly affective emotions, artists attempted to break through the *mimetic* layers of flickering television and computer screens to induce *real* feelings in recipients. Disgust was employed for different reasons: to shock, break taboos, to liberate suppressed feelings, or for mere entertainment.[2] Despite diverging agendas and formats across the media, the inflationary presence of disgust in (pop)cultural products nevertheless seems to point to a general social yearning for strong feelings and experiences. We could refer to this yearning as a 'hunger for the real', which seeks to feed on a Dionysian kind of reality that lies beneath the various screens of digital technology. A quote by the painter Francis Bacon, whose visceral work influenced many artists of the time, expresses the relation between art and screens as follows:

---

1   The last decade of the twentieth-century is a time of dramatic technological advances. With the affordability of personal computers and the arrival of the internet, alongside globalisation and rising capitalism, consumerist ideologies and new information media enter into the living rooms of the majority of Western families. These developments have since profoundly altered our modes of communication, ways of acquiring knowledge, and our perception of world events (cf. Brockett and Hildy 539; James and Imre ix).

2   The functions of disgust will be discussed in detail in the next chapter (V.ii).

When talking about the violence of paint, it's nothing to do with violence of war. It's to do with an attempt to remake the violence of reality. We nearly always live through screens – a screened existence. And I sometimes think, when people say my work looks violent, that I have been able to clear away one or two of the veils or screens. (qtd. in Critchley and Webster 218)

Disgust can be regarded as a violent aesthetic means, which proves particularly potent in enabling a transgression of *mimetic* boundaries, or can in fact be considered as a kind of 'weapon' that pierces through *mimetic* layers, as already Kant noted in his description of disgust as a particularly *real* and 'vital' emotion (cf. II.ii).

The omnipresence of disgust in the arts and the various media of popular entertainment is mirrored in an increased academic interest in the sensation from the late nineteen-nineties onwards, which has recently led to an "explosion of research on all aspects of disgust" (Chapman and Anderson 62) in the natural sciences, and progressively also made its entry into the humanities. But before turning to theoretical approaches to disgust in general and in its aesthetic manifestations in particular, we shall first briefly survey some of the most famous Western examples from the 'high' arts as well as from largely global formats of popular entertainment of the nineteen-nineties and the first decade of the twenty-first century that made use of the 'vital' aesthetic potential contained in disgust.[3]

Sensational Disgust & *Abject* Art: "Sick Stuff"

In the nineties, there were a number of art exhibitions displaying pieces that caused repulsion among their visitors. Some of these shows drew inspiration from Kristeva's notion of the *abject* or Bataille's concept of the *informe* (cf. Noys 33; cf. III.i), such as the Whitney Museum's exhibition on "Abject Art: Repulsion and Desire in American Art" (New York, 1993);[4] the Tate Gallery's "Rites of Passage. Art at the End of the Century" (London, 1995), which included a range of highly visceral pieces, such as John Coplan's *Self-Portrait* (1994) consisting of four panels depicting close-ups of the artist's ageing naked body, or Mona Hatoum's *Corps Étranger* (1994), a

---

3   The overview is not exhaustive, as each genre's developments during this period would amount to a study of its own. For a more detailed overview cf., for example, Rina Arya's study on *Abjection and Representation. An Exploration of Abjection in the Visual Arts, Film and Literature* (2014).

4   The curators' emphasis is on taboo subjects relating to sexuality and gender. In this context, they define *abject* art as "a body of work which incorporates or suggests *abject* materials, such as dirt, hair, excrement, dead animals, menstrual blood, and rotting food" as a means to "confront taboo issues" (in Henry n.p.).

video installation which displays a journey through the artist's body with an endoscopic camera;[5] or the Centre Pompidou's "The Formless: Instructions for Use" (Paris, 1996). The "Formless" show contained works ranging from Robert Smithon "dump[ing] tons of dirt on a hill" to Andy Warhol's "oxidation paintings", which the artist created by urinating on large pieces of canvas (Grauer n.p.). According to Victor Grauer, the aim of the show was to "get viewers 'down and dirty,' inviting them to experience 'formlessness' on its own [...] terms" (*ibid.*).

Despite some institutional warming to *abject* art, social acceptance regarding the display of disgust-evoking works, however, was still largely restricted to a confined group of academics and avant-garde artists.[6] Towards the end of the century, the 'high' arts in general, and disgusting works of art in particular, nevertheless increasingly began to become more mainstream and merge with forms of popular entertainment (cf. Jones n.p.). In the UK, this merging also had great political significance because it was much enforced by New Labour's 'branding' of a new 'Cool Britannia', which endorsed many young artists working at the time. If one specific point in time had to be chosen to signal this development, it would have to be the opening of the "Sensation. Young British Artists" exhibition at the Royal Academy in London in 1997,[7] an art show sponsored by media-mogul Charles Saatchi. The exhibition attracted a large number of visitors[8] and caused much controversy over the inclusion of Marcus Harvey's *Myra* (1995), a portrait of child murderer Myra Hindley composed of children's handprints, and Christopher Ofili's *The Holy Virgin Mary* (1996), a painted collage showing a black Mary amid material such as cow dung and snippets of pornographic images. The show later toured Berlin and New York, and Rudolph W. Giuliani, mayor of New York at the time, was so upset about Ofili's work, which he described as "sick stuff", that he threatened to cut off subsidies to the Brooklyn Museum of Art should they continue to show it (qtd. in Goodnough n.p.).

The controversial exhibition brought to fame many of the so-called 'YBAs', such as Damien Hirst, Tracey Emin, and Sarah Lucas, who are all known for their shocking and often repulsive artworks, and to some degree rooted *abject* art in the establishment, but it also gave rise to critical disapproval. Cultural theorist Angela

---

5   The show's catalogue includes an interview with Kristeva, where she critically reflects on the rising practice and social need for *abject* works of art (cf. Morgan and Morris).
6   In a review of the exhibition in the *New York Times* art critic Holland Cotter for example devaluates the show by likening it to a pubertal rebellious impulse to shock the audience. He claims that the show does little more than "give evidence of an instinct for provocation" with a "reliance on off-the-rack academic theory and an all-purpose, in-your-face 90's pique" (n.p.).
7   Art critic Jonathan Jones states that: "Two events changed the face of Britain in 1997. One was the landslide victory for New Labour [...]. The other was *Sensation: Young British Artists*" (n.p.).
8   According to the BBC News "[a] total of 284,734 people visited the three-month exhibition. On average, 2,800 people per day" ("Sensational Hit for Royal Academy" n.p.).

McRobbie, for example, compares these artists' pieces to the sensational topics discussed in the American Jerry Springer television talk show. In her view, YBAs' art is a "lite" and entertaining form of art with little or no political or intellectual agenda (6f.). McRobbie's comparison mirrors a common form of critique voiced against viscerally engaging forms of art. This critique, however, does not do full justice to artists working with visceral media and contents, since it rests on two logical shortcuts, where 'being visceral', or 'affecting the senses' is equated with 'sensational', and 'sensational' is equated with 'lite', 'un-intellectual', and 'unpolitical'. This kind of criticism is not only brought forward against visual artists, but against artists of all genres who work with viscerally effective sensations like disgust.

In-Yer-Face Theatre

A rise in challenging and extremely visceral artistic contents and styles could also be observed in the dramatic arts of the nineties. Critic and journalist Aleks Sierz coined the label '*in-yer-face*' theatre to identify a group of young and provocative British playwrights. On a webpage devoted to *in-yer-face* theatre, Sierz lists the dramatists Sarah Kane, Mark Ravenhill, and Anthony Neilson as the "hot shots" of this style of dramatic and theatrical practice.[9] Sierz defines '*in-yer-face* theatre' as an experimental form of theatre that implements the agenda set out by early twentieth-century avant-garde artists, "shock[ing] audiences by the extremism of its language and images; unsettl[ing] them by its emotional frankness and disturb[ing] them by its acute questioning of moral norms" (ibid.). Despite the brashness of *in-yer-face* plays, Sierz argues that these contain "much more than a collection of shock tactics" (ibid.). He states that taken together these elements "represent a consistent critique of modern life" (ibid.).

In German director-oriented state theatres, works of *in-yer-face* artists were highly valued from their first appearance onward and featured prominently across most of the country's major stages, which soon led to a heated debate in the arts sections of national newspapers over the omnipresence of visceral and nauseating actions and elements such as excretion, blood, and 'aberrant' forms of copulation on stage, for which critics coined the term '*Ekeltheater*' (=disgust-theatre; cf. Lottmann n.p.).[10]

---

9   I will give a detailed analysis of *in-yer-face* dramatist Sarah Kane's plays and their relation to disgust later, which is why I only roughly outline *in-yer-face* theatre here (cf. VI).

10 British *in-yer-face* plays were delivered by famous German directors such as Peter Zadek and Thomas Ostermeier. In a 2005 review of British drama from the past decade, Aleks Sierz notes that Kane was "recently [...] more often staged in Germany than Schiller" ("Beyond Timidity" 55).

Ekelfernsehen & Viral New Media Content

By the turn of the century, disgust-related contents and topics were no longer limited to academic and artistic discourse and practice, but had entered numerous channels of mainstream popular culture. This became especially evident throughout the cultural sphere of television and the new media, where formats presenting repulsive content enjoyed great popularity, many of them globally.

In television, disgust was a central topic in many of the so-called 'reality TV shows', such as *Jackass* (2000), *Fear Factor* (2001), *I'm a Celebrity…Get Me Out of Here!* (2002), or medical documentaries like the UK show *Embarrassing Bodies* (2007). The display of gruesome anatomical procedures in programmes like *Autopsy: Confessions of a Medical Examiner* (1994) also increasingly began to enter into other popular television genres like medical drama (e.g. *Nip/Tuck*, 2003) and crime series (e.g. *CSI: Crime Scene Investigation*, 2000). In Germany, the presence of television shows involving disgusting content like dismembered bodies, the consumption of appalling animals, or gruesome moral indecencies led to the coinage of the term '*Ekelfernsehen*' (=disgust-TV), which was listed in fifth place on the German 'word-of-the-year list' in 2004 (*GfdS* n.p.).

The popularity of disgust-eliciting contents across the (pop)cultural spheres of art, theatre, and television was also reflected in the new media. Websites like Rotten.com enjoyed great popularity in the early noughties. Rotten.com is a website devoted to the collection of highly disturbing and appalling images and videos, such as gruesome illnesses and diseases, forensic photography, or aberrant sexual practices. The website calls itself an "archive of disturbing illustration" presenting the "soft white underbelly of the net, eviscerated for all to see" (n.p.). Another phenomenon that illustrates the popularity of disgusting contents in new media formats was the case of a trailer for a porn movie called *2 Girls 1 Cup* (originally *Hungry Bitches*) which shows two young women eating each other's excrements, then kissing and finally throwing up into each other's mouth. In 2007, the trailer for the porn movie became one of the most-watched internet videos of the year, with YouTube clips of people's reactions to the trailer going viral (cf. Cusack 7; Heine n.p.).[11] In an explanation that sounds very similar to Plato's elaboration on the effects of *mimetic* works of art (cf. I.i), Elise Moreau points to the significant role that emotional responses play in contents that go viral: "On the internet, a piece

---

11   It is interesting that the expression 'going viral' is itself drawn from the medical field of infectious disease, which points to the health-harming and contagious capacity of a virus. According to the *English Oxford Living Dictionaries*, in common modern usage the term 'viral' simply indicates that "an image, video, piece of information, […] circulated rapidly and widely from one internet user to another" (n.p.). In this context, the term loses most of the negative connotations of being associated with infectious diseases, but instead represents a state of popularity that is highly desirable, yet almost impossible to willingly achieve.

of content can spread just like a virus if people become 'infected' when they see it. The infection usually comes from evoked emotions that spur the viewers to share it" (n.p.).

IV.i Contemporary Approaches to Disgust in the Natural & Social Sciences

Considering the rising use of disgust in numerous artistic genres from the nineteen-nineties onward and its 'viral' entrance into the various realms of popular culture in ever-increasing formats of the new and 'old' media, the sensation can be argued to have clearly left the confines of avant-garde aesthetic practice and theory. Disgust's omnipresence in high and popular culture at the beginning of the new millennium was also mirrored in an increased interest from scholars across different disciplines. Important publications on disgust predominantly came from the Anglo-American world. In the fields of biology, psychology, and the neurosciences, psychologists Paul Rozin and Paul Ekman are viewed as pioneers in the study of disgust and have published numerous books and articles on the subject. Other relevant publications from these fields of study include neuroscientific research of so-called 'mirror neurons'[12] (e.g. Wicker et al., "Both of Us Disgusted in My Insula", 2003), as well as Susan Miller's *Disgust. The Gatekeeper Emotion* (2004), Daniel R. Kelly's *Yuck! The Nature and Moral Significance of Disgust* (2011), and Rachel Herz's *That's Disgusting. Unraveling the Mysteries of Repulsion* (2012).

In the humanities, the first seminal publication on disgust was William I. Miller's socio-political study on *The Anatomy of Disgust* (1997), followed by Winfried Menninghaus' historical and aesthetic investigation in *Ekel. Geschichte und Theorie eines starken Gefühls* (1999),[13] which opened the ground for a long-neglected investigation of disgust's role in works of art by scholars from the fields of aesthetic and literary studies. These specific aesthetic approaches, however, shall be the topic

---

12 Mirror neuron theory is generally attributed to the Parma group around neurophysiologists Vittorio Gallese and Giacco Rizzolatti, who have been working in the field since the 1980s. Gallese states that: "Mirror neurons provide the neurophysiological basis for the capacity of primates to recognize different actions made by other individuals: the same neural motor pattern that characterizes the action when actively executed is evoked in the observer. [...] Furthermore, new empirical evidence suggests that the same neural structures that are involved in processing felt sensations and emotions are also active when the same sensations and emotions are to be detected in others" ("Mirror Neurons and Art" 422).

13 Menninghaus' study was translated into English and published under the title *Disgust. The Theory and History of a Strong Emotion* in 2003. All future references to Menninghaus unless otherwise indicated refer to the English edition.

of the next sub-chapter.[14] First, we want to take a look at recent approaches from the natural and social sciences to the sensation of disgust, which have largely informed its contemporary aesthetic debate. As it is not possible to elaborate on all of these different approaches in detail, I restrict my selection of theories discussed in the following section to those that have had a substantial impact on the evaluation of aesthetic disgust.

Psychology & Disgust

Since the so-called "affective revolution" (Chapman and Anderson 62) or "turn to embodiment" (Shilling ix), emotions and their manifestation in our bodies and interplay with cognition have increasingly become a subject of interest in the humanities. Most of the recent publications on disgust from these fields of study take a decisively interdisciplinary approach, and all of the authors mentioned in the preceding section work, in one way or another, with the propositions made by psychologist Paul Rozin.[15]

Until Rozin and his colleagues started investigating the nature of disgust in the nineteen-eighties, the sensation had hardly received any attention from scientists or academics outside the confined circle of scholars who were occupied with the particular post-WWI European avant-garde movements discussed in the previous chapter.[16] Up to that point, Charles Darwin's first scientific definition of disgust in *The Expressions of Emotions in Man and Animals* (1872) as one of six basic emotions, which functions as an aversive mechanism against anything that is perceived to be offensive to the taste (cf. 257f.), was basically undisputed among scientists. Rozin and his colleagues agree with Darwin's assumption that disgust originates from a biological or instinctive "response to bad tastes" ("Varieties of Disgust" 870). Still, they also incorporate Freud's counter-claim, which states that disgust is a learned and thus cultural emotion, into their approach. This was motivated by experimental results that showed that neither animals nor young children exhibited disgust-

---

14   Extracts of an earlier version of the ensuing summarising passages on psychological and sociological research on disgust were also used as background information for an article on the repulsive Other in Tim Crouch's play *I, Malvolio* (cf. Ablett, "Malvolio" 47-51).
15   The studies of the other famous pioneer of disgust research, Paul Ekman, though interesting, are less relevant for aesthetic investigations. For example, he examined the facial expressions involved in our disgust-reactions and argues for the sensation's evolutionary biological base (cf. 169-200).
16   One of the few exceptions is psychologist Andra Angyal's article on "Disgust and Related Aversions" (1941) from which Rozin and his colleagues took their first cues. This study, however, can be argued to have only come to the attention of a wider circle of scholars through its presence and discussion in publications of Rozin and his associates (cf. "Varieties of Disgust" 870).

reactions when faced with typical elicitors like faeces or insects.[17] Rozin and Haidt thus argue that disgust developed "biologically *and* culturally" from its biological predecessor 'distaste' ("Domains of Disgust" 367; my emphasis).

Rozin claims that through preadaptation,[18] the physiological sensation of distaste as a mechanism to protect the body from harm in the form of pathogenic foods expanded to the more complex realm of human disgust, which functions as a "system to protect the soul from harm" ("Food for Thought" n.p.). He maintains that disgust as a uniquely human sensation thereby represents "an entirely new category of ideationally based, contamination-sensitive revulsion or withdrawal" (*ibid.*). Together with his associates, Rozin identifies the following main categories of disgust-elicitation to have developed through processes of preadaptation from the biological instinct of distaste:

(1) 'Core disgust': foods that are perceived as harmful (cf. *ibid.*)
(2) Reminders of animal origin: protection against association with animalistic drives, including "body boundary violations, inappropriate sex, poor hygiene, and death" ("Varieties of Disgust" 870)
(3) Moral disgust: directed at the protection of "what are perceived to be sacred values and objects"; including for example cases of "incest, blasphemy, treason, betrayal, and actions that are seen to be 'sleazy' or 'subhuman'" ("Domains of Disgust" 367).

Rozin and his colleagues also noticed disgust's particular potential with regard to fears of contamination that easily transgress between physical and metaphysical realms, which had already been a determinant factor in the ancient Greek notions of *miasma* and *dyschéreia* (cf. I). According to Rozin et al., a fear of "potential biological contamination and infection" forms the base of all of the above-named manifestations of disgust ("Disgust" 761). This fear of contagion and the associated often illogical idea of transference from physical to metaphysical realms or vice versa are theoretically conceptualised by Rozin et al. with reference to what they call the two "laws of sympathetic magic":[19] "The first law, *contagion*, holds that 'once

---

17   The findings of Rozin et al. were: "The percentage of children under 2 years of age who put disgusting things in their mouths were as follows: 62% for imitation dog feces (realistically crafted from peanut butter and odorous cheese); 58% for a whole, small, dried fish; 31% for a whole sterilized grasshopper; and 8% for a sterilized lock of human hair" ("Conception of Food" 145).
18   Rozin and Haidt define "preadaptation" as a process "by which the structure or system that evolved for one purpose is re-used in a new context" ("Domains of Disgust" 367).
19   These so-called "laws of sympathetic magic" are adopted by Rozin and his colleagues from James George Frazer's *The New Golden Bough. A Study in Magic and Religion* (1889) and Mar-

in contact, always in contact.' That is, there can be a permanent transfer of properties from one object (usually animate) to another by brief contact" ("Sympathetic Magic" 703; original emphasis). The second law is based on *"similarity"*, which in its most basic sense means that "'the image equals the object'" (*ibid.*). The second law helps to explain why people would refuse to eat a chocolate dessert shaped in the form of dog faeces (cf. *ibid.* 705). These laws also elucidate why, for example, violators of moral norms are commonly deemed 'polluted' in the same way as if they suffered from some contagious disease: "people often do not want to touch them or touch things they have touched" ("Domains of Disgust" 367).

Mirror Neurons, Disgust, & Art

Rozin's and his associates' insights into disgust caught the interest of many cognitive psychologists and neuroscientists. Neuroscientists active in the fields of disgust generally work with the propositions made by Rozin and his colleagues and seek to find proof in the recordings of brain functions. A specific branch of the neurosciences, generally referred to as 'mirror neuron theory', posits that watching certain actions or emotions performed or experienced by others activates the same areas in the brain that would be activated if the action or emotion were actually carried out or experienced (cf. Gallese, "Embodied Simulation" 78ff.).[20] With regard to disgust, Bruno Wicker and his colleagues have found that the focal neurological site for disgust processing is the anterior insula, which is also the primary taste cortex (cf. Wicker et al. 655f.); an observation that could confirm the assumption that disgust originates from an aversive food reaction. Wicker et al. also found that the activation of respective brain areas is particularly strong when test persons are confronted with *mimetic* representations of people experiencing disgust (*ibid.*), which seems to confirm Kant's contention that disgust, more than any other emotion, allows for a transgression of *mimetic* boundaries in that the feeling it evokes is always *real* (cf. II.i).

Vittorio Gallese has furthermore proposed that the process of mirror neuron mapping of real or even imagined actions and emotions (via visual, auditive, or linguistic stimuli) to a great extent explains the mechanisms involved in humans' engagement with works of art: "[A] crucial and fundamental element of aesthetic

---

cel Mauss' *A General Theory of Magic* (1902), which both looked at magical belief systems in traditional cultures (cf. "Sympathetic Magic" 703).

20 The activation of mirror neuron simulation is strongest when real, albeit simulated actions or emotions are being observed, as opposed to the same actions or emotions being watched on video (cf. Gallese, "Mirror Neurons and Art" 444).

response to works of art consists of activation of embodied mechanisms encompassing simulation of actions, emotions, and corporeal feeling sensations" ("Mirror Neurons and Art" 444.; cf. also Wicker et al. 655).[21] On the basis of these findings, Gallese claimed to have found a valid argument against the "primacy of cognition in our responses to art" (444; cf. also Gallese and Freedberg: "Motion, Emotion and Empathy in Esthetic Experience" 197-203).[22]

Moral Disgust & Socio-Political Hierarchies

The first book-length study on disgust outside the natural sciences is W. Miller's socio-political study on *The Anatomy of Disgust*, which draws its insights from "history, literature, moral philosophy, and psychology" (xii) and has greatly influenced the contemporary academic debate on disgust and its role in the arts.

W. Miller's most important contribution to a theorisation of disgust is his evaluation of the sensation's socio-political meaning. He rejects Rozin's Darwinian understanding of disgust's origin in food rejection ('core disgust') by claiming that the idea of disgust as primarily related to matters of food and consumption only became a significant defining feature in the wake of seventeenth- and eighteenth-century aesthetic theories, when taste became "a metaphor for an aesthetic and social sense of discernment" (11; cf. II).[23] W. Miller maintains that disgust first and

---

21 The mirror neuron approach is not undisputed, especially with regard to their findings concerning morality and the arts (e.g. embodied simulation as the basis of empathy; cf. for example "The Embodied Simulation and its Role in Intersubjectivity", or Freedberg's and Gallese's "Motion, Emotion and Empathy in Esthetic Experience"). For a critical discussion cf. Pierre Jacob's "What Do Mirror Neurons Contribute to Human Social Cognition" (190–223).

22 The trend of conducting neuroscientific research to support or empirically validate theories on what motivates human emotions, behaviour and thoughts has not left the humanities untouched. Together with the rising interest in emotions and embodiment, scientific findings that are sought to confirm assumptions about emotional responses have increasingly made their way into the field of literary, cultural, theatre and performance studies. Yet none of the scholars who have been forging the area of cognitive approaches to literature have dealt with the aesthetically most interesting sensation of disgust in any detail. Cf., for example, Lisa Zunshine's (ed.) *The Oxford Handbook of Cognitive Literary Studies* (2015), *Introduction to Cognitive Cultural Studies* (2010); Alan Richardson's and Ellen Spolsky's (eds.) *The Work of Fiction: Cognition, Culture, and Complexity* (2004), Frederick L. Aldama's (ed.) *Toward a Cognitive Theory of Narrative Acts* (2010), Elizabeth Hart and Bruce McConachie: *Performance and Cognition. Theatre Studies and the Cognitive Turn* (2006).

23 W. Miller explains the common conflation of matters of taste (as related to food) and disgust as follows: "There is a certain attractiveness to the suggestion that the notion of taste as a capacity for refined discernment gave rise to a taste-based word to describe its 'negative essence' that is, disgust. The gust in disgust was very early on, in both English and French, not a narrow reference to the sense of taste as in the sensation of food and drink, but an

foremost "ranks and orders us in hierarchies" (4) through an underlying mechanism of negative evaluation. In his view, disgust at certain foods and habits of eating is a consequence of this mechanism of putting things in order and structuring our surrounding, rather than its cause.

For W. Miller, cases of moral disgust also fall into this category. He contends that actions or thoughts which defy clear categorisation, or placement into systems and orders, are evaluated negatively as 'low' and 'base' and hence disgusting. According to W. Miller, moral repulsion too is thus caused by "things for which there could be no plausible claim of right" (36; cf. discussions on *miasma*, *dyschéreia*, and *abjection* in I, III). As examples of actions that cause moral disgust he lists: "rape, child abuse, torture, genocide, predatory murder and maiming" (36). While these examples probably give little rise to questioning their appalling nature, other instances of moral disgust are not so clear-cut. Homosexuality, for example, is a classical case that demonstrates the flexibility of what can be perceived as morally disgusting (cf. Jones 39f.). Whereas some cultures and specific cultural groups (e.g. Orthodox Catholics) would regard homosexuality as something morally repulsive "for which there could be no plausible claim of right" (W. Miller 36), since from their perspective the only 'plausible' justification of sexuality (i.e. procreation) cannot be achieved by homosexual partners, in most Western societies and governments, homosexuality has increasingly come to be perceived as 'normal' or 'natural' on a continuous scale of sexual identities.

W. Miller distinctly points to the dangers that lie in using disgust-reactions as a compass for the evaluation of surroundings or people's moral transgressions (which Plato and Kant had advocated; cf. I.i, II.i). In an argument that mirrors Kant's assessment of disgust being an all too 'vital' or 'real' emotion, W. Miller claims that we are particularly prone to *not* questioning feelings of being appalled by something, because disgust "has the look of veracity about it. It is low and without pretence. We thus feel it trustworthy, even though we know it draws things into its domain that should give us pause" (180).

W. Miller also finds that due to the sensation's close link to imagination, disgust is unduly prone to overgeneralisation and breaching of different categories, which can for example result in a conflation of the aesthetic and the moral realm. One could thus, for example, be inclined to "judg[e] ugliness and deformity to be moral offences" (21).[24] Throughout history, this conflation of categories under the

---

homage to the broader, newly emerging idea of 'good taste.' The new expanded taste was about distinction, class, education, wealth, talent; it was the ability to reject the ugly in art, architecture, speech, and dress, to disapprove of glib music and poetry" (170).

24   In *Hiding from Humanity: Disgust, Shame and the Law* (2004), Martha Nussbaum makes a strong case of exhibiting the dangers that lie in basing our judgments of things on our disgust-reaction. She argues that disgust should be explicitly excluded from any involvement in legal proceedings, claiming that "its thought-content is typically unreasonable, embodying mag-

rhetoric of disgust has functioned as a powerful social and political tool of discrimination. In racist rhetoric, for example, different outer appearance, such as darker skin colour, is often used to signify 'low' or 'barbaric' behaviour and 'sullied' minds, and in Nazi Germany, images of Jews with rat-like features were a virulent tool of dehumanisation. These examples show how disgust can play a major role in social and political acts of discrimination (e.g. racism, misogyny, ageism, etc.), which have been used by political leaders throughout history to turn societies against minorities and foreign 'influence' in order to elevate their own group's status.

IV.ii   Aesthetic Disgust in the Humanities

In *Stay, Illusion! The Hamlet Doctrine* (2013), Simon Critchley and Jamieson Webster make a strong case for the inclusion of disgust in contemporary aesthetic practice as well as in theory since they regard the sensation's visceral nature as an instrumental tool to counterbalance our increasingly "screened and distanced" mode of existence (219). For them, disgust is one component of art's potential violence, which they see as reflecting "the task of tragic poetry" *per se* (218). They maintain that aesthetic disgust not only "repulse[s] or repel[s]" us, but that it "might also wake us up" through its "force of the uncontainable" (218; cf. the Dionysian principle in II.ii). The authors' reflections on this topic unfortunately come to an end here, which is why we need to look to other places for a theoretical elaboration on aesthetic disgust.

The main publications available on aesthetic disgust are: Menninghaus' *Disgust. Theory and History of a Strong Emotion*, Robert Wilson's *The Hydra's Tale. Imagining Disgust* (2002), Sianne Ngai's *Ugly Feelings* (2005), and Carolyn Korsmeyer's *Savoring Disgust. The Foul and the Fair in Aesthetics* (2011). To my knowledge there exists only one publication that treats the specific relation between disgust and the dramatic genre, which is Robert Douglas-Fairhurst's chapter on "Tragedy and Disgust" in Sarah A. Brown's and Catherine Silverstone's (eds.) *Tragedy in Transition* (2007: 58-77).

All of these contemporary studies on aesthetic disgust are highly interdisciplinary in their approaches, drawing their insights from the historical theories discussed in the previous chapters as well as from the more recent psychological and sociological findings of Rozin and his associates and W. Miller's *The Anatomy of Disgust*. Since these approaches have already been discussed in detail (I–IV.i), I shall refrain from re-iterating at length what is said about these, but instead offer a cursory overview of those historical approaches that have had the most prominent

---

ical ideas of contamination, and impossible aspirations to purity, immortality, and non-animality, that are just not in line with human life as we know it" (14).

impact on contemporary scholarship or have found scientific validation in recent empirical studies.

Disgust in Art as a Matter of Life & Death

One of the most important features of disgust that has found its way into contemporary aesthetic studies is the sensation's intricate link to liminal states of in-between life and death, which Nietzsche first brought to the fore through his notion of a Dionysian spirit in *The Birth of Tragedy* (cf. II.ii), and which Kristeva investigated in detail in her analysis of *abjection* in *Powers of Horror* (cf. III.ii). Menninghaus' definition of disgust, for example, largely overlaps with Kristeva's understanding of the *abject* as "death infecting life" (4). He defines the essence of disgust to be an expression of, and warning against, states of crises involving matters of life and death: "Everything seems at risk in the experience of disgust. It is a state of alarm and emergency, an acute crisis of self-preservation in the face of an unassimilable otherness, a convulsive struggle, in which what is in question is, quite literally, whether 'to be or not to be'" (1). Menninghaus' description bears much resemblance to Nietzsche's claim that disgust is basically a reaction to the Silenian wisdom (i.e. being born to die), which famously evoked a feeling of existential disgust in Shakespeare's Hamlet character (cf. II.ii; cf. also W. Miller 41.). W. Miller, too, sees a direct connection between disgust and humans' inability to grasp their mortality:

> What disgusts, startlingly, is the capacity for life, and not just because life implies its correlative death and decay: for it is decay that seems to engender life. Images of decay imperceptibly slide into images of fertility and out again. Death thus horrifies and disgusts not just because it smells revoltingly bad, but because it is not an end to the process of living but part of a cycle of eternal recurrence. The having lived and the living unite to make up the organic world of generative rot — rank, smelling, and upsetting to the touch. (40)

W. Miller offers a more complex explanation of the inherent ambiguity that lies between life and death by referring to their mutual dependency and natural circularity (cf. 76f.). In an example which he quotes from Shakespeare's *King Lear*, the nauseating interdependency of life and death is vividly exemplified in Lear's association of the female sexual organs with death:

> KING LEAR: [...] *There's hell, there's darkness, there is the sulphurous pit, Burning, scalding, stench, consumption; fie, fie, fie! pah, pah! Give me an ounce of civet, good apothecary, to sweeten my imagination: there's money for thee.*
> GLOUCESTER: *O! let me kiss that hand!*
> KING LEAR: *Let me wipe it first; it smells of mortality.* (IV.vi)

Lear refers to the vagina (the ultimate place of procreation and life-bearing) as a dark and smelly "sulphurous pit" (*ibid.*). However, this passage not only depicts Lear's struggle to come to terms with the Silenian wisdom, but also exhibits two further closely related features of disgust that are crucial in contemporary investigations of the sensation in general and its aesthetic manifestation in particular, namely the intricate relation between disgust and imagination. Lear acknowledges that the cause of his repulsion lies in his imagination alone ("sweeten my imagination", *ibid.*), yet he nevertheless seems convinced that these thoughts have polluted his body, which he now conceives of as contagious ("Let me wipe [my hand] first; it smells of mortality", *ibid.*).

Disgust & Imagination

The idiosyncratic relation between disgust and imagination is crucial in a majority of theoretical reflections on aesthetic disgust, and there is little dispute among scholars that there does in fact exist a strong link between imagination and the evocation of disgust. In *The Hydra's Tale*, Robert Wilson refers to imagination as disgust's "primary residence" (xix), and already Darwin pointed to this intrinsic relation when he remarked how "readily [...] retching or actual vomiting is induced in some persons by the *mere idea* of having partaken of any unusual food" (259; my emphasis). The contention that even imagining something repulsive can provoke a real feeling of nausea not only lay at the base of Kant's argumentation for disgust's exclusion from the aesthetical realm (cf. II.ii), but has also found some recent confirmation from scientific and psychological studies of disgust (cf. Wicker et al. in IV.i).

The conclusions which scholars draw from disgust's 'vital' potential to break through *mimetic* boundaries, however, differ. While some argue in line with Kant's contention that disgust's *realness* makes it *per se* anti-aesthetical (cf. II.i), others see its aesthetic value to lie precisely in this ability to strongly affect recipients' feelings. Ngai's discussion of disgust in the 'Afterword' to her publication on *Ugly Feelings* (cf. 332-54), for example, shows that Kant's evaluation of disgust as an un-aesthetic emotion is far from outdated. While Ngai states that the aim of her study is to "expand and transform the category of 'aesthetic emotions'" through the inclusion of "sentiments of disenchantment" (5f.), she seems to conceive of disgust as rather *too ugly* to be included in the main body of her text, when she states that the sensation, "in its intense and unambivalent negativity [,...] brings us to the edge of [her] project [,...] marking the furthest it can go" (354). Like Kant, Ngai considers disgust's visceral charge to indicate an "endpoint of mimetic art" (348).

Most scholars forging the field of disgust, however, tend (unsurprisingly) to argue in favour of aesthetic disgust's presence in artistic practice and its integration into theoretical approaches. They mainly regard aesthetic disgust as an effective and affective antidote to the "screened and distanced" (Critchley and Webster 217) modes of existence in post-industrial societies (cf. also Menninghaus 14).

Art & the Laws of Sympathetic Magic Belief

The intricate relation between imagination and the sensation of disgust, which Rozin and his associates explained with reference to the 'laws of sympathetic magic belief' ("Sympathetic Magic" 703), makes disgust a particularly interesting sensation with regard to its manifestations and effects in works of art. In Wilson, for example, we find a vivid example of this relation from Shakespeare's *The Winter's Tale*, where Leontes reflects on the idea of swallowing a spider (Wilson 38 f.):

> [...] There may be in the cup
> A spider steep'd, and one may drink, depart,
> And yet partake no venom, for his knowledge
> Is not infected; but if one present
> The abhorr'd ingredient to his eye, make known
> How he hath drunk, he cracks his gorge, his sides,
> With violent hefts. I have drunk, and seen the spider. (II.i)

In this speech, Leontes offers a fitting description of the prominent and potentially unreasonable role imagination plays when considering something disgusting.[25] The imagination (ultimately a fiction) of having drunk the spider suffices to cause severe symptoms of physical disgust in Shakespeare's Leontes: "[H]e cracks his gorge, his sides, / With violent hefts" (*ibid*.). This passage also contains the idea of contagion from a physical to a metaphysical realm (i.e. 'sympathetic laws of magic belief'), which also has its roots in the imagination since ideas and thoughts should theoretically not be able to physically afflict us (cf. also *miasma* in I). The idea of having become polluted is mirrored on a stylistic level in this passage as well, since Leontes does not refer to his knowledge as having become *af*fected, but instead conceives of it as having caught the pollution and hence become "*in*fected" (*ibid*.; my emphasis).

The example from Shakespeare not only demonstrates how powerful disgust-reactions to imagined sources can be, and how well these can be modelled into a

---

25 Wilson aptly notes that Shakespeare does not use the word 'disgust' once (cf.4). Shakespeare's non-usage of the word 'disgust', however, is not surprising, since the term was not in common usage at his time (cf. Menninghaus 3f.).Yet Shakespeare's plays offer an extraordinarily rich source of matters of repulsion being used as an effective dramatic device (cf. V for further examples).

potent aesthetic device, it also illustrates the potentially irrational nature of these assessments. While this feature of disgust may serve to initiate fruitful discussions on questions of rational and irrational modes of judgment when encountered in works of art, it can become a dangerous mode of assessment in real life, as W. Miller indicated in *The Anatomy of Disgust*. Because feelings of repulsion, even at imagined elicitors like Leontes' spider, feel very *real* and have "the look of veracity about [them]" (W. Miller 180), their legitimacy (i.e. their perception as a logically reasonable response) is generally not questioned. These relations between disgust and imagination are not only mirrored in aesthetic practices (e.g. literary style: "affected" being turned into "infected"), but also in the debates surrounding disgust's presence in works of art. Already Plato had feared the 'infection' of the mind through the *mimetic* arts, and Kant, too, took the sensation's ability to provoke real feelings at the mere thought of something appalling as his cue to position it as antipodal to what he conceived of as the *sublime* effect of art (cf. II.ii).

The Aesthetic Effect of Disgust

Whereas Nietzsche and Kristeva argued that aesthetic representations of revolting contents and styles can promote the evocation of an aesthetic pleasure in form of the *sublime* (cf. II.ii; III.ii), the general trend in recent scholarship tends towards the Kantian position of viewing the effect of aesthetic disgust as diametrically opposed to that of the *sublime* (cf. II.i).

However, instead of using this as an argument to expel the sensation from the aesthetic realm, as Kant proposed, they generally value its ability to transgress *mimetic* boundaries. Wilson describes the antipodal relationship between the *sublime* and the effects of aesthetic disgust as follows: "[D]isgust names that which cannot be represented or which lies beneath the possibilities of representation. [...] What is sublime cannot be represented because it transcends the possibilities of representation. It is above the beautiful just as the disgusting is beneath the ugly" (5). Critchley and Webster conceive of disgust's aesthetic effect in the same way. They explicitly ground their support of an "*art of the monstrous*" (217; original emphasis) on this 'anti-*sublime*' effect, since they see it as the most powerful way to aesthetically confront the challenges Western societies have had to face since the beginning of the twentieth century (cf. III; IV):

> If we look back at much of what is most radical and interesting in the art of the last century, we can see that we are no longer dealing with the sublime or indeed with art as the possibility of aesthetic sublimation but with an art of *de-sublimation* that attempts to adumbrate the monstrous, the uncontainable, the unreconciled, that which is unbearable in our experience of reality. (217; my emphasis)

In *Savoring Disgust. The Foul and the Fair in Aesthetics*, Carolyn Korsmeyer presents a similar approach. She too regards aesthetic disgust's effects as antipodal to the *sublime*. But instead of talking about *de-sublimation*, she appropriates the term '*sublate*' into the debate, which in chemistry describes the opposite process of *sublimation* (i.e. solid to gas), namely, the event of substances passing directly from gas to solid (cf. 131ff.; I.i). Korsmeyer sees here a fitting metaphor to describe what happens when we experience aesthetic representations of disgust: "Just as the experience of sublimity is likened to an elevation and expansion of spirit – free from earthly weight – so the sublate offers aesthetic insight in a bodily, visceral response" (132). The idea to introduce a term that captures the aesthetic experience of the brute and nauseating 'materiality' of being (cf. the Sartrean In-Itself, III.i) in juxtaposition to the well-established notion of the *sublime* looks constructive at first sight, yet to conceptualise the effect of aesthetic disgust as antipodal to the fear-induced *sublime* falls prey to some logical fallacies, which shall be discussed in more detail in chapter V.

IV.iii Summary

With the rapid technological developments and proliferation of the new media, the last decade of the twentieth century marked the dawn of a post-industrial era that dramatically altered Western societies' modes of communication and perception of world events. Progressively 'screened' and thus physically distant forms of social interaction were combined with an unprecedented 'bombardment' of global information and imagery via the various new and 'old' media channels. This changed mode of experiencing the world was countered by an increased presence of highly visceral disgusting elements across the Western art scenes as well as the popular media.

The artistic engagement with matters of disgust towards the turn to the new millennium was also mirrored by an increased academic interest in the emotion which led to "an explosion of research on all aspects of disgust" in the noughties (Chapman and Anderson 62). Research on disgust was pioneered by the psychologist Paul Rozin and followed first mainly by scholars from the cognitive sciences and sociology, and gradually also by academics from the aesthetic and literary fields of study. The most important publications concerned with aesthetic manifestations of disgust were Menninghaus' *Disgust. Theory and History of a Strong Emotion*, Wilson's *The Hydra's Tale*, and Korsmeyer's *Savoring Disgust. The Foul and the Fair in Aesthetics*. These investigations into the sensation's mechanisms were generally interdisciplinary in their approach and to a great extent informed by Rozin's and his associates' groundwork in the field.

Empirical research supplied scientific evidence for some of the historical hypotheses concerning humans' interaction with art. Plato's claim, for example, that the *mimetic* arts encourage an imitation of the perceived actions and emotions in the recipient's mind is supported by studies from the field of mirror neurons, which suggest that when test persons observe emotional states or actions in others, their own brains 'mirror' the brain activities of the persons they observe (cf. Gallese "Mirror Neurons and Art" 422). Gallese's assertion that an "aesthetic response to works of art consists of activation of embodied mechanisms encompassing simulation of actions [and] emotions" (*ibid.* 444) also concurs with Aristotle's argument that recipients of the *mimetic* arts experience a kind of simulated training of their emotions (cf. I.ii).

Gallese furthermore concluded from these results to have found a valid argument against the "primacy of cognition in our responses to art" (444). This claim, that aesthetic engagement is not a predominantly cognitive action, is however by no means a new argument. It has been paramount to aesthetic discourse ever since Plato first formulated his concerns about the *mimetic* arts for precisely this reason and eighteenth-century aesthetic approaches placed the sensual interaction with works of art at the centre of their theoretical reflections (e.g. Kant's 'aesthetic ideas'; cf. II.i). Nevertheless, it can be argued that these philosophical propositions have now also found scientific validation.

Cognitive science also found possible proof of an intrinsic relation between disgust and taste from the observation that both are processed in the same area of the brain: the anterior insula (cf. Wicker et al. 655f.). These findings align with the assumption that the sensation of disgust originated from the biological (i.e. natural) instinct of distaste. This is a position that has been held by most scientific scholarship since Darwin (e.g. Rozin et al.) and that to larger and lesser degrees also played an important role in historical approaches to disgust and art, such as Plato's connection between the appetitive part of the soul, *miasma* and the *mimetic* arts, or Kant's close examination of the role of taste in engagements with art, for example (cf. I.i; II.i). Disgust's link to the biological instinct of distaste, however, cannot be viewed as evidence for disgust likewise being a purely physiological reaction, as some scholars still maintain (cf. McConachie 18f.). Various experiments by Rozin and his associates have indicated that Freud was right in his contention that disgust is a primarily cultural and thus learned emotional response (cf. III), which has led them to conclude that disgust must be both a "biological [...] *and* cultural [...]" emotion ("Domains of Disgust" 367; my emphasis).

Rozin's findings reconnect disgust back to its ancient predecessors *dyschéreia* (as defined by Plato to inhabit a space in-between humans' natural instincts and rational faculties) and *miasma* (cf. I). According to Rozin, disgust developed from a physiological mechanism to protect the body from harm (i.e. distaste) into a complex "system to protect the soul from harm" ("Food for Thought" n.p.). This 'system' largely overlaps with the notion of *miasma* in that it represents a "category of ideationally based, contamination-sensitive revulsion or withdrawal" (*ibid.*). The fear of contagion and the associated often illogical idea of transference from physical to metaphysical realms are theoretically explained by Rozin et al. with reference to the "laws of sympathetic magic", which contain (a) the idea of contagion from one object to another in terms of 'once in contact, always in contact', and (b) the idea of similarity, namely, that 'the image equals the object' ("Sympathetic Magic" 703).

Empirical studies furthermore showed that the sensation of disgust, more than other emotions, provokes strong 'mirrored' feelings in test persons (cf. Wicker et al. 655f.), which indicates that Kant's assumption regarding disgust's particular potential to transgress *mimetic* boundaries was correct (cf. II.i). The idiosyncratic quality of disgust's inherent 'vitality' could partly explain why depictions of repulsive contents became so popular across the arts and media with the advent of an increasingly "screened existence" (Critchley and Webster 219) of forms of personal interaction and modes of communication towards the turn to the new millennium. Aesthetic disgust's ability to induce strong experiences seemed to address a 'hunger for the real' prevalent in Western post-industrial societies of the time, which to some degree mirrored the artistic agenda of early twentieth-century avant-gardes who sought to offer an affective antidote to the emotional numbness that afflicted Western societies after WWI (cf. III).

Aesthetic studies on the topic of disgust around the millennium generally agree with the proposition that disgust is a particularly "strong vital sensation" (Menninghaus 1). One concern that arises from this proposition is the question of how to evaluate this effect and how to conceptualise and refer to it. Here approaches diverge: Whereas most scholars who have been forging into the field of aesthetic disgust welcome its ability to produce strong feelings in recipients (cf. Menninghaus 14; Critchley and Webster 217f.), Ngai's evaluation of disgust as marking the "endpoint to the mimetic art" (348) demonstrates that the Kantian position which holds disgust to be antipodal to the aesthetic realm is far from outdated. Where most scholars also seem to agree with Kant is in the evaluation of aesthetic disgust's effect to be oppositional to the *sublime*, which shall be discussed in more detail in the next chapter.

V. Theorising Disgust for Drama Analysis

The aim of this chapter is to establish a comprehensive approach to aesthetic disgust that incorporates and synthesises the previously discussed different schools of thought on *miasma/dyschéreia*, *Ekel*, *abjection*, and disgust. In scholarly discourse on disgust and its cognates, which comes from various academic disciplines such as philosophy, the natural sciences, psychology, sociology, and psychoanalysis, these different historical approaches are rarely discussed by means of differentiating comparison. The more recent terms 'disgust' and '*abjection*' are seldom contrasted or addressed in relation to each other, and the ancient notions of *miasma* and especially *dyschéreia* find hardly any mention in contemporary approaches to disgust[1] – despite the fact that they can in many ways be viewed as encapsulating the multifarious and complex facets of disgust much better than the in many ways misleading term of 'disgust' itself with its close linguistic association to the biological instinct of 'distaste'.[2] This procedure of comparison and integration of the different terms that have been used in scholarly discourse on matters of disgust will form the backbone for determining the particular forms, functions, and effects of aesthetic disgust in dramatic works of art which will be presented in the two ensuing sub-chapters.

Insights from Ancient Disgust

The 'story' of disgust and its manifestation in works of art dates back much further than eighteenth-century as Menninghaus contends in *Disgust. Theory and History of a Strong Emotion* (cf. 3f.) – the most influential contemporary study on aesthetic disgust. The disgust-related ancient Greek notions of *miasma* and *dyschéreia* are not

---

[1] The first publication on *The Ancient Emotion of Disgust*, edited by Donald Lateiner and Dimos Spatharas, was published in 2017.
[2] As a matter of fact, the term 'dis-*taste*' is in itself as deceptive as its linguistic synonym 'disgust', seeing as 'taste' likewise invites associations to the uniquely human notions of 'refined' taste as developed in eighteenth-century aesthetic approaches (cf. II).

only present in famous works of ancient drama, but also discussed in the seminal philosophical treatises of Plato and Aristotle (cf. I).[3] Physiological as well as moral forms of pollution, contagion, and transgressions of boundaries were not only important topics of social, political, and ethical reflection, but also already reflected on with regard to their aesthetic manifestations in works of drama. A look into disgust's ancient history greatly enhances our understanding of this complex sensation, not only with regard to changing manifestations of what is deemed repulsive over time, but even more so with regard to what has *not* changed and thus may point to the sensation's more general or even universal characteristics.

Family Resemblance

In terms of family resemblance, *dyschéreia* and *miasma* share most features with 'disgust' as defined by Rozin and his associates (cf. IV.i) as well as with Kristeva's notion of *'abjection'* (cf. III.ii). *Dyschéreia* and *miasma* are both used to refer to: improper categories of food and ways of eating; diseases and wounds linked to impurity, lack of hygiene, and death; animalistic behaviour and features, inappropriate sex, and disregard or transgression of social rules. *Dyschéreia* and *miasma* can furthermore both be applied to objects, actions, or persons that challenge rational thinking, because they represent liminal states of in-between, such as life/death, human/animal, inside/outside, etc. (cf. I.iii). They share this characteristic with Kristeva's notion of *abjection* in that they refer to states that defy assimilation into what Kristeva construes as the 'symbolic order' (cf. III.ii). Jonathan Lear argues that Aristotle's usage of *miasma* in the context of differentiating between (dramatic) actions that would cause pity and fear, and those that would evoke repulsion does in fact help us to understand an essential component of common disgust reactions: "Disgust is something we feel in response to what we take to be a total absence of rationality" (329; cf. I.iii).

Magical Contagion

Associated with *dyschéreia* and even more so with *miasma* are fears of contamination and contagion, which according to Rozin et al. also form the base of all domains of

---

3   Following Meinel's finding that *miasma* plays a central role in all but two tragedies that have survived from Greek antiquity, with one of these being Sophocles' *Philoctetes*, which is also clearly concerned with matters of disgust as the analysis in the first chapter demonstrated, one could even speak of an omnipresence of disgust in Attic drama (cf. Meinel 2). These findings clearly contradict Menninghaus' claim that disgust was only "occasionally portrayed" in literary texts of Greek antiquity, and only took on "'a life of its own'" in the eighteenth century (3).

typical disgust-elicitation (cf. IV.i).[4] The intrinsic correlation between ideas of pollution and contagion (i.e. *miasma*) may partly explain why the sensation of disgust is so prone to the 'laws of sympathetic magic' (cf. IV.i), which one could also call the 'laws of magical contagion'. The common conflation of physical and moral forms of repulsion and the concomitant fear that a mind polluted by immoral thoughts may 'infect' the body, or a deformed physical appearance points to a deformed state of mind was prevalent in the ancient notion of *miasma* (cf. Plato's fear of the 'infectious' *mimetic* arts; I.i). To this day, this mechanism still underlies a great amount of disgust reactions, as Rozin et al. showed in their experiments (cf. IV.i). The fact that these 'laws of sympathetic magic' are often illogical was also to some degree acknowledged in ancient times, as Aristotle's student Theophrastus' reflection on the "Superstitious Man" in *Characters* demonstrates. Here he labels the behaviour of a man who avoids physical proximity to a *miaron* woman (having recently given birth) because he fears contagion, as 'superstitious'. Theophrastus' text thus exhibits a clear understanding that these fears do not stem from a real threat, but are rather based on magical thinking (cf. I).

In-Between Nature & Culture

Long before Rozin and his associates concluded that disgust cannot only be understood as a natural aversive response, but rather as one that developed "biologically *and* culturally" ("Domains of Disgust" 367; my emphasis), Plato already suggested that *dyschéreia* should be conceived of as a sensation located in-between humans' natural drives (appetitive part of the soul) and their rational faculties (cf. 435c-444a; I.i). Plato's theoretical construction of a tripartite structure of the soul and disgust's role therein in many ways anticipated the Freudian model of the soul and his conception of disgust as the culturally infused emotion *per se* in charge of keeping animalistic drives at bay (cf. III). Plato argued that these kinds of base and *miaron* desires were likely to be present in all humans, "even in some of us who seem to be so very measured" (571d), because *miaron* actions like instinct-driven excessive food and drink consumption, sexual intercourse with family members and animals, or "foul murder" (571b-d) commonly surface in people's dreams. He thereby also presented an early version of the Freudian notion of the subconscious (cf. I.i, III). Due to his acknowledging and incorporating the attracting allure of disgusting objects into his theoretical reflection (cf. Leontius-narration, I.i), Plato's discussion on the

---

4   In her study on *Sexual Pollution in the Hebrew Bible*, Eve L. Feinstein points out how central ideas of pollution, contamination, and contagion are to the sensation of disgust. She finds that disgust and the sources of pollution in the Hebrew Bible "show [...] striking correlation" (*ibid.*). This similarity leads her to the conclusion: "Disgust and pollution are two facets of the same phenomenon: When we consider one, we *ipso facto* contemplate the other" (25).

topic can even be argued to surpass contemporary psychological and scientific investigations of the sensation since these generally focus exclusively on its aversive function (cf. IV.i).

Contemporary Disgust in Relation to Distaste & *Abjection*

The most elaborate theoretical reflection concerning the question why objects, actions, or persons that are found repulsive are commonly also a source of fascination and even attraction can be found in Kristeva's psychoanalytical investigation of states of *abjection* (cf. III.ii). In a next step of synthetisation, I thus aim to integrate Kristeva's notion of *abjection* into a model of disgust that sees its evolutionary base in the biological instinct of distaste (cf. IV.i).

Unlike the ancient notions of *miasma* and *dyschéreia*, the terms 'abjection' and 'disgust' are both commonly used in contemporary academic discourse. Yet, these two more recent terms are rarely discussed in relation to each other (cf. Arya 33ff.). As the previous elaboration on Kristeva's theoretical layout of *abjection* in *Powers of Horror* has shown (cf. III.ii), her poetical academic style of writing is not always easily accessible, which may partly explain why her notion of *abjection* is "often misconstrued [... or] marginalized", if not "ignored completely", especially in "Anglo-American studies on disgust" (Arya 33).[5] Some scholars, such as Menninghaus, seem to view *abjection* to be basically synonymous with disgust, calling the former a "buzzword" and "the newest mutation in the theory of disgust" (365).

The conflation of *abjection* and disgust, however, is not an easy answer to a complex question, as Rina Arya shows in her discussion of the two terms. Before Arya, Korsmeyer and Smith had already attempted a distinction between *abjection* and disgust on the basis of their relation to the sensation of fear, claiming that while *abjection* involves fear, disgust does not (cf. 18f.). Arya rejects this differentiation by arguing that disgust, as an aversive reaction that protects body and mind from harm, is clearly linked to the sensation of fear (cf. 39). She maintains that both notions are related to fear, yet that they differ in regard to the *kinds* of fear they

---

[5] Rina Arya accords the "neglect of abjection in studies on disgust" to the "still unbridgeable gap between the analytic and continental traditions in philosophy" (36). The notion of *abjection* does in fact find no mention in Daniel R. Kelly's *Yuck! The Nature and Moral Significance of Disgust*. W. Miller refers to it in merely two footnotes in *The Anatomy of Disgust*; and Ngai only mentions it briefly and in passing in *Ugly Feelings*. And even where the *abject* is mentioned, as is the case in Menninghaus' study on the aesthetics of disgust, where he devotes a whole chapter to Kristeva's concept of the *abject* (365-402), it does not become a constitutive part of a general approach. Menninghaus' chapter on *abjection* follows only *after* his literary analysis of the aesthetic manifestations of disgust in authors such as Sartre and Kafka, and thus finds no concrete application.

entail (cf. 37). She claims that while *abjection* involves a specific fear regarding the loss of self-hood, the "self remains intact" in experiences of disgust (38). Arya thus concludes that disgust must be regarded as the broader category of which *abjection* is a "proper subset" (39; cf. also Wilson 93).

Disgust as a Subset of *Abjection*

I agree with Arya's finding that *abjection* cannot be differentiated from disgust on the basis of the latter term's non-relation to fear, yet I would suggest that *abjection* rather than disgust forms the broader category. If we agree with Kristeva in situating *abjection* at the core of what it means to become a human subject (cf. III.ii), it seems evident to view *abjection* as the fundamental category and disgust, which has been shown to be a predominantly learned emotional reaction (cf. IV.i), as the subset. I would furthermore argue that both notions entail a fear regarding threats posed to our sense of self-hood, because if we understand disgust as a discriminatory cultural marker against our animalistic ancestry, then any evocation of it through association with the base and instinctive natural world signifies a potential impairment of our integrity as cultivated human beings (whether we conceive of this consciously or not). As Menninghaus states with reference to Shakespeare's Hamlet, disgust always presents "a state of alarm and emergency, an acute crisis of self-preservation in the unassimilable otherness, a convulsive struggle, in which what is in question is quite literally, whether 'to be or not to be'" (1). *Abjection* and disgust thus share a concern regarding the integrity of one's sense of self-hood. Yet *abjection* presents the broader category of which disgust can be viewed as one particular subset. States of *abjection* can, but must not necessarily, induce disgust; they can also give rise to other feelings such as fear or the pleasure of border transgression as conceptualised in Kristeva's notion of *jouissance* (cf. III.ii).[6]

Overconsumption

Arya seeks to support her argument for disgust's non-identity-threatening essence with the example of a disgust reaction evoked by overconsumption of food (cf. 39f.). I would argue that also in these cases (which may well result in the physiological urge to vomit), the feeling of disgust can be derived from a threat to the sense of self-hood. Even if we are not at all times conscious of it, our identity can in fact be viewed as being highly threatened by excessive food consumption: uncontrolled sounds and smells such as farts and burps may exit from our orifices, and our bodies become deformed: our stomachs bulge immediately and obesity may result in

---

6   In the realm of sexuality, for example, otherwise repulsive body parts (orifices, etc.) and their excretions commonly become a source of attraction and pleasure.

the long term. In contemporary society, the 'disease' of obesity is most commonly linked to excessive food consumption and is highly charged with associations surrounding disgust: uncontrolled 'animalistic' gorging (pig-like, etc.), soft and flabby flesh, audible heavy breathing, sweating, non-adherence to the social ideal of slim bodies, lack of self-control needed to 'keep in shape', to name just a few.[7]

Besides the above-mentioned predominantly culturally induced associations, overeating can also simply lead to the physiological necessity to vomit, because of having brought the stomach's capacity for intake to a limit. However, I would argue that even in this case, there is (for humans at least) more at stake than a purely physical purging of surplus substances, because for humans vomiting is not only an experience of limits (stomach/intake), but also poses a threat to the self in the sense of: 'cannot *take* anymore', 'need to expel', 'will lose part of oneself', which explains why even watching someone else vomit, or smelling vomit can be a sufficiently strong stimuli to provoke feelings of nausea in others. When we vomit, we not only throw up food, we throw up a slimy mash of substances including saliva and stomach acids – ultimately a part of ourselves. And it is a highly 'unrepresentable' and smelly part of ourselves that splashes into the toilet, the bucket, or onto the ground at our feet.

Distaste: The Vomiting Cat

In viewing disgust evoked by overconsumption as non-identity-threatening, Arya seems to conceive of the sensation as a primarily physiological instinct that simply protects the body from harmful incorporation. This purely physiological instinct, however, is in Rozin's terminology not disgust, but its evolutionary ancestor 'distaste', which is also present in animals and young children (cf. IV.i). A 'purely' physical act of vomiting, which can be observed in animals who have eaten unhealthy substances, generally differs from human vomiting, as the section above illustrated. We may imagine a cat throwing up as a result of having eaten something harmful, because its instinct (i.e. distaste) protects its body from such incorporation. But according to scientific research by Rozin et al., animals like this cat will not feel disgusted (cf. IV.i).

For humans, however, even if we subtract all the cultural associations linked to excessive eating or incorporation of harmful substances, the act of vomiting itself, and even the fear of having to vomit, is enough to re-connect us to our essentially

---

7   Obesity is furthermore popularly associated with the lower classes and a lesser degree of intelligence (cf. Roger et al. "The Relationship between Childhood Obesity, Low Socioeconomic Status, and Race/Ethnicity" and Goswami's "The Greater Your Weight the Lower Your IQ"); not to mention the actual life-threatening diseases that can result from obesity, such as diabetes, types of cancer, osteoarthritis, and cardiovascular diseases, which according to the World Health Organisation were the leading cause of death in 2012 ("Obesity" n.p.).

abject-inflected core: "during that course in which 'I' become, I give birth to myself amid the violence of sobs, of vomit" (Kristeva 3). Thus, if we agree with Kristeva's psychoanalytical placement of *abjection* at the origin of the process of humans' subject formation, we can even conceive of 'natural' aversive reactions, such as vomiting caused by overconsumption, as psychosomatic reminders of our first act of rejection, the painful *abjection* of the mother: the process which allowed us to become who we are (i.e. conscious human subjects), but which also always continues to threaten the fragile concept we establish of ourselves (cf. III.ii).

Model of Synthetisation: Distaste, *Abjection*, Disgust

We can conclude from the reflections made in the previous sections that disgust like *abjection* stems from perceived threats to our sense of self-hood, whether we are consciously aware of it or not. Establishing disgust as a sub-category of *abjection* does not mean that these notions are necessarily incompatible with psychological findings which suggest that disgust developed from the biological instinct of distaste. It is not inconceivable to view *abjection* and disgust both as evolutionary offspring of distaste. Most scientific scholarship since Darwin has claimed that distaste and disgust share its evolutionary root in a protection of the body which by means of preadaptation developed into a mechanism to protect the soul from harm (cf. IV.i). The same applies to *abjection*, which may well have originated from an ability to reject the m/other's food via the archaic mechanism of distaste, whereby the process of becoming a subject (i.e. self-conscious and independent human being) is first played out physically in the rejection of incorporating 'foreign' substances (i.e. vomiting). Disgust features at a last stage in this setup, as a reaction which humans adopt and culturally train in social structures to control states of *abjection*. The model of the relation between these three categories would look as follows:

Distaste
- aversive
- biological, instinctive, physiological reflex
- present in animals and humans
- protection of the body against harmful substances in nature, above all incorporation of health-threatening food
- can cause vomiting

Abjection
- aversive/attractive
- unique to humans
- psychosomatic mode of rejection that constitutes humans' subjectivity
- at the same time poses a threat to humans' sense of selfhood

- protection of the soul against nature (animalistic drives, death, ambivalence)
- initiator/safeguard of culture
- connector to nature (pre-symbolic mode of existence)
- can cause disgust but: can also cause feelings of *jouissance*, fear, etc.
- can cause vomiting
- vomiting can function as a reminder of *abjection*

Disgust
- aversive
- unique to humans
- learned reaction
- psychosomatic manifestation or symptom of *abjection*
- protection of the soul against nature (animalistic drives, death, ambivalence)
- connector to nature (animalistic drives, desires, etc.)
- can cause vomiting
- can be caused by vomit or vomiting

In this model distaste is represented as the purely biological ancestor of *abjection* and disgust, and disgust as a particular and concrete psychosomatic reaction to experiences of *abjection* – *one* of several possible reactions (*jouissance*, fear, etc.). Disgust and *abjection* both represent uniquely human experiences which should be differentiated from the biological instinct of distaste, regardless of similar physiological responses such as vomiting. What supports this setup is the fact that whereas the instinct of distaste is inborn and the experience of *abjection* constitutes, in Kristeva's understanding, a very early stage in the infant's development, disgust cannot be observed in children younger than two years of age (i.e. prior to language acquisition/toilet training; cf. Rozin et al., "Conception of Food" 145). To place the psychoanalytical notion of *abjection* in-between the biological instinct of distaste and the culturally motivated feeling of disgust can furthermore help to explain why the complex sensation of disgust should have developed from distaste in the first place. Rozin et al. suggest that the biological instinct of distaste protects the body from dangers prevalent in nature, whereas disgust by means of preadaptation developed in the human as a "system to protect the soul from harm" ("Food for Thought" n.p.; cf. IV.i).

Ekel & Aesthetic Disgust

Having clarified the general relation between distaste, *abjection*, and disgust, and shown how closely they resemble the ancient notions of *dyschéreia* and *miasma*, we shall now turn our attention to disgust's German cognate *Ekel* as well as to the implications of the propositions made above for disgust's role in aesthetic practice and theory. From the discussion of *Ekel* in the context of the aesthetic discipline established in eighteenth-century Germany, we can extract insights into humans' ratio-affective engagement with works of art and the mechanisms of disgust therein. We are also equipped with some suitable terminology to refer to these phenomena.

Eighteenth-century aesthetic approaches were the first to fully develop and conceptualise the crucial role that emotions play in the apprehension of artworks and how these interact with the cognitive facilities, a position which has recently been supported by neuroscientific research (cf. Gallese "Mirror Neurons and Art" 422; IV.i). Kant introduced the notion of an 'aesthetic idea' to describe the sensual insights that can be gained from engagement with works of art, arguing that it "stimulates so much thinking that it can never be grasped in a determinate concept" (§49). He used the term '*sublime*' to refer to the pleasurable experience which may arise from such encounters (cf. II.i).

Nietzsche followed Kant in this regard when he described how engagement with works of art can induce a "certainty of something directly apprehended" (14), an experience which he, like Kant, connected to the notion of the *sublime* (cf. II.ii). Yet whereas Kant singled out *Ekel* as antipodal to the *sublime*, for Nietzsche the insight into "the true essence of things" (40) always addresses the most basic human conflict: the Silenian wisdom which he views as intrinsically linked to *Ekel*. For Nietzsche, 'ideal' or *sublime* works of art (i.e. Attic tragedy, cf. II.ii) essentially engage with metaphysical *Ekel* in two ways, first as a cause, and then as a remedy. He maintains that art provokes existential disgust by confronting humans with their inherently ambiguous condition through the interplay of Apollonian and Dionysian forces. Yet art is for Nietzsche at the same time the only kind of "medicine" available to offer consolation (75). According to Nietzsche, only art can "re-direct those repulsive thoughts about the terrible or absurd nature of existence" and turn them into something *sublime* through a process of *katharsis* in the Aristotelean sense, where "disgust at absurdity is discharged by artistic means" (40). Nietzsche's model of an aesthetic engagement with disgust-eliciting topics (i.e. the Dionysian in-between; above all the Silenian wisdom, cf. II.ii) in a homeotherapeutic sense corresponds with Kristeva's understanding of *abject* art's ability to provide a *katharsis* and thus "protect [...] from the abject [...] by dint of being immersed in it" (29). The systematic distinction made above between the terms '*abjection*' and 'disgust' helps us to describe this particular aesthetic effect: representations of *abjection* in art via disgust-eliciting contents or forms can induce the contradictory feelings of *jouissance* and disgust and via confrontation in the *mimetic* realm release these difficult feelings from the recipient's mind and body in the form of a *katharsis*, which constitutes the aesthetic experience of the *sublime*.

The Aesthetic Effect of Disgust: *Sublime* or *Sublate*?

To follow Nietzsche and Kristeva in conceptualising the aesthetic effect of appalling artistic representations as *sublime* contradicts Kant's contention that the effect of *Ekel* in art needs to be perceived as antipodal to the *sublime* (cf. II.ii) as well as the position which the majority of contemporary scholars working with aesthetic disgust have adopted (cf. Korsmeyer, Wilson, Critchley and Webster, Ngai, IV.ii). Korsmeyer, for example, introduced the notion of the '*sublate*' to capture this supposedly oppositional effect, arguing that "just as fear can be the foundation for encounters with the sublime, so disgust can achieve its own aesthetic counterpart" (132). In order to justify the proposition that the *sublime* may also be evoked by representations of disgust, we thus need to challenge the arguments brought forward by those who consider the aesthetic effect of disgust to be 'anti-*sublime*'. Korsmeyer metaphorically conceptualised the presumed antipodal relation between the *sublime* and *sublate* by drawing on the terms' usage in the field of chemistry, where '*sublimation*' describes the process of substances passing directly from solid to gas, and '*sublation*' denotes the direct passing from gas to solid (cf. ibid., IV.ii). From my point of view, this metaphorical transferal (and by inference the claim that these effects need to be understood as antipodal) does not adequately capture the experience of disgust (aesthetic or real). While the chemical term of '*sublimation*' aptly approximates the experience of a de-materialisation of world and knowledge, as in the Kantian sense of presenting an 'aesthetic idea' which cannot be grasped in its magnitude by means of rational reasoning alone (cf. II.ii), the metaphorical implications of the term '*sublate*' do not lend themselves as fittingly to describe aesthetic encounters with disgust. To conceptualise the effect of aesthetic disgust in terms of matter passing directly from a vaporous state into a kind of solid materiality fails to acknowledge the ambiguity or in-betweenness that is inherent to encounters with things that are deemed disgusting. While Korsmeyer's contention that the *sublate* offers insight into an 'earthy' kind of materiality in the sense of a physiological 'realness' (cf. Sartre's notion of the 'facticity' of the In-itself, III.i) can be considered to be a crucial component of what it means to be disgusted, this 'materiality' can, however, surely not be conceived of as being solid. As Sartre elaborated at length, the essential core of this materiality (i.e. the In-Itself) is slippery, slimy, and ungraspable (cf. III.i). If we are to agree that 'solid' is not a suitable description of the effect of aesthetic disgust, it follows that whatever the effect of aesthetic disgust may be, it should not be perceived as being antipodal to the notion of the 'vaporous' *sublime*. There is another argument to be brought forward against the claim that aesthetic disgust's effect should be understood as oppositional to the *sublime*. As the discussion concerning the differentiation between disgust and *abjection* has shown, both notions incorporate some sense of fear since they both function as aversive protection mechanisms against real or perceived harm (cf. Arya 39). If disgust is intrinsically related to fear, the aesthetic effects evoked by fear and disgust can hardly be conceived of as antipodal. In conclusion, I suggest that there is little evidence for us to regard the aesthetic effect of disgust as different, never mind oppositional, to the aesthetic effect of the *sublime*. If we furthermore agree with Kant's description of the sublime as a state where "the mind is not merely attracted by the object, but is also always reciprocally repelled by it" (§23, cf. II.ii), which aptly describes the ambivalent feelings provoked by encounters with *abjection*, it seems productive to hold on to the term *sublime* to describe the aesthetic effect of disgust (despite Kant's oppositional position).[8]

V.i Forms of Dramatic Disgust

The historical background and theoretical reflections of the previous chapters have shown how drama and especially tragedy is a genre that lends itself particularly well to the depiction of universal human conflicts, of which our coming to terms with mortality can be regarded as the most important one. In accordance with the model established in the introductory section of this chapter, the evocation of disgust in drama can be viewed as an aesthetic mode of representing the universal experience of *abjection*.

An aesthetic representation of *abjection* in drama can become manifest in various forms of disgust-evoking elements, either on the level of content, literary style, or both. The most instructive and exemplary insight into the specific forms of aesthetic and specifically dramatic disgust can be drawn from Douglas-Fairhurst's study on "Tragedy and Disgust" and Kristeva's analysis of Louis-Ferdinand Céline's writing in *Powers of Horror*.[9] Even though Kristeva's analysis deals with the narrative genre, many of the features of *abject* writing she identifies are congenial to the analysis of drama. I will extract the specific characteristics that apply to dramatic forms of disgust from Kristeva's and Douglas-Fairhurst's analyses and supplement

---

8   This is not to say that it is unthinkable to mark out differences between purely fear-inflected aesthetic effects and those that are accompanied or dominated by the sensation of disgust, or that the latter do not pass through some kind of intermittent state (i.e. slimy; cf. III.i) before turning into the vaporous state of the *sublime*. Yet if we were to describe any particular aesthetic effect of disgust in terms of chemistry at all, we would need a term denoting the particular state of a substance in-between the different aggregate states of solid, liquid, and gas to capture the intangibility (cf. *dyschéreia*; I) of things we experience as repulsive. I will have to leave this question open, since the evaluation of aesthetic effects is to a large degree recipient-based and would thus need empirical data which I am not able to provide in this theory-based study.

9   Kristeva regards Céline as "a privileged example" of *abject* writing, since he "does not, within the orb of abjection, spare a single sphere: neither that of morality, or politics, or religion, or esthetics, or, all the more so, subjectivity or language" (207f.).

these with relevant contributions from other previously discussed studies on the topic by W. Miller, Menninghaus, Wilson, Korsmeyer, as well as my own findings.

I will first present an overview of semantic fields of typical disgust-elicitation as they may become manifest in dramatic writing and which comply with the categories of disgust defined in recent scientific scholarship as well as with disgust's historical cognates *miasma*, *dyschéreia*, *Ekel*, and *abjection*.[10] In the second sub-section, I will turn to the particular linguistic forms and structures in which disgust can be communicated in the theatrical text. To illustrate how these semantic fields and semiotic manifestations of disgust can be used in drama, I will provide examples from previously discussed plays like Sophocles' *Philoctetes* or Euripides' *Bacchae*, as well as from the dramatic works of Shakespeare. Shakespeare's plays offer an extraordinarily rich source for exemplifying the aesthetic employment of appalling actions and viscerally effective language. Using examples from Shakespeare not only shows, once again, that dramatic disgust was a potent aesthetic device before the term 'disgust' itself came to be commonly used in the English language (cf. Wilson 4), it also provides readers with a contextualising background since most will be familiar with the text.[11]

1. Semantic Fields of Disgust-Elicitation

Abjection, whether in real life or aesthetically mediated, represents states of ambiguity which destabilise and thereby question the rules and norms set up by society in the 'symbolic order' (cf. III) and give rise to feelings of repulsion. These states are experienced as a loss of control over meaning; they threaten humans' sense of self-integrity (cf. V). In ancient tragedy, these states of ambiguity were commonly

---

10   These categories are merely intended to serve the facility of inspection for drama analysis; a strict separation into a clearly defined categorical system is difficult to accomplish because most categories of disgust-elicitation tend to overlap, as the elaborations on the semantic fields will show. Also, disgust with its highly imaginative potential and its underlying 'sympathetic laws of magical belief' (cf. IV.i) rarely stays within the boundaries of one category. Especially in aesthetic manifestations of disgust, it is common that two or more of the related categories are mixed to enhance the aesthetic effect.

11   There are a number of other authors and dramatic genres that would be interesting to investigate with regard to their employment of dramatic disgust, such as Roman tragedy (Lucius Seneca, etc.), Gothic plays (Joanna Baillie, etc.), *Sturm und Drang* (Friedrich Schiller, etc.), Jacobean revenge tragedy (Thomas Middleton, etc.), 'angry young men' (Edward Bond, etc.), Holy theatre (Peter Brooks, etc.), Actionism (Hermann Nitsch, etc.), or immersive theatre (Gob Squad, etc.), to name but a few. Since any mention of particular examples from these authors or genres would necessarily appear eclectic within the realm of this general overview, the decision was taken to use only previously discussed examples and supplement these with generally accessible citations from Shakespeare's plays.

associated with the Greek god Dionysus and the ritualistic practices involved in his celebration (cf. I; II.ii). Representation of *abjection* in drama can be accomplished by drawing on a wide range of categories that typically elicit disgust, which largely overlap with the Dionysian realm. As the historical discussion of disgust and its cognates have shown, at the core of humans' disgust reactions lies the essentially tragic knowledge of having been born to die and the resulting struggle to come to terms with anything that calls into question the provisional structures that are employed to 'cover up' this Dionysian truth (cf. I; II.ii). Drama can make use of *abjection*'s 'powers of horror' (cf. III.ii) in different ways. On the level of content, the most commonly encountered literary devices are metaphors and similes that 'feed' on the rich semantic fields available for the evocation of disgust.

Food & Consumption

Loathsome foods and appalling modes of consumption have been employed in drama ever since the genre's origin in Greek antiquity. Across the academic disciplines, food-loathing and specific modes of consumption represent an undisputed category of disgust-elicitation, which according to psychologists developed from an instinctive distaste as a protective mechanism to prevent us from incorporating "rotted and toxic food" (Herz 6, cf. IV.i). Consumption-disgust can, however, also be evoked by a broad range of non-toxic foods. As already Darwin noted, any food that appears 'foreign' in form, smell, texture, or mode of preparation can cause repulsion (cf. 257ff.).

Another source of disgust via modes of consumption is linked to surfeit and excessive eating. Plato had already linked this phenomenon to the base, instinctive, animalistic *appetitive* part of the soul (cf. *miasma* in I.i). Excessive and improper ways of eating are to this day commonly conceived of as marking a blurring between the categories of animal and human. The semantic category of food and consumption in association with disgust is thus commonly employed to degrade individuals or groups on the basis of their different eating habits (cf. V.ii Order & Other). The underlying mechanism of establishing social hierarchies via negative assessment translates well into drama, where dramatic disgust can be used to either solidify or question these hierarchies (cf. reversal in *Philoctetes* and *Bacchae* in I). In both of the previously discussed ancient plays, Sophocles' *Philoctetes* and Euripides' *Bacchae*, the eating of raw (i.e. bloody) flesh, for example, is used to reduce the social outcasts Philoctetes and the Bacchean *maenads* to a 'sub-human' animalistic state (cf. I).

Consumption elicits the most intense feelings of repulsion when it is directly linked to the dichotomous pair of life/death.[12] This is for example the case when rotten or waste products (especially bodily waste products such as excrements) are being consumed,[13] or when the consumption of one creature's decaying body sustains the life of another (e.g. parasites). In these cases, the conflation of the oppositional life/death categories, which Bataille conceptualised in terms of oral consumption (the *homogeneous*: life affirmation, assimilation) and excretion (the *heterogeneous*: waste, death, cf. III.i) reaches a nauseating climax. We find a vivid example of such a scenario in Philoctetes' address to the parasites feeding on his wounded foot: "This is your chance to feast, fix your teeth in vengeance upon my mottled meat" (1155, cf. I).

Another action that falls into this category and functions as an even stronger elicitor of disgust, because it also implies moral transgression, is cannibalism, especially when it occurs within family ties (cf. Segal, *Tragedy and Civilization*). This atrocious act has found its way into some of the most famous works of drama.[14] In Euripides' *Bacchae* (where the act is only imagined), Agave not only brutally murders her son, but also fantasises about the preparation of a festive meal from his remains. Killing her own son reverses Agave's traditional role as 'life-giving' mother. By expressing the wish to consume his body, she also reverses her motherly role as nurture-provider for her son into the role of a 'nurture-taker' from his flesh. She now wants to take *into* her body (to nurture herself) that which she has as mother *brought out* of it.

Animality

Disgust as a mechanism to demarcate humans' distance from their animalistic ancestry forms the second most commonly agreed-upon category of disgust-elicitation (cf. IV.i) that has featured prominently in works of drama since its origination from the Dionysian cult (cf. I-IV). The patron of drama, Dionysus himself, is classically associated with beastly physical features, savage manners, and instinctive sexual drives (cf. I). In Sophocles' *Philoctetes*, we find a wide-ranging application

---

12   The meaning of the term 'consumption' itself is already indicative of this ambiguity since it not only denotes 'eating' but in the passive also 'death' as in "wasting of the body by disease; wasting disease" (cf. "Consumption" n.p.).
13   A famous example that makes use of this category of disgust-elicitation is Luis Buñuel's surrealist film *Le Fantôme de la liberté* (1974), where people are sitting defecating on toilets around a dining table and retreat to small cabins whenever they need to eat.
14   Famous plays in which cannibalism features are, for example, Seneca's *Thyestes*, where Thyestes is unknowingly served his sons' heads for dinner, or Shakespeare's *Titus Andronicus*, where Titus serves Tamora her sons for dinner in a pie. Cf. Wilson for a more detailed discussion of this latter example (27f.).

of this category to mark the protagonist's abysmal state as something in-between human and animal. Philoctetes has been reduced to a creature that not only eats like an animal, but also has to move like one. Because of his infected foot he cannot sustain an upright walking position, but has to "crawl" (295, 701) to move forward (cf. I).

Another category of disgust-elicitation associated with animals relates to the material quality of softness and/or sliminess (cf. slime in III.i). Exemplary cases are toads, slugs, worms, and maggots. Many of these animals are not only difficult to literally 'get a grip on', but they are also difficult to conceptually grasp (cf. *dyschéreia*: 'difficult to handle', I). Where is the front of a worm and where is its back? Where does it eat and where does it excrete? If the worm was cut in half, would both sides live on? The worm figures prominently in Shakespeare's *Hamlet*, where Hamlet not only uses it to depict life as being determined by the knowledge of death: the un-graspable and 'wormly' essence of our existence (cf. Silenian wisdom in II.i), but also to destabilise the social hierarchies he finds himself to be part of (cf. IV.i). Hamlet equates the King to the beggar and the worm, in that they will all suffer the same fate of dying and being consumed by other creatures. Once again there is a conflation of different categories of typical disgust-elicitation through the supplementation of the animal category with that of food and consumption. Hamlet answers Claudius' question concerning the whereabouts of the recently deceased Polonius with: "At supper", yet "[n]ot where he eats, but where he is eaten" by worms and maggots (IV.iii). Hamlet further dismantles common hierarchical structures by reversing the order of the Elizabethan 'great chain of being' (cf. *Britannica* n.p.) and raising the worm up to the status of "emperor": "[W]e fat all creatures else to fat us, and we fat ourselves for maggots: your fat king and your lean beggar is but variable service; two dishes, but to one table: that's the end" (IV.iii).

Hamlet continues by taking the imagery another step further, by indicating that the King may finally end up as the beggar's waste product: "A man may fish with the worm that hath eat of a king, and eat of the fish that hath fed of that worm. [...] Nothing, but to show you how a king may go a progress through the guts of a beggar" (*ibid.*). Hamlet's description not only makes an indirect reference to cannibalism, which relates back to the category of food and consumption discussed above; by downgrading the King to the gut products (excrements) of a beggar, he also employs a third category of disgust-elicitation, namely bodies and their (waste) products.

Body Boundaries

In drama, body metaphors feature regularly as a stylistic device. Since all humans share the experience of having a body, body metaphors are a particular potent device in drama (as well as in language in general) to structure and make sense of the world (cf. Heinz 80f.). Disgust that is evoked by specific body parts or bodily functions is generally related to violations of the body's integrity (dismemberment, deformation, injury, etc.) and thus mainly to 'zones' that are prone to endanger this integrity. Body-disgust is predominately evoked by the body's orifices and substances related to these: blood, urine, sweat, mucus, as well as excrement, vomit, etc. Orifices, wounds, and their emissions make the inside of the body appear outside of it, and, according to Kristeva, cause repulsion because they represent the instability of the border between object and subject, which calls "the autonomy or substance of the subject [...] into question" (in Morgan and Morris 22). Deformed bodies or dismemberment can give rise to feelings of disgust for the same reason.

Of the substances that depart through the bodies' orifices, excrements are those that are generally perceived as the most appalling (cf. Rozin et al., "Varieties of Disgust" 870, IV.i). Defecation is considered as defilement and excrements as waste products that need to be "jettisoned from the 'symbolic system'" to guarantee the stability of "social rationality" (Kristeva 65). According to Kristeva, excrements and other bodily waste products cause repulsion because they are associated with a pre-symbolic (pre-cultural) state of quasi animalistic existence. Like Bataille in his conception of the *heterogeneous* (cf. III.i), Kristeva also regards faecal matter as an ultimate reminder of humans' death-born condition: "Such wastes drop so that I might live, until, from loss to loss, nothing remains in me and my entire body falls beyond the limit – *cadere*, cadaver" (3; original emphasis). Sophocles' Philoctetes offers a vivid rendering of his *abject* condition when he describes himself as a "corpse among the living" (1018). In social systems, physical reminders of our mortal condition are strictly held at bay by rules of hygiene and social conduct. Disregard of these rules, whether this happens voluntarily or involuntarily, is viewed as highly appalling, as Theophrastus' characterisation of the offensive man (*dyschéreia*) demonstrated (cf. I), and can lead to those inflicted being excluded from the social *body*, as was the case with Philoctetes (cf. I; Heinz 81).

Closely related to the violation of physical boundaries and body fluids are sexual actions, which supply rich material for possible disgust-association. Besides sexuality's direct relation to breaching physical boundaries via the orifices, it is also strongly linked to most of the other classical semantic fields of disgust-elicitation: animality (sexual instincts, drives), pollution (sexual diseases, etc.), and moral transgression (incest, paedophilia, etc.).

Often it is the woman's body (especially the vagina) that becomes associated with disgust, which is likely to stem from its relation to the process of birth.[15]

---

15 What is important to note here is the fact that it is almost exclusively men who put forward the opinion that it is women (especially the ageing woman; vetula) who register particularly high on a scale of disgust-elicitation. Feinstein finds this gender bias to be a logical result of a "male controlled discourse" on disgust: "To the extent that disgust protects the self from

From Shakespeare's "birth-strangled babe / [d]itch-deliver'd by a drab" (*Macbeth*, IV.i) to Samuel Beckett's "It's abominable! [...]. They give birth astride of a grave" (*Waiting for Godot* II), imagery pertaining to humans' tragic condition with reference to the process of birth or the female body are common and often give rise to theatrical characters' disgust. The previously mentioned example from Shakespeare's *King Lear* illustrates this point particularly strongly, when Lear in his state of existential crisis expresses his utter disgust at the female vagina (and via its procreational function also to life in general): "There's hell, there's darkness, there is the sulphurous pit, / Burning, scalding, stench, consumption; fie, / fie, fie! pah, pah!" (*King Lear*, IV.vi).

Pollution

As already discussed in detail in relation to the ancient concept of *miasma*, we conceive of something as polluted when matter falls out of categories and is regarded as contaminating the 'purity' of a given (logical) system (cf. I). The idea of pollution can become manifest in many forms ranging from dirt, filth, and waste products to diseases and non-observance of cultural and social conventions, especially ones that are related to sexuality (e.g. rape, incest). Illnesses and diseases that are associated with pollution are mainly contagious and commonly related to sexuality (e.g. the plague, syphilis, AIDS, etc.). Diseased bodies are often perceived as a signifier of "death infecting life", *abjection* (Kristeva 4, cf. III.ii). Polluted bodies turn their sufferers into potentially contagious matter, which often results in their social exclusion (e.g. Sophocles' *Philoctetes*). Because of the 'laws of sympathetic magic' physical states of pollution, be they due to lack of hygiene or a result of specific illnesses and diseases, are commonly perceived as an indication for an equally 'polluted mind'. The fear of contagion inherent in pollution, which travels so freely between physical and metaphysical realms, makes this category of typical disgust-elicitation a particularly salient dramatic device. In Shakespeare's *A Winter's Tale*, for example, Polixenes uses the language of pollution and disease to give testimony

---

contamination by the other, a male perspective, which naturally regards females as 'other,' may also regard them as more disgusting and contaminating than males, leading to a fear of female sexuality and a heightened aversion to female emissions" (36). Since I do not see much plausible reason, besides the gender-bias forwarded by male writers, to view (elderly) women as essentially more appalling than (elderly) men (whose abilities to procreate also greatly diminish over time), I refrain from dealing with this aspect at any length and thus avoid contributing to a continuation of the 'vetula-story', which posits the (ageing) woman's body as a prime signifier of repulsion. For a more detailed elaboration on the vetula motif you may cf. Menninghaus, who discusses the topic at some length, especially in his analysis of Franz Kafka's work (cf. 87ff., 178ff., 203ff., 227ff.).

of his loyalty towards his friend Leontes. He claims that if he had committed adultery (as Leontes assumes):

> O, then my best blood turn
> To an infected jelly, and my name
> Be yok'd with his that did betray the Best!
> Turn then my freshest reputation to
> A savour, that may strike the dullest nostril
> Where I arrive; and my approach be shunn'd,
> Nay, hated too, worse than the great'st infection
> That e'er was heard or read! (I.ii)

The vocabulary from the field of pollution ("infected jelly") is used by Polixenes to give evidence of the 'purity' of his soul by means of contrast.

Meinel argues that pollution "is ubiquitous and central" to Greek tragedy (1; cf. *miasma*, I), and it has become a dominant motif in many well-known dramatic works since then. Creon's statement that "[t]here is an unclean thing [...] polluting our soil" in the opening scene of Sophocles' *Oedipus the King*, for example, closely resembles Marcellus' statement that "[s]omething is rotten in the state of Denmark" (I.iv) in Shakespeare's *Hamlet*; both illustrating the corruptness of the states the characters inhabit.

Moral Transgression

Scientific research has confirmed the Freudian claim that disgust cannot only be elicited by potentially harmful entities from the physical realm, but also by transgressions of social and moral norms and rule (cf. III, IV.i). As Rozin et al. state, disgust not only functions to protect the body, but also the soul from perceived harm (cf. IV.i). According to Wilson, "[d]isgust can be [...] a psychomotor agent of social taboo, a personal police force that patrols the boundaries of social exclusion, censoring violation" (29).

The question of cause and effect is two-fold in the domain of moral disgust. Social norms and cultural taboos (dietary restrictions, toilet training, etc.) are, on the one hand, established to keep humans' association with typical disgust-elicitors from the previously listed categories at bay. In this case disgust is not only the effect but also the motivator for the establishment of social rules (cf. Freud 'cultural feeling'; Kristeva 'safeguard of my culture'; III) and thus functions as a kind of second-order (or double) aversive mechanism. Moral disgust can, however, also be induced by entirely non-physical actions. Kristeva argues that anything which "does not respect borders, positions, rules. The in-between, the ambiguous, the composite. The traitor, the liar, the criminal with a good conscience, the shameless rapist, the killer who claims he is a savior" (4) can cause *abjection* and thus provoke feelings of repulsion. In these cases, the underlying fear of pollution and contagion is transferred to the metaphysical realm where it denotes "matter out of place" in terms of instances that cannot be entirely grasped, things that are *abject* because they defy assimilation in a 'symbolic order' (cf. *miasma* and *dyschéreia* in I; *abjection* in III).

Appalling forms of moral transgression lie at the heart of numerous classic works of drama, ranging from the incest motif in Sophocles' *Oedipus the King* to acts of cannibalism in Euripides' *Bacchae* or Shakespeare's *Titus Andronicus* (cf. Food and Consumption) or violent forms of child abuse in Lessing's *Miss Sara Sampson* (cf. II). In Sophocles' *Philoctetes* we find a revealing exemplary case of an instance of 'pure' moral disgust when Neoptolemus expresses utter self-disgust (*dyschéreia*) at having attained Philoctetes' trust and friendship by means of lies and deception. For Neoptolemus this is the most appalling kind of transgression (worse than Philoctetes' physiologically ambiguous state as in-between human and animal), because it represents a breach with what he conceives to be human 'nature' (cf. I).

2. Structures & Semiotic Modes of Disgust

States of disgust-evoking *abjection* in drama can become manifest not just on the level of content, but also on the level of syntax and literary style. Mirroring the transgression of boundaries that is intrinsic to the notion of disgust, an *abject* style of writing is also commonly characterised by a dismantling of linguistic rules, a "perversion" of language as Kristeva calls it (15ff.). This can be achieved in various ways by the use of specific vocabulary, which either because of its content (commonly drawn from the above-named semantic fields of disgust-elicitation), its corruption of socially acceptable linguistic norms (e.g. slang, swear words), its visceral onomatopoetic charge, or through unusual or 'foreign' combinations of words, can have an unsettling effect on recipients.[16] Linguistic or grammatical 'perversions' function to enhance the disgust-eliciting effect of depicted contents to a degree that can literally turns recipients' stomachs.

Lists

Lists are a stylistic feature frequently used in dramatic works to order and arrange repulsive items. Lists share a distinctive characteristic with the sensation of dis-

---

16 As Aristotle's example, discussed in the first chapter, demonstrated, exchanging the one 'common' word "eat" with the more unusual term "feast" in the context of Philoctetes' rotting foot being consumed by parasites (cf. 1458b) enhances the affective charge of the image by adding two further ambiguous categories (animal/human; joyful life sustainment/painful decay) to the already appalling description (cf. I.ii).

gust. They can induce a sense of order and structure, while at the same time displaying the inability to form a coherent narrative around the items presented. Douglas-Fairhurst claims that lists "respond to the worry that the world is falling apart with a form of grammar that is both symptom and therapy" (71). For Douglas-Fairhurst, lists provide "an illusion of control over the unstable and contingent mess of the world" (72; cf. also Kristeva 136).

In Shakespeare's *Macbeth*, we find a vivid example of the effectiveness of lists when the witches describe the ingredients of a soup they are preparing. These include, besides various slimy animals and animal parts (toad, snake, frog toe, tongue of a dog, etc.), human body parts such as the "liver of [a] blaspheming Jew", the "nose of Turk", "Tartar's lips", and the "finger of [a] birth-strangled babe / Ditch-delivered by a drab" (IV.i; cf. Douglas Fairhurst 71; Wilson 164).

Listings of appalling contents not only mirror a simultaneous loss of and need for control, they can also greatly enhance the disgust-eliciting effect of the objects presented. Since lists lack causal connections between the items they present, they provide a form that encourages our imagination to conjure up further revolting associations to accomplish cohesion.

Onomatopoeia & Interjections

Onomatopoeia and interjections serve as a powerful tool to inscribe disgust into dramatic language. Wilson coins the expression "semiotics of revulsion" (10) to refer to these stylistic devices. With reference to Shakespeare's use of these semiotic layers, he states: "An affect such as disgust is seldom named, no markers point directly towards it, but it can be felt. [...] One of Shakespeare's very physical terms for moments of repulsion and loathing is 'gorge'" (Wilson 8). The example Wilson uses to illustrate this point is taken from Shakespeare's *Hamlet*, where Hamlet holds Yorick's skull in his hands and reflects how he had been "on his back a thousand times; and now, how abhorred in my imagination it is! my gorge rises at it" (V.i; cf. Wilson 8). Wilson argues that the word 'gorge' contains the somatic dimension of vomiting or being close to vomiting, which evokes

> a strikingly concrete image from which it is possible to infer a physical, although only imaginary, feeling of disgust. Yorick['s] skull in Hamlet's hands, his rotted body in Hamlet's imagination, dissolves before the mind's eye, stinks in the mind's nose. (Wilson 8)

Other terms that mimic actions of retching, vomiting, or spitting and thus supply signifiers with a particularly graphic and vivid semiotic layer of repulsion are words such as: 'maggots', 'gagging', 'goo', 'gunk', 'dung', and interjections like 'yuck' or those with front plosive sounds like 'pah', 'fie', and 'fut' (cf. W. Miller 85, Darwin 256ff., Wilson 8). Wilson argues that "you can hardly cry out 'pah!' without narrowing the nose and pursing the mouth as if in vomiting" (8). The plosive interjections named here are often used by Shakespeare and commonly given extra charge by repetition like in Lear's outcry of repulsion when pondering the female genital: "fie, / fie, fie! pah! pah!" (*King Lear*, IV.vi). W. Miller regards these exclamations also as an indication of the characters uttering them being so strongly afflicted by disgust that they are "beyond speech" (167).

Other onomatopoeia that reflect features of disgust are those derived from the material quality that is ascribed to objects of repulsion: the ungraspable (i.e. 'difficult to handle' (*dyschéreia*); cf. I) soft and slippery texture of slime (cf. III.i). Allusion to this quality can be found in words like 'slug', 'sludge', 'slush', 'slither', 'slobber', and 'slime' itself. Shakespeare uses terms from this category to mirror the 'slimy' texture of the soup the witches are preparing in *Macbeth*: "slips of yew, / [s]liver'd in the moon's eclipse, [...] [m]ake the gruel thick and slab" (IV.i).

Slang

Colloquial language and slang draw widely from the semantic fields of disgust and commonly supplement these with the aforementioned layers of 'semiotic revulsion'. Slang is a mode of communication that shares many characteristics with the sensation of disgust and the underlying structure of *abjection*. It is often highly affectively charged by making use of vivid vocabulary (cf. "Slang" n.p.) and thus discloses emotional states particularly well. As Kristeva states: "[E]motion, in order to make itself heard, adopts colloquial speech or [...] slang" (191).

Slang defies the rules of standard or socially acceptable language and is commonly employed as a linguistic tool for the degradation of others. It can also be used to offend and display discontent with personal, social, or cultural values. At the same time, the use of colloquial and slang potentially places its speaker fairly low in the social hierarchy (beneath the respected norm; cf. IV.i).[17] But, as noted in the *Cambridge Dictionary*, this mode of communication can also be used to form "close personal relationships with others" within particular groups or settings (cf. "Swearing and Taboo" n.p.).

According to Kristeva, slang in its often violent and strange forms functions as "a radical instrument of separation, of rejection" (109). The ambivalence inherent to states of *abjection* is also mirrored in slang, in that it likewise "produces a semantic fuzziness, if not interruption, within the utterances that it punctuates and rhythmicizes" (191). Like disgust, slang is thus a potent device for the construction of social orders and hierarchies by means of negative evaluation (cf. IV.i).

---

17 In one of the earliest recordings of the word 'slang' itself in 1765, the term is used to denote the "special vocabulary of tramps or thieves" ("Slang" n.p.).

In drama, as the genre of the spoken word, colloquial language and slang can be employed most effectively to strongly affect recipients. As Kristeva notes: "Excitement and disgust, joy and repulsion – the [...recipient] deciphers them very fast [...] where emotion does not allow itself to be dolled up in flowery sentences" (204). Aristotle had already advocated the usage of authentic as well as highly affective language (cf. 1458b, I.ii). Jeffrey Henderson notes that obscene language was used in Greek tragedy to highlight "dereliction from respectable norms" like "predatory male behaviour [...], savagery [...], disruptive violence or indiscipline" (2). In Shakespeare too, we find numerous illustrative examples of slang and cursing such as: "ye fat-guts!" (*Henry IV Pt. 1*, II.ii), "whoreson" (*Hamlet*, V.i), or "bunch-back'd toad" (*Richard III*, I.iii).

Another common feature of degrading language is association with pollution and bad smells (cf. *Philoctetes* and *Bacchae* in I), which can also be found in Shakespeare's works: "More of your conversation would infect my brain" (*Coriolanus*, II.i), "[T]he rankest compound of villainous smell that ever offended nostrils" (*The Merry Wives of Windsor*, III.v). Eighteenth-century playwrights of the German *Sturm und Drang* movement also effectively employed this characteristic of colloquial language. Richter describes Goethe's use of slang elements in *Götz von Berlichingen* (1773), where the main character asks a messenger to report back to the Hauptmann that "he can kiss my ass" (III),[18] an expression which he regards as "emblem[atic] of the storm and stress play's confrontation with the audience", where "[m]oral improvement is still on the agenda, but through an in-your-face encounter with sexual desire and the body" (443). This could also be considered as an accurate description of a majority of plays listed as examples of 1990s' theatrical *in-yer-face* aesthetics, where the use of brash colloquial language is a defining feature (cf. Sierz, "in-yer-face" n.p.).

V.ii   Functions & Effects of Dramatic Disgust

Aesthetic representation of the various disgust-elicitors listed in the previous subchapter can take on a number of important functions in works of drama. Aesthetic disgust can function on three different yet interdependent levels as a dramatic device, which can be roughly divided up into the ancient notions of *poiesis*, *mimesis*, and *aisthesis* (cf. Balme 43ff.). With *poiesis* I refer to the ways in which disgusting

---

18   The German original expression, which would literally translate into "He can lick me in the ass" ("er kann mich im Arsch lecken", III), is much stronger in its potentially appalling effectiveness, since licking the inside of someone's orifice transgresses the body boundaries of both participants, whereas kissing could theoretically occur without the violation of anyone's boundaries (cf. V.i).

contents and forms are linguistically employed as artistic tools for creating dramatic elements such as setting scenes or building characters. *Mimesis* in this context relates mainly to the specific theatrical mode of actual embodiment of disgust-eliciting actions and events on stage. The third category, *aisthesis*, pertains to the potential effects dramatic representation of disgust may have on recipients.

Mimesis: Bodies on Stage

I will begin with this mainly performance-oriented category, which is included for the sake of completeness. The emphasis, however, will be on the other two categories since the focus of this study lies on the functions of aesthetic disgust as they prevail in the dramatic text. *Mimesis* as a category nevertheless proves instrumental for the differentiation between implementations of dramatic disgust either in a *diegetic* mode (e.g. messenger reports of appalling incidents) or in form of *mimetic* enactment on stage (e.g. stage directions indicating violations). While *diegetic* modes evoke a 'playing out' of appalling events primarily in the recipients' imagination, *mimetic* modes offer a great potential for non-linguistic portrayals of disgust-eliciting actions or character traits. In sum, drama as a text intended for performance on stage offers the unique possibility to include non-linguistic elements of disgust-elicitation, which can greatly enhance the experience of repulsion in recipients. *Mimetic* modes of communication are especially potent in representing states of *abjection* that defy articulation in plain language (cf. III.i). Examples of disgust-enhancing *mimetic* elements include, for example, silences demonstrating shock, awe, or speechlessness, paralinguistic features in which feelings of repulsion can be fully felt or enhanced by further associations in the characters' as well as in the recipients' minds. Other elements are: facial expressions exhibiting disgust, or voice and intonation which amplify disgust-related sounds such as spitting, gagging, or interjections like "eww", "pah", etc. (cf. V.i Onomatopoeia).

Body Metaphors

The strongest non-linguistic signifiers and elicitors of dramatic disgust, however, are body images of wounded, sick, or deformed bodies, symbolising, for example, the disintegration of characters' moral convictions (e.g. Cadmus being turned into a snake in Euripides' *Bacchae*; cf. I). Body metaphors relating to disgust can either be used to confirm social mechanisms of discrimination against others, or they can function as an effective device to question the discrimination of others on the basis of their perceived 'defiled', 'deformed', or simply 'foreign' appearance or behaviour (cf. V.ii Order & Other). As Sarah Heinz states: "By staging the sick, damaged, or dying bodies of the protagonists [...], the audience is [...] confronted with their own disgust and their sense of individual and social hygiene" (82). According to Heinz, these kinds of depictions "give a voice, a physical presence, and a stage to those who are dehumanized as the other" (*ibid.*; cf. V.ii Social Critique).

Poiesis: Scene, Atmosphere, Character, Plot

Poiesis is etymologically derived from the ancient Greek verb 'to make' and has since ancient times been used to refer to the specific mode in which creative texts are 'made' (cf. Aristotle, 1447a). In drama, *poiesis* is concerned with all elements that conceptionally and linguistically create the dramaturgy of the play and influence the perceptions and interactions of characters within the story world (and by implication the perception of recipients). Disgust can serve as a powerful dramatic device in the realm of *poiesis*, either on the level of *diegesis* (i.e. narrating appalling events) or on the level of literary style which can enhance the effect of gruesome contents (cf. V.i). Dramatic disgust can be used to mark tragic conflicts, drive the plot, build characters, or create setting and atmosphere. In Shakespeare's *Hamlet*, for example, Marcellus' statement that "[s]omething is rotten in the state of Denmark" (I.iv) introduces the issue of moral decay that lies at the heart of the play. The allusion to disgust in the image of a rotting state functions not only to set the scene, but also as a foreshadowing device (cf. Wilson xxiv).

Order & Other

As in real life, disgust in drama is commonly used to designate the social hierarchical positions of characters in relation to others and can thus be employed as a marker of distinction or discrimination against individuals or groups (especially minorities; cf. IV.i). Prominent examples of characters' discrimination via association with disgust are the previously discussed cases of Philoctetes' and the Bacchae's social exclusion (cf. I). A classic case of discrimination on the basis of constructing a revolting image of 'otherness' can also be found in Shakespeare's *Othello*, where Iago 'warns' Brabantio about his daughter Desdemona's intimate engagement with the army general, the Moor Othello:

> Even now, now, very now, an old black ram
> Is tupping your white ewe. Arise, arise! [...]
> Or else the devil will make a grandsire of you. [...]
> I am one, sir, that comes to tell you, your daughter and the Moor
> are now making the beast with two backs. (I.i)

Iago utilises Othello's 'otherness' (dark skin colour) to evoke a number of degrading associations from the animalistic category ("ram", "beast with two backs") to fuel

Desdemona's father's rejection of her partner. By also describing Desdemona as a "ewe", he further indicates that her association with the Moor turns her equally 'sub-human'. Iago's repetitive "now, now, very now" not only indicates the urgency of his message, but also rhythmically imitates the sexual intercourse he reports on in the next lines with an equally onomatopoetically charged choice of wording ("ram", "tupping"). The evoked image of Othello's supposed animalistic hypersexuality is supplemented by the idea of sexual pollution through the indication that the Moor's "black" blood and semen not only 'soil' Desdemona's purity ("white ewe"), but also pollute the family's "white" bloodline (i.e. miscegenation). The conflation of both semantic fields of typical disgust-elicitation comes to a climax when Iago describes the young couple's sexual intercourse as "making a beast with two backs" (*ibid.*). This image does not only provoke the father to again vividly imagine his daughter's sexual exploits (i.e. two bodies united into 'one' with two backs), but also alludes to the animalistic and 'wild' nature of the encounter.

Simply by associating Othello with revolting animalistic and polluting behaviour, Iago manages to debase the powerful general to a sub-human state, and thereby significantly meddles with the existing social hierarchical order (based on birth right and power). He uses this strategy to move up the social ladder. By the end of the play, Iago has accomplished this mischievous task. The noble Moor, who had previously stood even above Brabantio, has been led to internalise Iago's racist character ascriptions and turned into a murderer, which places him at the bottom of the social hierarchy. Seeing no worth in his person or existence any longer he kills himself after claiming to be no more than a "turbanned turk", a "circumcised dog" (V.ii).

Aisthesis: Disgusted Recipients

Aisthesis is concerned with the effects dramatic disgust can have on recipients. My understanding of the term '*aisthesis*' is based on the classical Aristotelean meaning as being concerned with the interaction between perceived objects and the person perceiving them (cf. Shields n.p.). Since the development of aesthetics as a distinct academic field in eighteenth-century Germany, scholars have been primarily interested in the specific interaction of emotions and cognition at work (cf. Kant's 'aesthetic idea' in II.i) in the engagement with artistic products, their effects, and the potential insights that can be gained from such encounters. By implication of characters predominantly being human, all of the functions and effects that apply extradiegetically to recipients can likewise affect characters within the story world as part of the dramaturgy (i.e. *poiesis*).

Shock

An effect that is commonly attributed to disgust-evoking artistic representations is shock. Generally, it depends on the artist's intentions and the recipient's inclination whether the shock-effect is perceived negatively as an offence or insult against prevailing social and cultural values (cf. Wilson 16), or positively as a provocation that invites the reconsideration of the presuppositions that informed the strong emotional response. As Wilson states, aesthetic disgust can "startle the audience out of its habitual complacency" (*ibid.*). In its ability to startle and shock, *abject* art invites (or rather, forces) its recipients to take a moment of pause, which allows them to afterwards revisit the presuppositions that caused their strong emotional reaction. According to Critchley and Webster, the shock effect of disgust can function to "wake people up" (218). This feature of aesthetic disgust became especially important in the agendas of Europe's early twentieth-century avant-garde artists, who radically implemented revolting contents and forms in their works to "touch the intimate nerve" (Kristeva 138) of a desensitised shell-shocked society and thereby offer an effective antidote to rising fascism.

Real Feelings

Closely related to the category of shock is aesthetic disgust's ability to induce strong emotional responses. As Kant already found and neuroscientific research confirmed, disgust is particularly capable of transgressing *mimetic* boundaries; it is a distinctly *real* and vital emotion (cf. II.i; IV.i). Supporters of the highly affective dramatic works of, for example, '*in-yer-face* theatre' argue that recipients' intense experiences of nauseating and violent elements bring them in contact with the most gruesome realities of the human condition, a feature that already Nietzsche considered to lie at the heart of tragedy (cf. II.ii), and which can be found in many of the classic examples of drama such as Sophocles' *Oedipus* or Shakespeare's *Titus Andronicus* (cf. Wald n.p.).

With its highly emotive edge, aesthetically evoked disgust in form of *abject* language is able to "grab hold of emotion by means of speech" (Kristeva 138). In its vitality, aesthetic disgust has proven to be a potent vehicle to catch recipients' attention, especially in post-Gutenberg societies, where people are continuously flooded with an infinite amount of textual and visual data from across the different channels of the new and 'old' media. As an "attention focusing device" (Wilson xxiv), it can be employed to lay emphasis on particular aspects that artists wish to bring to the fore. The idiosyncratic quality of disgust's inherent 'vitality' also appears to address a '*hunger* for *real* emotions' prevalent in post-industrial societies where personal contacts and modes of communication have become increasingly replaced by 'screened' forms of social engagement (cf. IV). According to Menninghaus, disgust in its viscerality furthermore allows for people's connection to their bodies and physical sensations: "the dark, 'dense' and 'intense' continent of elemental, bodily (self-)perceptions" (14). One could argue that to some extent the roles of art and everyday life have become reversed over the past two decades. As life progressively takes place in form of *simulacra*,[19] art in general, and the theatre in particular, seem to become increasingly sought out to offer *real* experiences; a trend visible in the increasing amount of contemporary participatory theatrical and performative formats (cf. Machon *Immersive Theatre*), or the strong performative emphasis of the world's leading contemporary art exhibition Documenta in 2017 (cf. Michalska n.p.). People might go to the theatre simply to look into the eyes of a stranger and experience a *real* moment.

Social Critique

By shock and strong emotional engagement of recipients, dramatic disgust is an effective tool to question norms and values of dominant social beliefs and convictions. As already discussed in the section on "Order & Other", disgust is especially potent to show the plight of individuals and cultural groups that are debased on grounds of their 'otherness'. A confrontation with aesthetically mediated *abjection* is instrumental to dismantle the 'symbolical order' on which social systems are based and thus lays bare the mechanisms involved in these processes of degradation and dehumanisation. What can be gained from these procedures of de-masking is an understanding of the role language plays in setting up the symbolical systems (belief, propaganda, etc.) that control our everyday lives. By taking a closer look at what disgusts us and how disgust is expressed through language, we can learn to question discourses and test the validity of underlying presuppositions and structures against rational or humanitarian convictions.

Confronting Death & Ambiguity

Through the aesthetic representation of states of *abjection*, which largely defy communication in straightforward referential language, drama's recipients are enabled to come in contact not only with the tragic core of existence (the Silenian wisdom), but also with the fact that their human intellectual and physical abilities are limited (cf. II.i, III). According to Douglas-Fairhurst, the concept of disgust "provides a set of ideas and a set of words for characters who are forced to come to terms with the fact that their physical capacities will never be adequate to their ideals or longings"

---

19   Cf. Jean Baudrillard's seminal work on *Simulacra and Simulation* (1994 [1981]). Cf. also Anette Pankratz' article on "Signifying Nothing and Everything: Extension of the Code and Hyperreal Simulations" (63-78).

(4). His example of Shakespeare's *King Lear*, where Lear answers Gloucester's appeal to kiss the King's hand with: "Let me wipe it first; it smells of mortality" (IV.vi), illustrates the *abject* core of all disgust reactions as "death infecting life" (Kristeva 4). Ambiguous dichotomous relations, as embodied in the Dionysian spirit of in-between, are not solved, but shown, allowing for acknowledgement and the possibility of reconciliation with the paradox facets of human life.[20] With *abjection* not only being a constituent part of each human subject's existence, but also a condition that we will ultimately meet at some point of life when body and mind enter the stage of decay, all humans will have to come to terms with their own contingency eventually. It might therefore be constructive to become acquainted with the idea early on within the 'safe' realms of art in order to get used to it and practice handling the associated feelings of disgust, in the same way that for instance doctors and nurses learn to deal with feelings of repulsion when engaging with sick or dying patients.

Attraction & Pleasure

Already Plato noted that objects or incidents that cause repulsion can also be perceived as attractive (cf. *dyschéreia* in I.i).[21] In the most simple sense, this general feature of disgust can be used to attract readers' or audiences' interest. Since disgust marks the boundary between socially and culturally constructed rules and orders and humans' basic animalistic instincts, an engagement with things that are deemed revolting can be experienced as liberating. According to Nietzsche, a Dionysian transgression of boundaries can even cause ecstatic states of bliss and joy (cf. II.ii), a kind of pleasure, which Kristeva later defined as '*jouissance*' (cf. III.ii). The attractive or pleasurable component of revolting objects, persons, or actions works particularly well when these are presented in works of art: "destructive or painful action[s], such as death on stage, bodily agony, wounds, and the like" (Aristotle 1452b) or "the most contemptible insects" (1448b) can cause pleasure when

---

20 Terry Eagleton offers a poetic summary of the relation between Dionysus, abjection, and the tragic genre when he describes it as "an orgy of un-meaning, before the dawn of subjectivity itself, in which bloody stumps and mangled bits of bodies whirl in a frightful dance of death. The orgy dissolves distinction between bodies, and thus prefigures the indifferent levelling of death. Indeed, in the terms of Freud's *Beyond the Pleasure Principle* this god of ease and self-gratification represents a pure culture of the death drive [...]. Dionysus is the saint of life-in-death, a connoisseur of the kind of energy we reap through reckless self-abandonment" (3f.)

21 Scott L. Knowles states with regard to the value of the employment of disgust for the theatrical performance: "If the [... performance] provokes the desire to stop horrific acts and with the theatrical context it also attracts spectators, then there is the potential to prevent the audience from simply stopping the experience (by leaving or not going) and instead focus on what the experience is highlighting outside of the theatre" (62).

encountered in their *mimetic* representation. According to Aristotle, one source of pleasure stems from the delight we take in the artistic craftsmanship (cf. 1452b). Nietzsche goes one step further when he contends that art can "heal" us by "re-direct[ing] those repulsive thoughts about the terrible or absurd nature of existence into representations with which we can live" (40).

But it is not only *jouissance* and admiration for the craftsmanship involved in creating artworks able to induce 'aesthetic ideas' (cf. II.i) which cause pleasure. Another source of aesthetic pleasure that was already present in Aristotle's approach, is the pleasure gained from learning and understanding the nature and setup of revolting items, persons, or actions depicted.[22] As mentioned above, by aesthetically confronting *abjection* via disgust-eliciting objects, recipients are powerfully brought in contact with their most essential human conflict. By addressing the issue of "death infecting life" (Kristeva 4) via art, recipients can learn to better grasp and thus deal with the contingency of human existence. They enrich their lives by incorporating and understanding this essential dimension; and, according to Aristotle, learning and understanding is pleasure.

Finally, engagement with *abjection* via the *mimetic* arts can lead to a release of negative energies in form of *katharsis*, a process of cleansing or healing that functions in the form of an immunisation. Kristeva describes *abject* art as an "impure process", which "protects from the abject only by dint of being immersed in it" (28). Through art appalling actions can to some degree be acted or 'thought' out within the safe realm of a sanctified institution. Kristeva thus talks of art as the "catharsis par excellence" (17):

> Through the mimesis of passions – ranging from enthusiasm to suffering – in 'language with pleasurable accessories,' [...] the soul reaches orgy and purity at the same time. What is involved is a purification of body and soul by means of a heterogeneous and complex circuit, going from 'bile' to 'fire,' from 'manly warmth' to the 'enthusiasm' of the 'mind.' Rhythm and song hence arouse the impure, the other of mind, the passionate-corporeal-sexual-virile, but they harmonize it, arrange it differently than the wise man's knowledge does. (28f.)

Kristeva argues that by purifying the *abject*, art fulfils a similar role that religions have played throughout human history. For her, however, art is better equipped to manage this task in contemporary Western societies, which are increasingly seen to lose trust in set values and Christian belief-systems. Kristeva regards modern Western societies to be generally in a state of crisis, which closely resembles states

---

22 Had Aristotle allowed human nature to be essentially ambiguous and potentially 'foul' (*miaron*) too, his *Poetics* would function well to offer a solution to the paradox of aversion also in relation to disgust (cf. I.iii).

of psychopathological psychosis and runs "deeper than anything since the beginning of our era, the beginning of Christianity" (in Morgan and Morris 27). She maintains that art offers a form of "masterful sublimation [...]" (in Meisel 131), which can defer the eruption of psychosis in real life (cf. Morgan and Morris 27). Kristeva's understanding of sublimation here goes hand in hand with the Aristotelean notion of *katharsis*, with sublimation describing the (positive) effect that an aesthetically mediated dose of that which is generally rejected (the *abject*) has for the balance of the soul of artists and recipients. By giving a form to those horrors of human existence that symbolical systems (religious belief, science, etc.) increasingly fail to convincingly contain, control, and make sense of, *abject* art allows a release of the negative feelings we as humans experience as a result of our tragic condition (in-between life and death).

By confronting *abjection* collectively in an audience (or museum; or in the mind of a reader who feels connected in being allowed to share in the author's aesthetic product), recipients are offered the possibility of a reconciling form of communion, because the *abject* is "[w]hat people do not acknowledge but know they have in common; a base, mass [..., an] anthropological commonality, the secret abode for which all masks are intended" (Kristeva 134). A shared experience of an essential human conflict within a safe institutionally sanctified aesthetic realm (e.g. reading, theatre, museum, etc.) can in this regard fulfil a similar function to religious gatherings at churches or other places. Kristeva describes recipients' possible experience of feelings of communion as follows: "When they look at these objects, their ugliness and their strangeness, they see their own regression, their own *abjection*, and at that moment what occurs is a veritable state of communion" (23). By allowing the communion-building element of drama to take full force through the often brutal engagement with states of *abjection*, drama becomes reconnected to its originary roots in the Dionysian cult, where the establishment of feelings of communion was of central importance (cf. I). Taken together, the difficult and pleasurable effects of dramatic disgust as they become manifest in 'aesthetic ideas' account for the aesthetic experience of the *sublime*.

V.iii Summary

This chapter set out to synthesise the previously discussed historical approaches to disgust and its role in works of art. A comparison of the different terms '*miasma*', '*dyschéreia*', '*Ekel*', '*abjection*', and 'disgust' showed that most of the complex features that have only recently been approached in scientific and aesthetic studies on disgust (e.g. attraction, magical contagion, in-between nature/culture), were not only already contained in the ancient notions of '*miasma*' and '*dyschéreia*', but also reflected aesthetically in Attic tragedies as well as in philosophical reflections of the time.

In a next step, the relation between the 'modern' terms *'abjection'*, 'distaste', and 'disgust' was clarified and a model established that places distaste as an instinctive aversive reaction against pathogenic foods at the origin of the evolutionarily later and uniquely human experiences of *abjection* and disgust. We found that *abjection* as intrinsically intertwined with the process of becoming a human subject must predate the sensation of disgust, which is a distinctly learned reaction. Also, *abjection* represents the broader category since it not only leads to feelings of repulsion, but can also induce other psycho-physical reactions such as the pleasurable feeling of *jouissance*.

From eighteenth- and nineteenth-century debates on aesthetics in general and the role of *Ekel* therein, we extracted some suitable models and terminology for a theoretical conceptualisation of aesthetic disgust, namely Kant's 'aesthetic ideas' and the *'sublime'* to denote the 'difficult' pleasure experienced when engaging with otherwise unpleasant subjects in their artistic forms.

Through the differentiation between the terms *'abjection'* and 'disgust', we were able to ascertain that the evocation of disgust in drama can be viewed as an aesthetic mode of representing the universal experience of *abjection*, which can become manifest on the levels of content, literary style, or both. In the first sub-chapter, we assessed forms in which aesthetic disgust can become manifest in the dramatic genre on the level of content (1. Semantic Fields of Disgust Elicitation) and style (2. Structures & Semiotic Modes of Disgust).

The established categories of typical disgust-eliciting semantic fields were: (a) food-disgust that protects the body from incorporating pathogenic foods, but also takes on an important role in distinguishing cultural groups on the basis of eating habits, (b) animal-disgust as a marker of humans' distance from animalistic ancestry, (c) body-disgust related to violations of physical boundaries, (d) pollution-disgust pertaining to fear of contagion and matter 'falling out of place', and (e) moral-disgust concerned with transgressions of norms, values, and rules set up by societies.

Stylistically, associations with these disgust stimuli can be effectively enhanced through particular syntactical structures and semiotic modes of abject writing. Especially potent are: (a) lists giving the illusion of order while at the same time failing to form a coherent narrative around the items presented, (b) onomatopoeia and interjections which mirror or enhance associations to disgust through emphasis or reflecting, on the level of sound, particular disgusting contents, and (c) slang which is a particular potent and affectively charged form of language.

In the second sub-chapter, we determined and discussed the particular aesthetic functions that pertain to dramatic disgust on the three interdependent levels of *poiesis*, *mimesis*, and *aisthesis*, with *poiesis* referring to dramaturgical and stylistic devices, *mimesis* looking at modes of non-linguistic representations, and *aisthesis* relating to dramatic disgust's potential effects on recipients. Several important aesthetic functions could be established for dramatic disgust, especially regarding their effect on recipients. These were: (a) shock, (b) the evocation of strong or *real* emotional responses, (c) social critique, (d) a confrontation with humans' most essential conflict ('death infecting life'; *abjection*), as well as a number of effects which taken together account for the 'negative' aesthetic pleasure of the *sublime* (e). The positive elements which determine this aesthetic experience range from: *jouissance* evoked by the transgression of social and cultural boundaries, to pleasures of learning about crucial aspects of human existence, and admiration for the craftsmanship involved in presenting such complex issues in a form able to provoke an 'aesthetic idea', to a release of the negative feelings involved in confrontations with *abjection* in form of *katharsis*. Experiencing such a strong ratio-affective encounter with art can furthermore induce feelings of consolation and communion among recipients.

VI. Case Study: Dramatic Disgust in the Works of Sarah Kane

The work of British dramatist Sarah Kane can be regarded as emblematic for late twentieth-century aesthetic engagement with issues of *abjection* and disgust. The staging of Kane's debut play *Blasted* at the Royal Court Theatre Upstairs in London in January 1995 can also be viewed as the starting point of what Sierz soon after came to define as '*in-yer-face* theatre' (cf. IV).[1] Kane's work is commonly viewed as the most famous example of *in-yer-face* theatre. In 2010, playwright Simon Stephens stated that looking back, *Blasted* could be considered "one of the most notorious plays of the last century" (n.p.) and the German director Thomas Ostermeier already assigned the status of modern classics to her work in 2006 (cf. Szalwinska n.p.). To this day, Kane's plays have been staged around the world to great success and received a large amount of scholarly attention.[2] Upon reviewing Philip Venable's award-wining musical adaptation of Kane's final play *4.48 Psychosis* for the Royal Opera House in 2016, Andrew Dickson of the *Guardian* stated that Kane had by then become "a canonical figure" (n.p.).

---

1   The media outrage to some degree resembled the public discussion provoked by Saatchi's exhibition of Young British Artists' work in the *Sensation* show two years later (cf. IV).

2   Popular and critical acclaim of Kane's work can in fact be argued to have increased over time. A simple search in the WorldCat online library catalogue in April 2017 produced more than 800 results for "Sarah Kane", with the number of entries peaking at approx. 70 in 2008 and 2012. For Kane's contemporary Mark Ravenhill, who has been actively writing since the 1990s, there are just above 300 entries (cf. WorldCat n.p.). Director Katie Mitchell's stagings of two of Kane's plays on major European stages, *Cleansed* for the National Theatre in 2016 and *4.48 Psychosis* in 2017 for the Schauspielhaus Hamburg, also signal this trend. On the homepage of the National Theatre, Kane, whose work only made its entrance onto the most important British stage with Mitchell's *Cleansed* in 2016, is now described as being "rightly recognised as one of the most important British playwrights of the 1990s, if not the 20th century" ("Five of the Best... Sarah Kane Plays" n.p.).

A "nauseating dog's breakfast of a play"

The attraction of Kane's work, however, was met with equally strong aversive positions held by some scholars (e.g. Luckhurst 107ff.) and especially by theatre critics who largely found her plays to be simply "disgusting" (e.g. Tinker n.p.). These oppositional attitudes and reactions to Kane's plays can be argued to be inherent consequences of the aesthetic features prevalent in all of her works, namely Kane's intense engagement with states of *abjection*[3] and her employment of stylistic devices that mediate disgust on all levels (i.e. *poiesis, mimesis, aisthesis*; cf. V.ii). Supporters of the highly affective potential of Kane's plays regard these gruesome and revolting contents and disgust-eliciting aesthetic devices as characteristic features of great classical works of drama (e.g. Sophocles' *Oedipus the King* or Shakespeare's *Titus Andronicus*) that bring recipients in contact with the 'darker sides' of the human condition (cf. Wald n.p.). By contrast, critics commonly take the evocation of their personal feelings of disgust as an indication for the 'low' aesthetic value of the work that provoked the reaction. The expression of theatre critics' personal feelings of repulsion dominated the reviews of Kane's early plays, as even the most cursory survey of critical reactions to her debut play *Blasted* illustrates.

In the *Daily Mail*, Jack Tinker described *Blasted* as a "disgusting feast of filth", which made him feel "utterly and entirely disgusted", and claimed that the play "knows no bounds of decency, yet has no message to convey by way of excuse" (n.p.). Morley Sheridan of the *Spectator* called *Blasted* a "sordid little travesty of a play" (n.p.), and John Gross of the *Sunday Telegraph* described the actions as a "gratuitous welter of carnage" (n.p.). Charles Spencer of the *Daily Telegraph* and Paul Taylor of the *Independent* went particularly far in describing the disgust reactions they felt were evoked by the play. Spencer called Kane's work a "nauseating dog's breakfast of a play", "entirely devoid of intellectual or artistic merit", "disgusting", and "pathetic", which made "hardened theatre critics look [...] in danger of parting company with their suppers" (n.p.), and Taylor maintained that watching *Blasted* was "a little like having your face rammed into an overflowing ashtray, just for starters, and then having your whole head held down in a bucket of offal" (n.p.).

The critical reception of Kane's ensuing plays *Phaedra's Love* (1996) and *Cleansed* (1998), as well as reactions to her screenplay *Skin* (1997), were not much warmer, which is probably why she initially used a pseudonym for the first public reading of her 1998 play *Crave* (cf. Saunders, *Love Me* 102). Critical discussion of Kane's final

---

3   It is surprising that comparatively few publications on *abjection* in Kane's work exist. Only in 2017 (after the completion of the present manuscript) was Eva Spambalg-Berend's monograph *Dramen der Abjektion: Der Umgang mit den "Mächten des Grauens" in den Theaterstücken Sarah Kanes* published. It is highly recommended as complementary reading to the following analysis.

play *4.48 Psychosis* (2000) was also tainted, albeit this time by the author's suicide in 1999 (cf. Saunders, *About Kane* 35).

The aim of this chapter is to take theatre critics' descriptions of Kane's plays as nauseating and disgusting at face value and to demonstrate how Kane employs the aesthetic potential of disgust to mediate states of *abjection* and thereby artfully and effectively accomplishes the communication of universal states of crisis and conflict. Kane's slim *oeuvre* of five theatre plays and one script for television offers a unique possibility for the analysis of the multifarious and complex forms and functions of aesthetic disgust in theatrical writing. In all of her plays, Kane addresses issues of *abjection* by employing literary devices of dramatic disgust, yet each play approaches this subject from a different angle and in a particular aesthetic form, ranging from the depiction of extremely graphical acts of violence and physical mutilation to more abstract engagements with the universal experience of *abjection* and its relation to mortality. Kane's work is thus not only invaluable with regard to the investigation of the meaning and implications of disgust-evoking contents, but also, and even more so, with regard to their manifestation and expression in form. Ken Urban, for example, describes Kane's dramatic style as a "continual collapsing of [...] simple binary structures" ("Ethics" 43), which is but one feature of Kane's idiosyncratic style that matches Kristeva's concept of *abject* writing (cf. III.ii).

For a deeper understanding of Kane's work, it is essential to read all layers of Kane's highly potent poetic language: its rhythms, breaks, onomatopoeia, and the orchestration of these elements. Especially Kane's later plays *Crave* and *4.48 Psychosis* demand a reading of the various semiotic modes of communication employed to emphasise, counterbalance, accommodate, or contradict the semantic meaning of spoken lines. The task in reading all layers of Kane's work is thus to also look for the performative value of her theatrical language: what do her words *do* besides communicating particular contents?[4] The analysis of Kane's work will be divided up into two parts, with the first part focusing on the dramatist's engagement with and utilisation of typical categories of disgust-elicitation in her early plays *Blasted, Phaedra's Love, Skin,* and *Cleansed,* and the second part taking a more detailed look at the literary style used to mediate dramatic disgust and communicate states of *abjection* in Kane's last two plays *Crave* and *4.48 Psychosis.*

---

4   Urban highlights the importance of form in all of Kane's work: "For Kane, content was nothing without form that best expressed such exploratory demands, and in this, each of her plays literally recasts dramatic form" ("Ethics" 40).

VI.i Kane's Early Plays: Manifestations of Disgust in *Blasted, Skin, Phaedra's Love* & *Cleansed*

Kane's early plays *Blasted, Phaedra's Love, Cleansed*, and her film script for *Skin* are notorious for their depiction of graphic scenes of violence and repulsion, which range from representations of defecation, diseased bodies, and violent dismemberment to physio-moral transgressions of social and cultural boundaries in acts of torture, rape, and cannibalism. These plays thus offer a particularly rich source for an analysis of the aesthetic manifestation of typical semantic fields of disgust-elicitation. Since the material for a disgust-focused analysis of Kane's work is so abounding, an inquiry into *all* manifestations of dramatic disgust in content and form could easily amount to a book-length study for each of her plays. I will therefore restrict the focus of analysis to selected categories established in the previous chapter that are particularly informative for each respective play.

I will begin with a detailed analysis of the ways in which two of the most classical and undisputed categories of disgust-elicitation, (a) food and consumption and (b) ideas concerning pollution, are employed in *Blasted*. The example of food and consumption is chosen because across the academic disciplines engaged with disgust and its cognates, this category is generally viewed as the most archaic manifestation of disgust. It not only connects humans to the most basic need of securing survival, but also functions as one of the most elementary markers of individuals' and cultural groups' social placement in hierarchical structures. Food, eating, and modes of consumption are, to a varying degree, essential elements in all of Kane's plays, especially in her early work. The same holds true for the second closely related category of pollution. Since antiquity, the notion of *miasma* has played a central role in dramatic works of art and Kane masterfully applies the rich aesthetic potential contained in fears concerning pollution and contagion in her dramatic language. As theatrical devices both categories are utilised in Kane's work to create setting and atmosphere, to build characters, signal relevant shifts in the plot structures, and to illustrate tragic conflicts from the Dionysian realm of dichotomous ambiguity with its *abject* core of "death infecting life" (cf. II.ii and III.ii).

I will treat Kane's script for *Skin* as her second play since it was completed shortly after the staging of *Blasted* in 1995 (cf. Saunders, *About Kane* 25). *Skin* is the only film script Kane wrote and scholars have almost entirely omitted engagement with it despite its highly poetic form and the complex discussion of racism and otherness.[5] In this play, food loathing also plays an elementary role and shall be

---

5 To my knowledge, only Mateusz Borowski looked at the play in more detail in his article "Under the Surface of Things: Sarah Kane's *Skin* and the Medium of Theatre" (184-194). *Skin* is neither mentioned in David Greig's introduction to Kane's *Complete Plays* (even though it is

discussed with a focus on how it functions to establish social identities and mobilise ideas of cultural difference in the form of racism.

The main character of Kane's third play *Phaedra's Love* can be regarded as representing the epitome of disgust, displaying features and actions from *all* of the semantic fields of disgust-elicitation presented in the previous chapter (cf. V.i). The focus of analysis for Kane's *Phaedra's Love* will, however, be placed on the *abject*-inflected relation between language and what we perceive as 'truth' as well as on the ambiguities inherent to states of *abjection*: simultaneous repulsion and attraction (i.e. *jouissance*).

The final play discussed in this section, *Cleansed*, has generally been regarded as Kane's most violent play, depicting the largest number of gruesome stage acts including various modes of torture and bodily mutilation (cf. Saunders, *About Kane* 29). The focus will lie on the strong body metaphors conveyed in the stage directions of the play. The category of disgust-elicitation via the body will provide the analytical frame to take a closer look at the physical and mental limits of the individual, and the individual's modes of transgression within social and cultural structures and restrictions.

Blasted: "This disgusting feast of filth"[6]

Kane's debut play *Blasted* is set in a hotel room in Leeds and centres around the abusive relationship between the 45-year-old journalist Ian and his former girlfriend, 21-year-old Cate. As 'war' breaks out between the couple (after Ian rapes Cate and she responds with resorting to violence against him as well), the domestic scenery changes into a state of civil war, marked by the entrance of a Soldier. Cate escapes, whereas Ian falls victim to the most atrocious violations at the hands of the Soldier. The Soldier ends up killing himself, and (after a brief visit from Cate) Ian is left on his own in a state of utter despair. Raped, blinded, and starving from hunger, Ian passes through a number of haunting experiences: frantic masturbation, attempted self-strangulation, defecation, cannibalism, and death. The play ends with Cate returning to the scene with food and sharing it with Ian, for which he expresses his gratitude.

Dramatic disgust plays an important role in *Blasted*: not only on the level of content, where various semantic fields of disgust-elicitation are employed as means of characterisation and setting the scene, but also on a formal level, where the sudden

---

included), nor is it part of most foreign language translations of her works. Cf. for example the German edition: *Sarah Kane. Sämtliche Stücke* (2002).

6   My apologies to Graham Saunders for using the same quote from Jack Tinker's review of *Blasted* (n.p.) as he did for the chapter heading of *Blasted* (cf. *Love Me* 37).

transition from a domestic setting to a scenery of war is mirrored in a change of style from a naturalistic depiction to surrealistic imagery, which can be described as an instance of what Kristeva terms *abject* writing (cf. III.ii).

Setting the Scene: "I've shat in better places"

Blasted opens with the description of the setting: "*A very expensive hotel room in Leeds – the kind that is so expensive it could be anywhere in the world. There is a large double bed. A mini-bar and champagne on ice*" (3). The atmosphere, which is created with the aid of the stereotypical Western hotel room elements of a mini-bar and a prepared bottle of champagne, is one of familiarity, comfort, security, and cleanliness, inviting exquisite and joyous modes of consumption in the form of drinks and the option of sexual intercourse (*large* double bed). Into the room enter the two main characters: middle-aged journalist Ian and his younger companion Cate. Their reactions to the room and its contents allow us to make some first assumptions about their social background, attitudes, and habits. Cate's admiration of the "*classiness of the room*" points not only to her "*lower-middle-class*" (3) background, but also marks her out as a highly appreciative and sensual character: "*She [...] bounces on the bed. She goes around the room, [...] touching everything. She smells the flowers and smiles*" (4). For Cate, the bottle of champagne represents a cultural object of luxury, a substance reserved for special occasions and celebrations. When Ian opens the bottle and pours her a glass, she thus enquires about the reason for celebrating (cf. *ibid.*; cf. V.ii Order & Other).

Ian does not answer Cate's question. For him the consumption of alcohol is far from being a ceremonial act. His excessive drinking of strong liquors at all times, despite serious health issues, clearly signals substance abuse, if not addiction. One of Ian's first actions on entering the hotel room is to pour himself a "*large gin*" (3) from the mini-bar, and gin is also the first thing he looks for when he gets up the next morning (cf. 24). His abusive attitude towards the consumption of alcohol foreshadows his equally abusive attitude towards sex, which he is soon to force upon his reluctant companion (cf. 7, 12, 13, 14f., 17, 24f., 27).[7]

Whereas the entire cultural setting of the hotel room is indicative of what we could call life-affirming forms of consumption in the sense of Bataille's notion of *homogeneity*, the human impulse for appropriation (cf. III.i), Ian not only upsets these expectations with his damaging attitude towards drinking, he furthermore immediately manages to 'defile' them with his initial comment on the room, the claim that he has "shat in better places than this" (3). By making direct reference

---

7   In her article on "Cruelty, Violence, and Rituals in Sarah Kane's Plays" Stefani Brusberg-Kiermeier briefly discusses the relation between food consumption and sexuality in ritualistic contexts (cf. 82f.).

to the act of defecation (i.e. the *heterogeneous* 'other' side of consumption; cf. III.i), Ian turns the logic of joyous consumption onto its head. His line, which is also the opening line of the play, introduces the *abject* agenda of *Blasted* from the start.[8] Not only does Ian's colloquial and derogative statement deviate linguistically from what is expected of a member of the middle class (cf. V.i Slang), the reference to the act of defecation is also greatly discomforting, especially in the context of the scenery suggesting the direct opposite (i.e. consumption). The mentioning of excretion unsettles what we understand as a 'symbolic order' (i.e. rules of social life).

What makes Ian's remark even more offensive is that instead of voicing his discontent in the more common (and abstract) manner of, for example, stating: "This is a shit place", his deviation from this common expression (in Aristotle's terms 'foreign'; cf. V.i Semiotic Structures) provokes a concrete image of Ian's act of defecation. Recipients are 'invited' to envision the explicit act of excretion, which not only involves a breach of bodily boundaries through the orifices, but also the production of smelly waste products which social systems have taught us to regard as polluting objects (cf. V.i Body). As a dramatic device, Ian's initial statement foreshadows his desperate actions in the final scene of the play, where, raped, blinded, and alone, he is shown "shitting" (59) in the worst place imaginable, among corpses in a room destroyed by war (cf. Ablett, "Approaching" 69).

Carnivorous & Rotten Characters: "It's only a pig"

Meat-eating in *Blasted* is strongly linked to brutish and violent (male) behaviour and symbolises a 'hunger' for dominance and sexual drives; a connection that had also been made in Euripides' *Bacchae*, where Pentheus had accused the Dionysian followers of such behaviour (cf. I). In *Blasted*'s main male character, Ian, the attributes of an instinct-driven and brutal 'meat-eater' are amplified in contrast to his companion Cate, a vegetarian and peaceful character, who reacts very sensitively to Ian's ham sandwiches, sausages, and bacon (cf. 6f., 34f.). For Cate, meat is a direct indicator of violence and death: "Dead meat. Blood. Can't eat an animal" (7). The mere idea of eating it makes her feel sick: "No, I can't, I actually can't, I'd puke all over the place" (*ibid.*). Ian provokes her by directly naming and degrading the animal that provided the ingredient for his sandwich: "It's *only* a pig" (*ibid.*; my emphasis). Later he fails to order a vegetarian variation for Cate's breakfast, causing her to retch at the sight and smell of sausages and bacon (cf. 35).

At first sight these "binaries [vegetarian/meat-eater] appear to correspond with gender stereotypes", as Helen Iball remarks in her analysis of *Blasted*: "Ian is the

---

8   Cf. my article on "Approaching Abjection in Sarah Kane's *Blasted*" (2014) where I used Kristeva's theory to demonstrate a stylistic development from the symbolic to the semiotic (63-71).

carnivorous red-blooded male", the "perpetrator/bad man", while Cate represents the archetype of the "victim/good girl" (23). This observation seems to find further evidence in the fact that in *Blasted* meat and its consumption is intrinsically linked to base and animalistic sexual drives. Ian finds Cate's loathing of meat immature and reacts to it by taking off his clothes and ordering her to perform oral sex on him; offering his 'meat' in this particular version of 'sexual education' (cf. 7). For Ian, sex represents just another form of 'meat consumption' instead of an intimate encounter between two people. His habit of reducing other people to 'pieces of flesh' not only becomes evident in his sexually abusive behaviour, but also in his debasing language about out-groups. He thus suggests that Cate only knows the service personnel's name because she is "[a]fter a bit of black meat" (17; cf. Knowles 71) and over the phone describes a woman who suffered rape as a "Scouse tart" who "spread her legs" (13).

Body Metaphors: "this lump of rotting pork"

Ian not only degrades those around him via association with typical disgust-elicitors, but also himself. This becomes especially apparent in his nauseating description of a lung operation he had to undergo: "[S]urgeon brought in this lump of rotting pork, stank. My lung" (11). In this statement we not only find the domain of meat-consumption ("pork"), but also a conflation of *all* other common fields of disgust-elicitation, which greatly enhances the emetic effect of these lines. Not only does the breaching of physical boundaries, with internal organs appearing outside of the body, violate the subject's integrity and typically give rise to feelings of nausea (cf. V.i Body), but by referring to his lung as a "lump of pork", Ian by implication further reduces his status to that of a pig (cf. V.i Animality) and his body to a diseased and "rotting" piece of meat, a waste product (cf. V.i Pollution). The association of the decayed lung with a substance intended for eating ("pork") provokes further stomach-turning sentiments since it suggests the consumption of a rotten vital organ (cf. V.i Moral). Ian's utterance thus contains at least three concrete disgust stimuli that are directly linked to the dichotomous pair of life/death: (a) decay and removal of a vital body organ, (b) consumption of a rotten substance, and (c) cannibalism.

Ian's disease is most likely lung cancer, which seems to be self-inflicted or at least aggravated by his excessive consumption of poisonous substances, namely tobacco and alcohol. His addictive behaviour is a defining feature of his character: "Whenever I think of you it's with a cigarette and a gin" (11), Cate states. Iball observes that: "Ian's cigarettes and gin are literally his 'props'" (23). Ian's abusive behaviour is paradoxical in common-sense logic since despite his great fear of death (cf. 10), he does everything to accelerate the process and intensify the symptoms, not unlike Theophrastus' "Offensive Man" (*dyschéreia*) who exacerbates the infection of his open wounds through carelessness (cf. I). Cate is appalled by Ian's self-mutilation. When he immediately pours himself a glass of gin and lights a cigarette after suffering a severe coughing fit ("*It looks very much as if he is dying*", 24) and provocatively asks Cate if she wants one too, she is speechless with disgust (cf. 25).

Ian's illness becomes manifest in coughing fits which bring up body fluids that he constantly has to spit out (cf. 4, 24f., 25, 33). In Kane's theatrical language, Ian's disease, however, registers on a more sophisticated level than solely demonstrating the dire consequences of substance abuse. According to Kristeva's theory, physiological symptoms are a mode of the body to express states of *abjection* that evade linguistic articulation (cf. III.ii).[9] Metaphorically, Ian's physiological symptoms can be argued to signify Ian's state of internal turmoil (cf. Saunders, *Love Me* 43) and thereby function as a powerful dramatic tool to counterbalance the character's verbally articulated convictions. Thus, while Ian does not show any remorse in words, his body communicates his moral ambiguity and a desire for purity and punishment. His coughing fits, for example, are the most severe after he has raped Cate. "*He begins to cough and experiences intense pain in his chest, each cough tearing at his lung. [...] It looks very much as if he is dying*" (24). Iball furthermore observes that Ian's coughing and retching is for the first time made visible in this scene; his suffering previously having been "hidden in the privacy of the en suite bathroom" (33). Ian's physical symptoms can be argued to act as a constant reminder that there is something poisonous inside of him that demands purification, a desire for *katharsis*.

Plot & Pollution: "Soiled Goods"

Graham Saunders maintains that "Ian is literally representative of a diseased male identity – a crude racist, misogynist and homophobe who is compulsively drinking and smoking himself to death" (*About Kane* 18). Ian can in fact be argued to embody the ancient idea of *miasma* on all levels (cf. I.). As compulsively as he poisons his own body with alcohol and nicotine, he causes harm and defilement to the people and objects around him. As the first section of this analysis already indicated, Ian's power to contaminate, degrade, and violate himself, his surroundings, and others through words, actions, and even his mere physical presence, was already foreshadowed in the play's opening line when Ian commented on the room in terms of excretion. Ian himself experiences his body as utterly defiled and polluted. He repeatedly claims that he "stink[s]" (cf. 4, 6, 8, 11) and wishes to wash himself (cf. 4, 25, 33), which can be regarded as a desire for a kind of *katharsis*. Cate indirectly

---

9   Kristeva describes the symptom as "a language that gives up, a structure within the body, a non-assimilable alien, a monster, a tumor, a cancer that the listening devices of the unconscious do not hear. In the symptom, the abject permeates me, I become abject" (11).

confirms Ian's self-assessment by ardently rejecting intimate contact. "Don't put your tongue in, I don't like it" (12), she states, and *"wipes her mouth"* (12, 17).

The diseased state of Ian's body can be argued to symbolise the impairment of his moral convictions; and both body and mind threaten to pollute those that come in contact with him. As a dramatic device, the imagery from the semantic field of pollution works most effectively with regard to the inherent 'sympathetic laws of magical belief', which allow for a rich metaphorical application. Through the rape, Ian forces his *miaron* condition onto Cate and consequently describes her as "[s]oiled goods. Don't want it, not when you can have someone clean" (52).[10] In Ian's logic they are now equals (in their states of pollution): "We're one, yes? [...] We're one" (26). Cate confirms the idea that Ian has 'rubbed off' on her (on more than one level) when she states: "I ache. [...] Everywhere. I stink of you" (33; cf. Ablett, "Approaching" 66). Her actions after the rape show that she has not only caught on Ian's smell, but also his patterns of behaviour. Cate's identification with defilement becomes linguistically apparent in the first word she utters in the morning after the rape. Previously a soft-spoken and gentle character, she now addresses Ian with the word: "[c]unt" (25), thereby adopting Ian's *'foul* tongue' in using derogative slang language as a tool of discrimination and degradation (cf. V.i Slang).

After another instance of sexual abuse, Cate too commits violent sexual actions by first seducing Ian and then biting into his penis. After the attack, Cate *"begins to cough and retch"* (33) – like Ian had done previously. In Cate's case, the coughing is caused by a pubic hair she must have swallowed in the process of the oral violation of Ian's genital: *"She puts her fingers down her throat and produces a hair. She holds it up and looks at IAN in disgust. She spits"* (33). Cate is appalled; she feels polluted and now for the first time also expresses a desire for a *katharsis*: "I'm having a bath and going home. [...] *We hear the other bath tap being turned on*" (35; cf. Ablett, "Approaching" 66).

Cate's state of pollution not only becomes manifest on an intradiegetic level through the character's changed mode of speech and behaviour, but it is also mirrored on a meta-level where Kane drastically breaks with the dramatic conventions (i.e. 'perversion'; cf. V.i Semiotic Structures). Despite unsettling actions and some linguistic deviations, the plot had up to the point of Cate's 'infection' still largely adhered to the conventions of a domestic drama, depicting the struggles and pains of an unequal couple. But, after Cate has become 'one' with Ian on the level of perpetual violence against each other, the play's scenery of domestic crime and pollution expands, like a disease that spreads from one house to a town, to a country. Now that the war has broken out between the couple, Cate looks out of the window

---

10   Ian's assessment of Cate as 'soiled goods' mirrors Biblical rhetoric on matters of sexual pollution. Cf., for example, the following passage from Numbers: "If any man's wife strays from him, betraying him, in that a man has lain with her [with] an emission of seed [...], she has made herself polluted" (5:11-31).

and sees this reflected outside as well: "Looks like there's a war on" (33; cf. Ablett, "Approaching" 66).

Blasting of the Symbolic Order: "No. It's Real"

With the Soldier's entrance into the hotel room in the middle of the second scene and the explosion of a bomb at the onset of scene three, the setting and with that the symbolic order of the play become literally 'blasted' (cf. Ablett, "Approaching" 66). Parallels can be drawn to Kristeva's analysis of Céline's novel *Journey to the End of the Night* (1934), where she describes the consequences of *abject* manifestations in fiction for the plot-structure:

> [W]hen narrated identity is unbearable [...], the narrative is what is challenged first. If it continues nevertheless, its make-up changes; its linearity is shattered, it proceeds in flashes, enigmas, short cuts, incompletion, tangles, and cuts. (Kristeva, *Powers of Horror* 14).

The strong effect of a similar structural collapse in Kane's *Blasted* and the resulting loss of orientation in recipients became evidenced in theatre critics' angry reviews. Jane Edwards of *Time Out* asks: "What war is being waged and why [...]. [A]re we really in Leeds?" (n.p.). Kane explained her motivation to break with the dramatic conventions by referring to the equally *logos*-defying mechanisms of war: "War is confused and illogical, therefore it is wrong to use a form that is predictable. Acts of violence simply happen in life, they don't have a dramatic build-up" (in Singer 141). The "transitionless cut" between the domestic and the battlefield can be argued to display the reality of "the existential absurdity of the war itself" (73), as Megan Becker-Leckrone states with reference to Céline's similar manoeuvre in *Journey to the End of the Night*.

After the bomb exploded in the hotel room, Ian is very much at loss without his usual frames of reference. "*He trails off confused*" (40) and finds it hard to believe that the situation he finds himself in is real. He thus considers that he "might be drunk", but the soldier sets him right by stating: "No. It's real" (*ibid.*). In states of war, social rules and expectations are commonly suspended.

The Soldier offers a vivid illustration of otherwise unacceptable taboo subjects, such as cannibalism and rape, which appear to have almost become a norm for him. The war situation is portrayed as indiscriminately tragic and the need to survive as the main motivation for violence. The Soldier reports that he saw a "starving man eating his dead wife's leg" and immediately afterwards asks Ian for food, claiming that he is "fucking starving" (50). He also tells Ian about the fate of his girlfriend: "Col, they buggered her. Cut her throat. Hacked her ears and nose off, nailed them to the front door" (47), which shows that he is not merely a perpetrator, but also a victim of war crimes. The Soldier demands that Ian take responsibility as a journalist by reporting on the gruesome events of war and thereby contribute to preventing further escalations of violence:

> Some journalist, that's your job. [...] Proving it happened. I'm here, got no choice. But you. You should be telling people. [...] Doing to them what they done to us, what good is that? At home I'm clean. Like it never happened. Tell them you saw me. Tell them ... you saw me (47f.).

Ian, however, does not feel any responsibility to report on the cruelties of war as a journalist who covers home affairs.[11] He furthermore argues: "No one's interested. [...] This isn't a story anyone wants to hear" (*ibid.*). To illustrate his point, Ian picks up a newspaper from the bed and reads out a 'story' that he says people would be interested in:

> 'Kinky car dealer Richard Morris drove two teenage prostitutes into the country, tied them naked to fences and whipped them with a belt before having sex. Morris, from Sheffield, was jailed for three years for unlawful sexual intercourse with one of the girls, aged thirteen.' (*He tosses the papers away.*) Stories. (48)

Ian argues that "stories" are intended for the reader's "joy" (*ibid.*). In his view, this requires them to be "personal" as well as "[s]oft and clean" (like the soldier's girlfriend who suffered most brutal violations, cf. *ibid.*). The Soldier responds to Ian's nonchalant attitude by making him *feel* what war and violation is *really* like and thus turning the story of the 'other' (i.e. foreign affairs) into a 'personal' one for Ian. The Soldier does so by enacting upon Ian what his girlfriend had suffered before (cf. *ibid.*). First he rapes him and then sucks out and eats his eyes, stating: "He ate her eyes. Poor bastard. Poor love. Poor fucking bastard" (50). As with Kane's other theatrical images, the soldier's consumption of Ian's eyes functions on more than one level: (a) literally as an act of cannibalism that can be viewed as a particularly dire yet 'logical' consequence of war; as a 'natural' act of last resort to secure survival once there are no other sources of food available; (b) psychologically as an act of revenge for the crimes suffered by the Soldier's girlfriend in the biblical sense of "an eye for an eye",[12] which on a meta-level functions as a device for driving the plot; and (c) metaphorically as a confrontation of Ian's myopia regarding the vicious circular logic of war, where the Soldier enforces Ian's in*sight* through a literal blinding. The metaphorical meaning furthermore functions as an intertextual reference to other famous tragic characters that were forcefully blinded, such as Sophocles' Oedipus

---

11 Ian thereby relegates all associations with actions and instances of war to the realm of the 'other', the 'foreign' – "I don't do foreign affairs" (*ibid.*).
12 The biblical imagery of an "eye for an eye" (Lev. 24:19-21) here not only becomes a literal metaphor; the Soldier's commitment to violence of this kind can also be read as him having become infected by the war crimes he had to witness and experience.

or Shakespeare's Gloucester in *King Lear* (cf. Iball 24).[13] It is no coincidence that *Blasted*'s Ian is a journalist. The play contains a complex debate on uses and abuses of language and contains a strong critique against sensational news reporting and modern society's ways of consuming such contents, as well as Western nations' interest in and responsibility towards 'other' countries in general. Ian's reluctance to tell the Soldier's stories point to Western nations' "culpability [...] in allowing [...] war[s] to continue" (Saunders, *About Kane* 18).[14] Through her dramatic imagery (i.e. stage directions) and employment of *abject* language, Kane finds an aesthetic mode to represent and to render *real* the kind of revolting and violent events and actions (wars, rape, etc.) which most people in Western society in one way or another come across daily in their encounter with television, online news, and print reports.

Skin: "English extra sausage" & Bananas

The short film *Skin*, to which Kane wrote the script, was first shown at the London Film Festival in October 1995 under the direction of Vincent O'Connell. In 1997 it was televised by Channel Four.[15] Public and critical reception of *Skin* mirrored the contradictory reactions that *Blasted* provoked. While the film was awarded a Golden Bear in the category Best Short Film at the 1996 Berlin International Film Festival, the *Daily Mail* described it as "one of the most violent and racially offensive programmes ever to be made for television in [the UK]" (n.p.). *Skin* picks up issues Kane already dealt with in *Blasted*, and in many ways precludes the ritualistic acts of violence and 'purification' experienced by the characters of her later play *Cleansed* (1998) (cf. Borowski 184-208).

---

13   Cf. Knowles' reading of the cannibalism depicted in this scene in *Dystopian Performatives: Negative Affect/Emotion in the Work of Sarah Kane* (68-70).
14   Kane stated repeatedly that her decision to introduce the topic of war to the play was motivated by the war in Bosnia and the ways in which the media (especially the tabloid press) approached the issue (cf. Saunders, *About Kane* 18f.). However, Kane distinctly decided to cut direct references to the conflict in Yugoslavia (e.g. in an earlier version the Soldier was called 'Vladek', cf. Saunders, *Love Me* 53). By cutting these direct associations, *Blasted* represents the universal mechanisms and structures of war rather than a political comment on one particular war fought at the time of writing. Kane's writing is thus far from unpolitical, quite the contrary. By looking at the general structures that underlie the eruption of wars and conflicts, Kane's *Blasted* fulfils a crucial criterion of classic tragic drama, namely the representation of 'universal' structures rather than the depiction of particular historical events (cf. Aristotle 'universal' in l.i).
15   In the following analysis, *Skin* will be read as a dramatic text, not discussing the specific performative manifestation of the piece in Vincent O'Connell's film version. I follow Saunders who suggests that *Skin* can be regarded as Kane's "second play [...] after *Blasted*" (*About Kane* 25).

Skin is set in Brixton, London. It deals with a young skinhead named Billy and a black woman called Marcia who lives opposite to him and to whom Billy feels attracted. The first scene introduces Billy in his flat drawing a swastika on his hand. He leaves the apartment to have breakfast with his comrades and to prepare an attack on an interracial wedding. After the bloody raid he goes home to take a shower. From his window he can look into Marcia's flat. He changes his clothes and goes over to see her. Marcia takes care of a wound he carried away from the assault and they have sex. Afterwards, she tears apart Billy's Union Jack boxershorts, ties him up, and starts hitting him, asking over and over again: "What's it like" (261). Then she bleaches and scrubs off the nationalistic tattoos from his body and carves her own name into his back. When Billy asks for a kiss, she demands that he eat from the bowl of dog food instead and tells him that things cannot work out between the two of them. Violated and broken, Billy leaves her flat and takes an overdose of pills. Having observed the scene through the window, his elderly black neighbour Neville comes in to save Billy's life by encouraging him to throw up the tablets he swallowed.

Skin is especially interesting for the analysis of the dramatic functions of disgust because it allows insight into one of the most socially relevant mechanisms of the sensation, namely the setting up of social hierarchies via negative evaluation (cf. IV.i, V.ii). Graham Saunders regards *Skin* as "Kane's most 'realistic' work in that it seems to overtly address issues of race politics [...,] advocat[ing] a message of racial integration" (*About Kane* 27). While this observation is certainly not false, it nevertheless presents a simplified interpretation of the play, overlooking some essential elements which tell a more sophisticated story – one that is not so much determined by realism, but rather by poetry and surreal imagery.

Food & the Other: Who Eats What

In *Skin* we find a highly complex engagement with issues of otherness and disgust played out symbolically between characters of different skin colours. We encounter a 'relationship' between a white skinhead and a black woman which moves between the extremes of love and repulsion. Kane renders this relationship in a highly stylised language that is dominated by the use of contrasting pairs: day/night, soft/hard, happy/sad, black/white, tenderness/brutality, dirty/clean, etc. These hyperbolic means of exhibiting differences and stereotypes (e.g. hard men/loving and soft women) are not only constantly established, but just as often broken – a feature of Kane's dramatic language that tells a more unfathomable story in its "continual collapsing of [...] simple binary structures" (Urban, "Ethics" 43).

The creative deconstruction of binary structures can generally be found on all levels of Kane's writing. In *Skin* it becomes most evident in the presentation of foods and modes of consumption. As in *Blasted*, the domain of food and consumption is used as an elementary dramatic device to psychologically and socially mark characters and set them apart; but whereas in *Blasted* this category mainly functions to mark gender distinctions and only marginally touched-upon issues of race (cf. 16f., 49), racial difference takes on the central role in *Skin*. In their struggle for power, the main characters of the play relentlessly draw from the semantic field of disgust to subdue the cultural 'other' by means of negative evaluation (cf. V.i Order & Other).[16]

English Breakfast & Racism

The second scene of *Skin* takes place in a café in South London where Billy and his comrades meet up to plan their violent attack on an interracial couple's wedding. The group orders: "Two English extra rasher, two English extra sausage, one double English" (251). The choice of dishes not only points to the group's ultra-national political standpoint ("extra", "double English"),[17] but also to their positive attitude towards excessive behaviour (food, sex, violence). The consumption of the meat-rich English breakfast in *Skin* functions in a similar way as the depiction of carnivorous male behaviour in *Blasted*, signifying violent, nationalistic, and sexist (stereotypically male) inclinations (cf. VI.i *Blasted*).

Skin's main character Billy, however, is a vegetarian, which immediately sets him apart from the rest of the group. Saunders reads Billy's vegetarianism as a clear indication of his ambivalence regarding identification with the fascist group (cf. *About Kane* 26). At the café, Billy chain-smokes while the others eat their meaty breakfasts. When his comrade Terry asks him if he wants a sausage, Billy *"looks disgusted"* (251). In *Skin*, as in *Blasted*, meat and its consumption are intrinsically linked to base and instinctive sexual drives. Billy's companions thus regard his as-

---

16   It is interesting to note here that even Darwin in his strictly evolutionary and brief discussion of disgust already illustrated the intricate relationship between food-loathing and racism (albeit probably unintended) in this example: "In Tierra del Fuego a native touched with his finger some cold preserved meat which I was eating at our bivouac, and plainly showed utter disgust at its softness; whilst I felt utter disgust at my food being touched by a naked savage, though his hands did not appear dirty" (257f.). The concern Darwin expresses here is related to the idea of contamination and the intensity of his repulsion towards his food after the 'foreigner' touched it is clearly marked linguistically by Darwin's drastic change in tone. While he first refers to the foreigner more objectively as a 'native', the latter immediately turns into a 'naked savage' from the moment he is perceived as a polluting agent – despite Darwin's awareness of the irrationality of his sentiments since the native's "hands did not appear dirty" (*ibid.*). This example indicates how powerfully the underlying 'laws of sympathetic magic', as defined by Rozin and his associates, function in this relation (cf. IV.i).

17   Kane had already associated the traditional English breakfast with a nationalistic and racist position in *Blasted*, where it is ordered by Ian (cf. 34) and later eaten by the Soldier (cf. 36).

cetic attitude towards meat as an indication for an equally ascetic attitude towards sex, as the following dialogue demonstrates:

TERRY: [...] Sausage, Bill?
BILLY *looks disgusted and all the others laugh at him.* [...]
TERRY: Wanna get yourself sorted, Billyboy.
BILLY: I'm all right.
TERRY: Not just your head, get some meat on your bones.
MARTIN: Your bone in some meat.
NICK: Your meat in her mouth.
TERRY: Your mouth round some meat. (251f.)

But Billy is not to be persuaded. Like Cate in *Blasted*, he is only too aware of the food's origin from a formerly living animal. "It's a pig's arse, Tel" (253), he says, burning his cigarette into a sausage skin (cf. V.i Animality; Body). Billy squeezes out the meat from the sausage and begins listing its ingredients: "Brain and bollock, innard and eyelid, toenail and teeth, all wrapped up in a pig's foreskin" (253). The nauseating effect of Billy's list of the pig's dismantled body parts (cf. V.i Lists) is further enhanced through the fact that these are partly drawn from the animal's sexual organs (bollock, foreskin). Also, the minuteness of the enlisted body parts (eyelid, toenail, foreskin) is rather 'foreign' in descriptions of animals and generally reserved for humans, whereby they indirectly turn recipients' attention to their own limited existence. Billy *"drops the empty sausage skin in disgust"* (254) and his elaboration on the sausage's ingredients does not fail to have an equally nauseating effect on his comrades: "MARTIN *spits out a mouthful of sausage and looks at it closely. He puts his fork down. Everyone stops eating*" (ibid.).

The authoritative café owner, a man called 'Mother', steps in to 'restore order' at the dinner table ("Good grub, that", ibid.), to which one of the men reacts with an apology; whereas Billy's action, of *"grind[ing] his cigarette into the meat"* (ibid.) and picking up a banana from the counter instead, can be read as a strong act of rebellion against the orders and rules of the 'carnivorous' group. Symbolically, this scene can be argued to represent the subject's initial experience of *abjection* in a rejection of the 'Mother's' food, which marked the beginning of the development of an autonomous identity (cf. III.ii). This psychoanalytical interpretation is further supported by Billy's succedent action of playfully pretending *"to shoot* [the others] *with the banana"* (254) – where his 'substitute sausage' (with equally phallic form) becomes a weapon of combat against the 'sausage order' of the group and Mother. Mother, however, tries to put Billy back in place (i.e. 'carnivorous order') by reminding him that the bananas are "not for eating" (ibid.). That Mother's remark is predominantly intended to restore his authoritative position is evidenced by the fact that Billy at no time shows any inclination to actually eat the banana.

It turns out that the bananas are intended as a tool of racial discrimination to provoke the interracial congregation that the group sets out to disturb. The skinheads use the bananas to signal that they view black people as 'savage' monkeys (cf. V.i Animality). Yet it is clearly the skinheads who behave like 'savage' monkeys: "BILLY *peels* [the banana] *slowly and eats it. He throws the skin at one of the men* [...]. *The distinctive sound of monkey noises begins from* BILLY", "*the skins doing ape impressions*" (255); the wedding guests are "*disgusted*" (ibid.) by their 'savage' behaviour (cf. V.ii Order & Other).

Underneath the Surface of Billy's Skin

Billy is, like Ian in *Blasted*, obsessed with personal hygiene. His preparation for the racist attack on the wedding bears some resemblance to an overly careful 'getting ready' ritual before a date.

> BILLY *shaving his head and chin, tipping shampoo onto his almost bald head, rinsing his head under the tap, scrubbing his neck, applying conditioner, cleaning his teeth, spraying deodorant under his arms, patting aftershave onto his face and neck and kissing his reflection.* (250)

Billy's usage of shampoo and conditioner on his hairless scalp reminds one of aching phantom limbs experienced after amputation. The action indicates that his identification as a 'skin' has not been wholly undertaken. His mother's message on his answer-machine supports the idea of a troubled or torn identity. Not only is Billy's mother worried about him, she also calls him by his full name "William" (250).[18]

After the attack, Billy takes another shower to try to ritually clean himself from perceived pollution. He is "[*vigorously rubbing soap*] *into every bit of himself except his right hand where the swastika is*" (256). The overt avoidance of washing away the swastika could point to Billy's feelings of insecurity, which need the strong symbol as a form of justification for his actions, a strength which he cannot muster from within (i.e. *under* the surface of the skin). After his shower, Billy defecates, which can be read as another act of purification. The following scene clearly diverges from realism despite the physical possibility of such an occurrence. Billy's neighbour Neville enters the bathroom and takes a look at Billy's excrements in the toilet. He shakes his head and Billy grins. In this highly symbolically charged

---

18 Saunders suggests that these instances indicate that Billy is either a "recent convert or an outsider to the group" (*About Kane* 26), but I would not necessarily go so far in making assumptions about Billy's 'history' or particular placement within the group. I rather read his problems with 'finding himself' amid the different forms of "[s]urface identit[ies]" (*ibid.*) available to him in his social surrounding as a more general exemplification of young people's difficulty in finding a 'right' place in the 'symbolical order' of social structures.

dreamlike scene, Neville takes on a paternal role showing disapproval at the open demonstration of faeces (i.e. 'toilet training'), yet by his mere presence in Billy's bathroom also signals that he acknowledges his 'accomplishment'. Like a young child Billy proudly shows Neville 'what he has done', enjoying the latter's disapproval of 'his shit'.

After Marcia rejects Billy, he feels his identity entirely scattered: "No more Billy" (266). He takes an overdose of painkillers with some beer and falls unconscious. Neville, who sees him fainting through the window, comes to save him. He *"kneels beside him, patting his back"*, while Billy *"is vomiting violently down the toilet"* (267). Neville calms him down "You're all right, white boy, you're all right", and encourages him to continue vomiting in order to expel all poisonous substance from his body: "That's it son, better out than in, you're all right" (268). Billy acknowledges Neville's kind and comforting gestures. Equally *cathartically*, he *"looks into the old man's face and smiles weakly. He begins to sob. Then rests his head on the toilet seat and cries his heart out"* (268).

Phaedra's Love: "fair is foul, foul is fair"

Kane's second play Phaedra's Love is a modern adaption of Seneca's tragedy Phaedra[19] which premiered at London's Gate Theatre in 1996. The play addresses contemporary Western culture, family relations, and the topics of love and honesty. It is set in an unspecified royal palace and focuses on the young prince Hippolytus whom his stepmother Phaedra is unhappily infatuated with. Because Hippolytus does not return her love, she commits suicide and leaves a letter accusing her stepson of having raped her. The prince does not deny the charges, because he can see a 'truth' in them. Neither his stepsister Strophe nor the Priest who offers him absolution can change his mind, so he is sentenced to death. Hippolytus' father, Theseus, returns from war and seeks revenge for his wife. In disguise he joins the mob who are out to vent their anger at the corrupt prince and helps to initiate a public onslaught on his son, who is then brutally torn to pieces by the crowd. Strophe, likewise in disguise, tries to come to her stepbrother's aid. Theseus rapes and murders her for defending a murderer. Once he realises that it is Strophe he violated, he kills himself. The play ends with Hippolytus in a near-death state seeing vultures descend

---

19   Seneca's play is itself an adaptation of Euripides' version of the tragedy; both are based on Greek mythology. Kane was commissioned by the Gate Theatre London to write a modern adaptation of a classic play and loosely based her writing on Seneca's version after originally having wanted to work on Georg Büchner's *Woyzeck* or Bertholt Brecht's *Baal* (cf. Saunders, Love Me 72).

from the sky. His last words are: "If there could have been more moments like this" (103); as he dies "[a] *vulture descends and begins to eat his body*" (ibid.).

While the ancient template focused on queen Phaedra's unrequited love for her chaste stepson Hippolytus, the young prince becomes the main character in Kane's version of the play (cf. Cohn 3). Hippolytus can be regarded as the epitome of disgust. He is introduced as the decadent prince of a contemporary royal family who spends his time eating fast food, watching TV, and masturbating into his socks (cf. 65f.). At first sight, Kane's Hippolytus seems to represent the opposite of the prince of the original version, who is portrayed as honourable and chaste. Closer analysis, however, shows that Kane's engagement with dramatic disgust in this play is far more complex than offering a simple conversion of values. *Phaedra's Love* lays bare some of the core mechanisms of disgust. Not only does the play illustrate how the repulsive can also be a source of attraction (i.e. *jouissance*), it also exhibits the instability of perceived conceptions of physical and moral states of purity as well as pollution and explores in depth the most basic questions and agonies of human existence: the meaning of love, life, and death.

A Foul Prince in a Foul World

In the first scene we are presented with the setting of a royal palace and the main character Hippolytus who "*sits in a darkened room watching television.* [...] *Sprawled on a sofa surrounded by expensive electronic toys, empty crisp and sweet packets, and a scattering of used socks and underwear*" (65). This introduction of a prince already unsettles recipients' expectations of encountering a 'noble' royal character (especially if they are familiar with ancient versions of the play), before a single line is spoken. In this modern version of the play, the prince is portrayed as a spoiled, yet dissatisfied member of a contemporary culture used to excessive consumption. He eats one hamburger after another while "*impassively*" watching a violent movie and masturbating into his used socks (*ibid.*). Hippolytus can be regarded as a hyperbolical, yet also stereotypical representative of a 'binge-generation' which tries to compensate emotional emptiness by excessive indulgences (cf. Szakolczai 25ff.). There are, however, more facets to Hippolytus: he not only embodies contemporary social *malaise*, he is also a tragic character in the most classical sense, with his melancholic condition bearing much similarity to Shakespeare's *Hamlet*.

Hippolytus' dis-ease (i.e. depression; cf. 65) is caused by his awareness of the fact that the world is not as it 'seems': "Always suspected the world didn't smell of fresh paint and flowers. [...It] [s]mells of piss and human sweat. Most unpleasant" (92). He is portrayed as a tired seeker and defender of the 'truth' and ardently yearns for the experience of something *real*. In Nietzsche's terminology, he is a classic example of a Dionysian man, who is, like Hamlet, disgusted by the fake and false 'Apollonian semblances' (i.e. *Schein:* superficial appearances) that dominate his life. He finds it "revolting" (75) that people come to the palace just to have their photo taken with him. Hippolytus is only too aware of the superficiality of the society he lives in and laconically voices his discontent with the priorities of news reporting when Phaedra asks him what he is watching on TV: "News. Another rape. Child murdered. War somewhere. Few thousand jobs gone. But none of this matters 'cause it's a royal birthday" (74). What becomes apparent is that Hippolytus is not primarily indifferent and disgusting because of his careless attitudes to matters of hygiene, health, and sexual encounters, but that he is himself someone who is highly appalled by society's superficiality and indifference (cf. V.ii Social Critique).

Language & Truth: Foul Language

In *Phaedra's Love*, we find the idea of language as a tool of harm in the image of a 'poisoned' tongue. After the scene where Hippolytus through his brutally honest words sends his love-sick stepmother Phaedra into a state of utter despair, we find him "*in front of a mirror with his tongue out*" (85). He examines the coating of his tongue: "Green tongue. [...] Fucking moss. Inch of pleurococcus on my tongue. Looks like the top of a wall. [...] Major halitosis" (*ibid.*; cf. V.i Pollution). Hippolytus uses language not only to express his radical honesty, but also (alongside his offensive disregard of rules of hygiene and other revolting habits) as a tool to keep people emotionally and physically distant from him.[20] He goes to great lengths to discourage Phaedra's strong feelings for him when she confesses her love to him. First, he tries to provoke her repulsion by describing himself and his actions as utterly appalling. His accounts range from his indifferent sexual encounters with a "[f]at bird" that "smelt funny" and "a man in the garden" (76) to explaining his habit of using his socks to collect his semen as well as for blowing his nose (77; cf. V.i Body). When these graphical statements fail to have the desired effect, he draws attention to the 'quasi-incestuous' nature of Phaedra's wishes by calling her "Mother" (78) and reminding her of the 'good' family's public image at stake (cf. V.i Moral). Finally, he explicitly tells her to "[g]o away. It's obviously the only thing to do" (80), but Phaedra is not to be persuaded.

After her "present" (*ibid.*) of fellatio to the disinterested Hippolytus, he takes the cruelty of his verbal assertions another step further, when he indicates that he not only previously had sex with Phaedra's daughter Strophe, but that the latter had also been intimate with Phaedra's husband Theseus, and was altogether a more skilful 'performer' than her mother (cf. 83f.), which leaves Phaedra speechless in shock and pain (cf. 84). Hippolytus continues his mental torture by asking: "Do I get my present now?", which renders Phaedra's 'gift of love' (i.e. fellatio) ultimately

---

20   Ironically this behaviour has the exact opposite effect – a feature to which we shall attend after the discussion of 'foul' language in the play.

worthless. Finally, he implies that she is likely to have caught a sexual disease from her actions when he tells her to "[s]ee a doctor", because he has "gonorrhoea" (85; cf. V.i Pollution). After his verbal abuse, he asks her for the third time if she "[h]ate[s] [him] now" (*ibid.*), to which Phaedra, despite the emotional torments she suffered from her stepson's words, replies in the negative.

Phaedra leaves the room and hangs herself (off-stage), leaving a note in which she accuses Hippolytus of rape. Strophe informs Hippolytus about the allegation and wants to know if it is true. When she asks her stepbrother whether he forced her mother into intimate contact, Hippolytus answers with the counter question: "Did I force you?" (87). Strophe replies: "There aren't words for what you did to me" (*ibid.*). Kane here effectively demonstrates the "inadequacy of language to express emotion" (qtd. in Saunders, *About Kane* 73). As she herself commented, "the English language doesn't contain the words to describe the emotional decimation [Hippolytus] inflicts. 'Rape' is the best word Phaedra can find for it, the most violent and potent, so that's the word she uses" (*ibid.*; cf. V.ii Social Critique). Kane has her Hippolytus become aware of the fact that the extent of pain Phaedra experienced on his behalf defies expression in everyday language and decide to accept the accusation of rape on account of its metaphorical truth value: "Then perhaps rape is the best she can do" (*ibid.*). He takes full responsibility for his actions: "I have no intention of covering my arse. I killed a woman and I will be punished for it" (96).

Jouissance: Attraction & Repulsion

Hippolytus in many ways exemplifies the characteristics of Theophrastus' "Offensive Man" (*dyschéreia* in I). His ultimate aim is to keep people emotionally distant by his self-fashioning as utterly loathsome.[21] Yet his appalling features and actions are also a great source of attraction to people around him. His character thus vividly demonstrates the paradox inherent to states of *abjection*. As Hippolytus himself states: "Women find me much more attractive since I've become fat. They think I must have a secret. (*He blows his nose on a sock and discards it.*) I'm fat. I'm disgusting. I'm miserable. But I get lots of sex" (77f.). Even when he indicates that he has a transmittable disease, the "bloke in the bogs, still wanted to shag [him]" (85; cf. V.i Body; Pollution). Strophe supports Hippolytus' self-assessment: "Everyone loves

---

21   In the conversation between Phaedra and Hippolytus prior to her suicide, we learn that Hippolytus is likely to have acquired this apathetic attitude after a past love relationship to a woman called 'Lena', whose mere mention provokes the strongest emotional response we see from Hippolytus throughout the play. Before Phaedra can say anything about Lena, Hippolytus "*grabs [her] by the throat*" and tells her to never "mention her again" or "even think about her" (83). This scene clearly indicates that Hippolytus is not as dispassionate as he seems, but rather fashions himself as detestable in order to protect himself from potentially painful emotional engagements with others.

him. He despises them for it" (72); her mother Phaedra's unwavering love for her stepson is the most eminent proof of his allure. When Hippolytus asks Phaedra why she loves him, she replies:

> You're difficult. Moody, cynical, bitter, fat, decadent, spoilt. You stay in bed all day then watch TV all night, you crash around this house with sleep in your eyes and not a thought for anyone. You're in pain. I adore you. (79)

Phaedra's love for Hippolytus shows that she does not love him *despite* his unfavourable features, but precisely because of them. When Hippolytus points out that her explanation is not "very logical", Phaedra replies that "[l]ove isn't" (*ibid*.; cf. V.ii *Abjection*). The reasons for Hippolytus' apparent attractiveness are manifold, but mainly stem from his radical liberation from any kind of social or moral restrictions (i.e. 'symbolical order'). Engagement with him, especially in the form of a quasi-incestuous love affair, seems to promise an exciting act of border transgression (cf. V.i *Moral*; V.ii *Jouissance*) that would allow Phaedra to break free from the manifold forms and rules of keeping up appearances (*Schein*) that she as a member of the royal family is required to stick to and which leave little space for *real* experiences. The attraction of potential border transgression is confirmed in Phaedra's statement that Hippolytus "thrill[s]" her (80). Hippolytus takes her reasoning as a sign of the superficiality of her feelings for him, assuming her vows of love to be stemming from a desire for adventure, so that he merely functions as a tool for her to attain her goals. This becomes clear in his statement "[t]his isn't about me" (82) and his apathetic remark "[t]here. Mystery over" (81) after Phaedra performs her 'gift' for him. Only after Phaedra's death does he realise that his assumption was false and that "[s]he really did love [him]" (91). He thus reacts to her accusation of rape and ensuing suicide not with fear or repulsion, but rather with bliss (i.e. *jouissance*), because he sees these as the expression of a 'higher truth' in the Nietzschean sense and as a *real* sign of Phaedra's love for him:

> This is her present to me. [...]
> Not many people get a chance like this.
> This isn't tat. This isn't bric-a-brac. [...]
> Life at last. [...]
> She really did love me. [...]
> Bless her. (90f.)

In Phaedra's sacrifice of her life for him, Hippolytus finds proof of her true feelings for him and that makes him willing to sacrifice his own life in return for her 'present'. In doing so, he can finally find a *real* meaning and reason for existence: "Life at last. [...] I'm turning myself in" (*ibid*.). It becomes apparent that underneath Hippolytus' overt indulgence in revolting practices, we find an idealistic fighter for honesty, a prince who is pure in thought. According to Urban, the ambivalent feelings Hippolytus conjures up in the other characters of the play likewise transfer to recipients of Kane's play: "That vertiginous sense we experience, fluctuating between disgust and tenderness for Hippolytus, is a trademark of Kane's theatrical universe" ("Ethics" 42).

Cleansed: "another bloody amputation"

Cleansed premiered at the Royal Court Theatre Downstairs in London in 1998. As with Kane's previous plays, theatre critics were quick to react to the "bags of disgustingness" (Gore-Langton n.p.) contained in *Cleansed*. Spencer considered the play to be "supping full of theatrical horrors' gore. Limbs are lopped off, tongues severed and penises transplanted with almost merry abandon" (n.p.) and Morley of the *Spectator* viewed *Cleansed* as a "shocker" and a "tacky, tawdry apology for a play, in which any real skill of characterisation or plotting is simply replaced by yet another bloody amputation" (n.p.).

In *Cleansed* the characters – the siblings Grace and Graham, the homosexual couple Rod and Carl, the young boy Robin, and the anonymous Woman – undergo numerous horrific experiences where their love, devotion, and sincerity are tried and tested by the authoritative figure of Tinker. The play relies heavily on theatrical images such as Carl performing a *"dance of love"* for Rod, after Carl's tongue and hands have been cut off (136). Spoken language is minimalistic and stage directions almost exceed the lines spoken by the characters (cf. Saunders, *Love Me* 88). The dramatic language Kane developed in *Cleansed* can be argued to present a stylistic borderline case in-between her early and her late plays. While the previously discussed plays still largely adhered to most of the classic conventions of play writing (e.g. setting, characters, plot development), Kane's final two plays, *Crave* and *4.48 Psychosis*, radically break with almost all of these framing structures. In *Cleansed*, highly symbolically charged surrealist scenes, which occurred in *Blasted*'s final scene and partly determined the aesthetics of *Skin*, dominate over naturalistic depictions of events throughout the play. We still find traditional characters,[22] but a conventional plot structure is replaced by a collection of twenty scenic fragments which are not embedded within a traditional story line.[23] The setting is equally obscure. All events take place within the confines of some university grounds enclosed by a *"perimeter fence"* (107). They are either outside or in spaces which are

---

22   Cf. Christina Delgado-Garcia's "Subversion, Refusal and Contingency: The Transgression of Liberal-Humanist Subjectivity and Characterization in Sarah Kane's *Cleansed*, *Crave*, and *4.48 Psychosis*" for a detailed discussion of Kane's progressive subversion of traditional characters from *Cleansed* onwards (230-250).

23   Kane names Georg Büchner's fragmentary play *Woyzeck* (1837) as a decisive influence for the dramaturgic structure of *Cleansed* (cf. Saunders, *Love Me* 87).

assigned specific colours or shapes: white (*"sanatorium"*, 112), red (*"sports hall"*, 116), black (*"showers of the sports hall"*, 121), round (*"library"*, 123). Whereas these indications of the setting are still suggestive of a naturalistic setting despite the symbolical supplementation of colours and shape, the events and actions that take place inside and outside of these rooms clearly defy straight-forward realism. In dreamlike scenes, the 'university' becomes a token for social institutions in general. Using Kristeva's terminology, we could refer to the various institutions that are being evoked in *Cleansed* (namely: hospital, prison, concentration camp, torture chamber, brothel) as power houses of the 'symbolical order', which 'guarantee' the implementation and perpetuation of social rules and cultural norms (cf. III.ii).

Gruesome life lessons

The 'university' with its etymological link to 'universal' and its social function as the most sophisticated institution of human learning (i.e. culture) works particularly well to collectively signify the universal conflict between the needs and desires of the individual and the demands and regulations of culture and society that not only lies at the heart of *abjection*, but also encapsulates one of the main concerns of the play.[24] Each character in *Cleansed* 'learns' in one way or another what it means to be human at the bare core of his or her existence. They 'learn' how easily their words, convictions, values, and feelings – and hence the general make-up of how they perceive themselves as individual subjects – can be annihilated at the hands of an authoritative power. The initially naively romantic Carl has to 'learn the hard way' that love is not an absolute. Traditional Western symbols of love, like the exchange of rings amid promises and vows that one would willingly die for the other (cf. 109), are no more than hollow gestures. In the rationale of the play, the authoritative figure Tinker comes to Carl's 'aid' and 'teaches' or 'cleanses' (i.e. 'heals') him of his immature and false beliefs. The first 'lesson' is conducted in *"The Red Room – the university sports hall"* (116), a space where typically young people's physical strength

---

24 Kane's statement that Georg Büchner's *Woyzeck* (1879) and George Orwell's *Nineteen Eighty-Four* (1949) were valuable sources for her thematic explorations in *Cleansed* (cf. Saunders, *About Kane* 38f.), supports the assumption that the conflict between individual and society plays a crucial role in the play. Orwell's novel and Büchner's play both show that there is a thin line between institutions that are meant for human support and those that have the power to destroy. The medical experiment that Woyzeck is subjected to, for example, can be argued to transgress the boundaries into torture – with the devastating effect of psychosis, which eventually leads to Woyzeck brutally murdering his partner Marie. The other sources of inspiration Kane names for *Cleansed* are August Strindberg's *Ghost Sonata* (1908) and Shakespeare's *Midsummer Night Dream* and *Twelfth Night*, (cf. Saunders, *About Kane* 38), which account for the dream-like form and the motif of love relations.

and stamina is tested. Carl seems to conceive of the brutal beating he has to endure as some kind of 'test' or a 'treatment of health' since he continues to address his violator Tinker as "Doctor" (*ibid.*). And also Tinker must regard Carl's (mal)treatment as helpful since he orders the "*unseen group of men*" who have beaten Carl into unconsciousness not to "kill", but to "[s]ave him" (*ibid*). When Carl wakes up, he receives the second lesson intended for his 'salvation', which is worth quoting at some length to show the monstrosity of the torture he endures:

> TINKER: There's a vertical passage through your body, a straight line through which an object can pass without immediately killing you. Starts here. (*He touches CARL's anus.*)
> CARL (*Stiffens with fear.*)
> TINKER: Can take a pole, push it up here, avoiding all major organs, until it emerges here. (*He touches CARL's right shoulder.*) Die eventually of course. From starvation if nothing else gets you first.
> *CARL's trousers are pulled down and a pole is pushed a few inches up his anus.*
> CARL: Christ no
> TINKER: What's your boyfriend's name?
> CARL: Jesus
> TINKER: Can you describe his genitals?
> CARL: No
> TINKER: When was the last time you sucked his cock?
> CARL: I
> TINKER: Do you take it up the arse?
> CARL: Please
> TINKER: Close your eyes imagine it's him.
> CARL: Please God no I
> TINKER: Rodney Rodney split me in half.
> CARL: Please don't fucking kill me God
> TINKER: I love you Rod I'd die for you.
> CARL: Not me please not me don't kill me Rod not me don't kill me ROD NOT ME ROD NOT ME
> *The pole is removed. ROD falls from a great height and lands next to CARL. Silence.* (116.f)

While there is, as a matter of fact, comparably little physical harm done to Carl in this scenario since the pole is 'only' "*pushed a few inches into his anus*" (117), the goriness of the scene results from Tinker's verbal descriptions. The violent transgressions of body boundaries are amplified by Tinker's vivid imagination and his insinuation of Carl being brutally "split [...] in half". The cruelty of this episode is further heightened by Tinker's mocking tone and his suggestion that he 'only' fulfils a sexual desire – "Rodney Rodney split me in half" (*ibid.*) – Carl may have exclaimed in moments of ecstasy. In this 'lesson', Carl's psychological integrity is broken, which is symbolically displayed on a physiological level, yet clearly predominantly a psychological issue since his physical integrity is only slightly violated, while the mental torture he is subjected makes him feel like he is being killed. And a part of him is in fact being killed in this scene. Like Winston in Orwell's *Nineteen Eighty-four*, Carl is subjected to his worst kind of fear, and like Winston Carl asks his torturer to perform the violent actions on his lover instead, breaking his promise that he would "never betray" Rod (110). Tinker's 'lessons' and 'cleansing' of Carl as well as the other characters continue in similarly gruesome or even intensified ways. Little is left as all characters are either killed or basically deprived of any form of physical or psychological integrity. Only a tiny spark of hope glimmers faintly in *Cleansed*'s bleak world of despair when in the final scene Grace/Graham reaches out to Carl and *"holds his stump"* (150), which is mirrored in change of setting as *"[i]t stops raining"* and the *"sun comes out"* (151). Yet this momentary suggestion of peace or even bliss is immediately eradicated as the *"sun gets brighter and brighter, the squeaking of the rats louder and louder, until the light is blinding and the sound deafening"* and the play closes with a *"Blackout"* (ibid.).

VI.ii   Kane's Late Plays: *Abject* Language in *Crave* and *4.48 Psychosis*

Kane's final two plays, *Crave* (1998) and *4.48 Psychosis* (2000), mark the author's radical break with a realist dramatic tradition.[25] Kane stated with regard to *Crave* that she "wanted to find out how a poem could still be dramatic" and that it was a deliberate "experiment with form, and language and rhythm and music" (qtd. in Saunders, *About Kane* 94). Urban summarises Kane's dramatic style in *Crave* and *4.48 Psychosis* as follows:

> While images were central to [Kane's] previous plays, these final pieces contain the images within the language of the plays, and she does this through the creation of a distinctly poetic style. Both plays are performance texts, with no stage directions, and in the case of *Psychosis*, no speaker designation. ("Ethics" 43)

---

25   Much scholarly attention has been payed to this stylistic change in Kane's work. Eckart Voigts-Virchow calls it a "linguistic turn" ("Anathema" 24). Christopher Innes labels *4.48 Psychosis* a "free-verse dramatic poem" (534), and David Barnett a "poetic meditation" (21). Some, together with Hans-Thies Lehmann (ix), locate Kane's final two plays in the realm of so-called 'postdramatic theatre' (cf. Diedrich 337). Cf. also the analyses of *Crave* and *4.48 Psychosis* by Voigts-Virchow ("Late Modernist" 205-220; "Anathema" 195-208), Pankratz (149ff.), Urban ("*Crave*" 496-498), Baraniecka (205-250), Deubner (155-218), Fordyce (103-110), de Vos (129-135), Tycer (23-26), Duggan (103-105), and Delgado-Garcia (230-250).

In *Crave*, classical characters are drastically reduced and merely indicated by single letters. No plot structure is discernible, stage directions are scarce, and the interaction between speakers (most of the time) does not follow the rules of coherent communication. In the introduction to Kane's *Complete Plays*, David Greig describes the effect of Kane's idiosyncratic poetic style as follows: "[I]n *Crave* one can almost feel the intoxicating release of Kane's writing as the borderlines of character evaporate entirely and her imagery moves from physical to textual realisation" (xiv). In Kane's last play *4.48 Psychosis*, all structural markers of traditional drama are reduced to nothing. Clues as to possible changes of space, characters, or time are merely indicated by orthographical signs such as spaces, dashes, hyphens, and slashes.

If we look at the development of dramatic language from Kane's debut *Blasted* to *4.48 Psychosis*, we witness an increasing destruction of familiar frames of reference and naturalistic means of representation, which reaches its formal peak in the surrealistic images conjured up by the polylogical voice/s of Kane's final play. The stylistic development can be aptly described with Kristeva's language as one of "approaching abjection" (cf.III.ii). One could argue that with *Crave* Kane initiates what Kristeva calls a "revolution in poetic language" (cf. III.ii); a process which is completed in Kane's final play *4.48 Psychosis*.

Using Kristeva's notion of *abject* language, I will show how Kane manages to find a dramatic style that is able to communicate the difficult and in many ways 'ungraspable' (cf. *dyschéreia* in I) themes addressed in her final two plays. For the analysis of *Crave*, I will focus on one of the highest and probably most appalling forms of moral transgression, namely sexual child abuse, and how this is communicated predominantly semiotically and on a structural level through an *abject* dramatic style in the interaction between the characters A(buser) and C(hild). The focus for the analysis of *4.48 Psychosis* will lie thematically on the confrontation with *abjection* via the Silenian wisdom and the speaker's experience of a complete breakdown of the 'symbolical order', which is mirrored on the level of form in a loss of and at the same time struggle for some kind of order.

Crave: "Maggots everywhere"

Crave premiered at the Traverse Theatre in Edinburgh in 1998. In this play Kane addresses similar topics as in her previous works such as the need for love, substance abuse, sexual assault, and states of existential crisis. Instead of depicting these events in actions on stage or suggesting any kind of spatial setting, Kane lets her voices report on their personal experiences and memories through language alone in this piece of "poetic drama" (Saunders, *About Kane* 32). Logical cohesion is replaced by choric and otherwise poetically interwoven mono-, dia-, and polylogues, which are mainly spoken on associative cues. The play is deeply influenced by T. S. Eliot's *The Waste Land* (1922), both in form and content, mirroring the latter's intertextual collage style with references ranging from the Bible to Shakespeare's *Hamlet* to Albert Camus' *The Plague* (1948) (cf. Saunders, *Love Me* 102ff.).[26]

The characters in *Crave* are merely indicated by the single letters A, B, C, and M. Every 'character' relates his or her 'story' of longing – which taken together form a powerful collage of deprivation and craving. All characters yearn for love and communion and appear to be unable to communicatively cross the distance to the desired (or hated) other, despite several appellative statements such as: "Please stop this" (157), "Listen" (162), or "I want you to leave" (166). The 'stories' in *Crave* are stories of identity and crisis (sexual abuse, addiction, etc.) and thus ultimately stories of *abjection*. Since states of *abjection* defy clear referential and coherent articulation in language, Kane lets her characters report on these experiences in a language that is determined by its poetic function. In Kristeva's terms we can describe the language in *Crave* as functioning predominantly semiotically (cf. III.ii). Meaning thereby becomes heterogeneous. Yet this does not mean that language in *Crave* is free of meaning or entirely open to interpretation,[27] but rather that it is elusive or evasive with regard to referring to a particular single meaning, which, despite the fact that it cannot be grasped in its magnitude, is nevertheless "always in sight" (Kristeva, *Desire* 34). The characters in *Crave* need to be understood in a similar way.

A, B, C, and M are not devoid of any form of identity (cf. Cohn 44).[28] In an interview with Dan Rebellato, Kane revealed how she saw A, B, C, and M: "To me A was always an older man. [...] The Author, Abuser, [...] and Antichrist. [...] M was simply Mother, B was Boy and C was Child" ("Brief Encounter" n.p.). Kane's understanding of these characters is unsurprisingly confirmed by their utterances in the play's text. A, B, C, and M are clearly gendered and aged.[29] They also each exhibit specific moods and speech patterns, and relate to particular narrative contents. Without any more notable or visually discernible characteristic features, however,

---

26 Saunders claims that Kane's decision to not include the staging of brutal and gruesome actions and her more overt usage of intertextual references from classical works of literature may have been the reason why the critical reception of *Crave* was much warmer than the responses to her previous work (cf. Saunders, *About Kane* 32ff.). For a detailed analysis of Kane's intertextual references in *Crave* cf. Voigts-Virchow ("Late Modernist" 205-220).

27 In this regard I disagree with Saunders who claims that the "poetic structure" of *Crave* "resists rational analysis" (*About Kane* 32).

28 Phyllis Naggis and Peter Morris have, for example, argued that A, B, C, and M are all part of one voice/character (cf. Saunders, *Love Me* 72f.).

29 When C for example comments on *her* monthly period, we may well deduce that she is female (cf. 156).

these personas can be viewed rather as archetypes than as specific (albeit fictional) individuals (cf. Saunders, *Love Me* 104).³⁰

As already indicated above, A, B, C, and M are not without 'stories', rather the contrary: They are all 'full' of memories and the desire to articulate these. From my reading of the play, A is a middle-aged or older man who struggles with his unrequited love for a child. B is a younger man who suffers from depression, substance abuse, and addiction. C is a younger woman who experienced sexual abuse in childhood and because of this finds it hard to cope with relationships and life in general. M is a middle-aged woman who agonizes over becoming older and feeling unloved. All characters struggle with language, especially when it comes to their efforts to recount their experiences of *abjection*.³¹ Since these experiences defy clear representation in coherent narratives, they are predominantly disclosed through semiotic modes of communication (cf. V.i Semiotic Structures). The heterogeneous dramatic structure of *Crave* deliberately leaves the relations between the characters open. We thus find no clear indication that A is the one who sexually abused C or that M is C's mother. This deliberate ambiguity is in accordance with the overall rationale of the play, which emphasises 'universal' or archetypical structures of dysfunctional relations (cf. Aristotle 1451a-b; I.ii) over 'factual' or particular relations. In the following analysis, I will concentrate on the characters A and C and the topic of sexual abuse as it becomes most readily detectable in an exchange of the characters towards the middle of the play. I will quote at some length in order to display the heterogeneous dimension at work in this dramatic polylogue, before taking a closer look at C and A in a wider context.

> C: I have this guilt and I don't know why.
> A: Only love can save me and love has destroyed me.
> C: A field. A basement. A bed. A car. [...]
> C: My bowels curl at his touch.
> A: Poor, poor love.
> C: I feel nothing, nothing. I feel nothing.
> B: I came back

---

30 The fact that the *dramatis personae* in *Crave* represent archetypes rather than specific individuals does in itself not yet present a radical break with the dramatic tradition as some have claimed (cf. Delgado-Garcia 237-241), but can be argued to actually fulfil one of the relevant dramatic requirements Aristotle laid down in his *Poetics* when he stated that dramatic characters should not depict individual 'histories', but rather 'universal' features and patterns of behaviour (cf. 1451a-b; I.ii). In the following, I will therefore continue to relate to A, B, C, and M as 'characters' instead of reducing them to 'voices'.

31 According to Shoshona Felman and Dori Laub, it is impossible for people having suffered trauma to form a linear and coherent narrative: "The trauma is [...] an event that has no beginning, no ending, no before, no during and no after [...], attained no closure, and therefore as far as its survivors are concerned, continues into the present" (11; cf. also Tycer 27).

C: If she'd left –
A: I'm going to die.
M: This abuse has gone on long enough.
C: Maggots everywhere.
B: There's no one like you.
C: Whenever I look really close at something, it swarms with white larvae.
A: Black folding in.
C: I open my mouth and I too am full of them, crawling down my throat.
B: Something happened.
A: So aghast.
C: I try to pull it out but it gets longer and longer, there's no end to it. I swallow it and pretend it isn't there. (174f.)

C: "it swarms with white larvae"

Crave's character C is prepossessed by her memory of sexual abuse which she never manages to articulate in 'plain' language, but relentlessly addresses through allusions. As a consequence of the traumatic experience she feels incapable of coping with the challenges of everyday life. C finds it impossible to trust anyone (cf. 163) and, like rape victim Cate in *Blasted*, she rejects physical advances: "My bowel curls at his touch" (175).[32] C also suffers from eating disorders ("Anorexia. Bulimia", 173) and depression (*ibid.*), and repeatedly expresses the wish to die (cf. 158, 189, 193). Overall, she is caught up between the contradictory desires to die or to find a way of managing to live on, with death increasingly gaining the upper hand. Her desire for life becomes apparent in her voracious fight to appropriate her past: telling her story, being listened to, making sense of it, and gaining control over her experiences by integrating them into a 'symbolic order'. What paradoxically keeps C alive and simultaneously causes her despair are her unceasing endeavours to articulate her experiences in language: "I write the truth and it kills me. […] I hate these words that keep me alive / I hate these words that won't let me die" (184).

Even though there is no clear plot structure framing C's utterances, there is a certain dramaturgy and development in her attempts to talk about her *abject* memories. Early on in the play she states that she "couldn't forget" (156). Later she appeals to the others to "[l]isten" (162), "[l]isten. […] I need to … remember. I have this grief and I don't know why" (171), and repeatedly tries to convey her needs but breaks off mid-sentence: "If I was / If I / If I was" (162), "I feel / I just feel" (167). At some point she interrupts the polylogical speech flow of the others (including the

---

32 C is afraid of and appalled by physical contact and intimacy in general. When B states: "Let's just go to/bed", she reacts with: "no no no no no no no no no" (161); and when M asks: "Do you want a massage?", she replies: "Don't touch me" (166).

sexual advances between M and B) with an unrelated narration from her childhood: "As a child I liked to piss on the carpet. / The carpet rotted and I blamed it on the dog" (167). This 'story' of a child's aberrant behaviour not only succeeds in catching the attention of the other characters (cf. V.ii Attention), but the action described, like the overt interruption, also clearly signifies that there is 'something wrong' with C that demands the others', especially the mother's attention (cf. V.i Body; Pollution). But M ignores and denies the needs of the child which becomes painfully blatant in the following exchange: M: "I'm unable to know you"; C: "Don't want to know me"; M: "I need a child"; C: "Mother" (167).[33] After considering that suicide is not an option because she does not "have the courage" (173), C makes another attempt at telling her 'story',[34] and finally manages to elliptically reveal parts of her *abject* experience through the image of maggots infiltrating her body.[35]

> Maggots everywhere. [...]
> Whenever I look really close at something, it swarms with white larvae. [...]

---

[33] The mother's inability to attend to the child's needs is later reinforced when C states: "No one to help me not my fucking mother neither" (179). The difficult relation between mother and child is another major topic addressed in *Crave*, where early on C declares: "I told my mother, You're dead to me" (155). The verbal interactions between C and M, however, point to a shared/collective/inherited memory regarding their relationship with men: "We pass these messages" (159). After A tells the story of a grandfather sexually abusing his granddaughter, which triggers strong aversive reactions in C (cf. 158), M's answer, "Haven't we been here before", not only demonstrates indifference regarding the victim and C's affective reaction but also displays a kind of recognition which hints at the likelihood of her having experienced similar forms of abuse. The nonchalant tone of her response furthermore indicates that, in contrast to C, who repeatedly actively rejects and confronts A's narration, M appears to take instances of abuse more or less for granted or as 'normal' facts of life. Her ardent desire to be loved at all costs and despite all circumstances can also be read as an indication for her having stayed on in an abusive relationship – another leitmotif of Kane's plays. C's repeated "If she'd left –" (157, 165, 175) recalls Cate's hallucinogenic utterance of "Have to tell her. [...] She's in danger" (9) – hinting at a pattern of women staying on with male abusers. C's "All things to all men" (156) and M's "I never met a man I trusted" (161) support this interpretation. C knows who is responsible for her mother's affective inabilities ("You killed my mother", 184) and consequently rejects both men as well as women, above all herself: "Be a woman, be a woman, FUCK YOU" (180; cf. Deubner 175ff.).

[34] The difficulty to capture in words what she intends to articulate is reinforced through her attempt to begin the 'story' with the phrase "One fine morning in the month of May" (175), which is an intertextual reference to Albert Camus' *The Plague*, where the struggling writer Grand relentlessly attempts to write down his story but cannot manage to get past the first sentence, which also begins with 'One fine morning in the month of May' (cf. Fisher, "Quotations" n.p.).

[35] The suggestion that this is a 'story' of sexual violation is supported by M's preceding statement: "This abuse has gone on long enough" (175), which directly introduces the overall theme of the ensuing depictions.

I open my mouth and I too am full of them, crawling down my throat. [...]
I try to pull it out but it gets longer and longer, there's no end to it. I swallow
it and pretend it isn't there. (175)

In this image we once again find the idea of *miasma* as a contagious form of pollution that freely transgresses between physical and metaphysical realms (cf. V.i Pollution). But other than in *Blasted*, where the semantic field of pollution is directly referenced ("I stink of you", 33) and the idea of contagion is made explicit through the character's change in language and actions (cf. I; VI.i *Blasted*), in *Crave* we find a highly condensed version of similar experiences encapsulated in a single but very potent metaphor, which employs imagery from the disease- and death-related category of swarming maggots (cf. V.i Animality, Pollution) infiltrating all areas of C's body and life (cf. V.i Body). The already appalling image of swarming maggots is intensified by the idea that something infectious enters the character's body through the mouth and crawls down her throat (cf. V.i Consumption). Not only does this image demonstrate a horrendous violation of the body's physical integrity but also a silencing of the sufferers' ability to speak or scream out against this infringement, which the onomatopoetic charge of the word "maggots" with its phonetic 'gagging' implication alludes to (cf. V.i Onomatopoeia; V.ii Vitality). Through the oral incorporation of the maggots as signifiers of disease and pollution we also once again find the disturbing conflation of the diametrically opposed Bataillean categories of the *homogeneous* (i.e. life affirmative consumption) and the *heterogeneous* (i.e. waste and death; cf. III.i).

The affective charge of the image of revolting maggots crawling down C's throat is further enhanced through its associative coupling to sperm and oral sex. C tells us that she "swallow[s] *it* and pretend[s] *it* isn't there" (ibid.; my emphasis). This subtle alteration or 'perversion' of grammar not only creates a feeling of unease in recipients, but, if read or listened to carefully, also reveals pieces of the character's experience of sexual violence which explains the link between the abuse she suffered, her attempts to keep silent about it, her inability to 'forget', and her prevailing difficulty to tolerate physical contact with others. This visual rendering of C's unwilling swallowing (i.e. incorporation) of appalling substances further offers a reasonable explanation for the eating disorders she says she suffers from: "Anorexia" (173) expressing her rejection of any kind of oral consumption, and "Bulimia" (ibid.) demonstrating the urge to free herself from what she had to "swallow" (175), her wish for a *katharsis* from the polluting substance inside of her (cf. V.i Pollution; V.ii *Katharsis*).

C's inability to rid herself of the polluting agent ("it", 175) also suggests that like Cate in *Blasted* (cf. VI.i *Blasted*), C has come to identify herself with the *abject*. Not only does she refer to herself in terms of self-disgust (cf. 180), she also states that she has "this guilt and [...] [doesn't] know why" (174). Ian Ward points out in his analysis of the "Rape and Rape Mythology in Sarah Kane's Plays" that the feeling of guilt is common in rape victims and indicative of the "myths" that they are themselves to blame for their abuse (cf. 227f.). Like rape victim Cate, C desperately seeks to be free from pollution and feelings of disgust: "I'm looking for a time and place free of things that crawl, fly or sting" (165). But instead of being able to discharge the defiling agent (i.e. memories), she has to "pretend it isn't there" (175). She experiences life as utterly appalling, painful, and false, which becomes powerfully perceptible in another strong image that encapsulates C's view on existence: "Shit on a plate. Look enthusiastic or your own mother will take you apart" (195). Receiving no help or acknowledgement of her 'true' story from the others, especially the mother who does all she can to avoid reaching down beneath an Apollonian surface existence (cf. II.ii; III.i) and confronting the painful truth (cf. 179),[36] C can find no way of appropriating the *abject* memories of her past in any tolerable manner, and thus comes to the final conclusion that there is no other way to 'forget' but death. At this point she moves beyond disgust, as the borderline between life and death, towards the latter: "I crossed a river, [...] [t]o be free of memory" (198).

> Let the day perish in which I was born
> Let the blackness of the night terrify it
> Let the stars of its dawn be dark
> May it not see the eyelids of the morning
> Because it did not shut the door of my mother's womb [...]
> Why did I not die at birth [...]
> That's me. Exist in the swing. Never still, never one thing or the other, always moving from one extreme to the furthest reaches of the other. [...]
> This never happened. (*A silence.*) [...]
> Darkness surrounds a collapsing star, [...]
> Into the light, [...]
> Beyond the darkness, [...]
> I don't dream any more, [...]
> I crossed a river, [...]
> To be free of memory, [...]

---

36 M employs a number of psychological strategies to keep control over herself, which locates her firmly in well-known realms of the 'symbolical order'. An example of these strategies are relaxation and imagination exercises intended to distract the mind from uncomfortable feelings or memories: "Control, control, relax and control. / Sunny landscapes. Pastel walls. Gentle air conditioning" (171), "Choose, focus, apply" (174). Another is using classical phrases of affirmative self-motivation: "Move on. [...] Move on. [...] Back to life" (189f.). In the end, however, M also "crosse[s] a river" towards death, where she will finally be able to leave the "truth" she so ardently avoids "behind" (197).

> Bright white light [...]
> Happy and free. (189-200)

The strong visceral and polysemic charge contained in the single image of C having to swallow the maggots can be argued to be a fitting example of an aesthetic form able to invoke an 'aesthetic idea', in that it "stimulates so much thinking that it can never be grasped in a determinate concept" (Kant §49, cf. V.ii Aesthetic Idea). We are here invited to apprehend a fraction of the *abject* horrors and feelings of repulsion that victims of rape experience and are unable to articulate in plain language (cf. V.ii Vitality, Aesthetic Idea, *Abjection*). The telling of C stands in stark contrast to the type of sensational reporting on rape stories as is common in the tabloid press, a topic already raised in *Blasted* through Ian's description of Samantha Scrace (12f.). Other than the glossy or even alluring tabloid stories (easily digestible or 'tasty'), C's rendering causes a great amount of unease and forms something akin to a formless lump that catches in your throat. Because the ambiguities and gaps readers or listeners receive from her narration cannot be easily solved and thus keep being turned over and over in their heads (with a nauseating effect), it becomes hard to find ready categories in order to gain control. To this is added the effect of the interwoven strands of narration from the other characters in the play, particularly A and M (cf. V.ii Social Critique).

A: "I'm not a rapist. [...] I'm a paedophile"

Early on in the play A 'introduces' himself with the two highly disquieting lines: "I'm not a rapist", "I'm a paedophile" (156). At first, the second statement appears like a step-up from the former one, suggesting that A is not only a sexual abuser, but worse, that he abuses children (cf. V.i Moral, Body, V.ii Shock). A literal reading, however, suggests that for A these two statements are intended as contrasts in the sense that he does not see himself as a person who violates others, but as someone who 'simply' loves children (i.e. *paedo*=child/*philos*=loving).[37] The tension created between A's self-description and C's and M's assertions, which by juxtaposition and association suggest that A was an abuser, creates an additionally nauseating effect for the recipient, as moral disgust at the paedophile may be transformed into something less clear-cut. What makes A's paedophiliac inclinations so difficult to

---

37 Common language conflation of the categories 'child abuse' and 'paedophilia' is actually highly inaccurate (despite possible convergence), since a paedophile is per definition someone who feels sexually inclined towards children without necessarily acting upon these desires, while the largest amount of child abuse is committed by non-paedophiles. According to a *Guardian* article on "Paedophilia: Bringing Dark Desires to Light" that appeared in connection to the Jimmy Saville revelations in 2012, "'true' paedophiles [...] account for only 20% of sexual abusers" (Henley n.p.).

handle (cf. *dyschéreia*, I) is that an 'easy' condemnation of his character cannot be as straightforwardly achieved as one might wish because his love appears to be so 'real' and sincere (cf. V.ii Ambiguity). The clearest evidence for the authenticity of A's love can be found in a monologue which continues over two pages (168ff.) and thus clearly stands out against all other utterances in the play which are rarely longer than one line.

> I want to [...] go to your party and dance till I'm black and be sorry when I'm wrong and happy when you forgive me and look at your photos and wish I'd known you forever and hear your voice in my ear and feel your skin on my skin and get scared when you're angry and your eye has gone red and the other eye blue and your hair to the left and your face oriental and tell you you're gorgeous and hug you when you're anxious and hold you when you're hurt (169).

As a recipient one can easily become immersed in (or even charmed by) A's long and often touching declaration of love. As a result, one may be all too easily inclined to 'forget' that there were clear indications that A's 'lover' may be a child. Only when C begins to violently interrupt A's speech flow with: "this has to stop this has to stop this has to stop this has to stop" (170) is the recipient shaken out of a state of possible romantic immersion, and the fact that A's love may well be experienced as torturous or harmful by others becomes apparent (cf. V.ii Shock).

As mentioned above, there are no overt indicators that connect A to C in the sense of A being C's actual abuser, but we find numerous subtle traces that indicate an abuser for which A can be regarded to stand as a token. C's elliptic statement: "A field. A basement. A bed. A car" (174) not only hints at locations of possible abuse, but semiotically also links these (stereotypical places of sexual abuse) to the 'token character' A. A's later memory of "[a]n empty car park which I never can leave" (189) further supports this connection. The interaction between A and C in the sequence where C narrates her experience of sexual abuse through the image of the maggots can also be read as representing a 'token relation' between the abuser and the child, which discloses two perspectives of a shared memory.

Defying easy condemnation once more, A is revealed as becoming increasingly aware of the fact that his love is not only destroying himself (cf. 174), but also causing harm to the one he loves. When C describes how her "bowel curls at his touch" (175), he expresses pity: "[p]oor, poor love" (*ibid.*), and when C begins telling her 'story' we can read his "[s]o aghast" as a memory of the child's face during the abuse, which makes him feel deadly ashamed ("[b]lack folding in", *ibid.*). In a later passage, the appalling associations with sexual child abuse are further enhanced through C's ambiguous statement: "Still sleeping with Daddy" (180), which can be read to refer either to the mother M or to herself (cf. incest in V.i Moral). In this context, the following utterances by A: "The games we play," and M: "The lies we tell" (180) become highly discomforting. For A the feelings of guilt, regret, and loss of love increase as the play progresses:

> My pain is nothing compared to hers. [...]
> We made love, then she threw up. [...]
> I despair of despair. [...]
> The thing I swore I'd never do, the thing I swore I'd – [...]
> On my children's lives, my children's love. [...]
> Throbbing between shame and guilt. [...]
> God forgive me I want to be clean. [...]
> Guilt lingers like the smell of death and nothing can free me from this cloud of blood. (177-184)

Like C (as well as B and M), A can find no other solution to handle life than to find consolation in the idea of death.

Confronting Ambiguity: "yes" "no"

In *Crave* we are presented with a heterogeneous collage of speakers that tells of love and abuse in a language of *abjection*. We learn for instance about the child C's difficulties of coping with life because she is haunted by memories of sexual abuse. We also get to hear the other side of the story through the voice of the abuser A. The actual event is never directly described by either of the participants, yet continuously alluded to in elliptical utterances that are not only multifaceted in meaning but through their onomatopoeic charge often also highly visceral, as C's image of the maggots infiltrating her body vividly demonstrated. As a recipient, the potential or 'token relation' does not become immediately clear, nor is the incident of abuse directly disclosed. The connections and insights into what *could* have happened are revealed over time and many are likely to register unconsciously before the fragmented pieces start coming together in a clearer yet still opaque picture (e.g. C's semiotic reference to A in "A field. A basement. A bed. A car", 175; and A's later guilty memory of "[a]n empty car park which I never can leave", 189). Nevertheless, 'meaning' continuously surfaces throughout the play and becomes perceptible on a non-semantic level in the form of feelings of unease – aroused, for example, by the change in grammar in C's descriptions of swallowing "it" (i.e. the maggots, 175) or by the structural interplay between C's continuous tone of rejection ("no", "this has to stop", 161, 170, 179, etc.) and A's affirmative "yes" (157, 166f., 169f., 186, etc.). When the recipient at some point of the play comes to realise that, for example, A's declaration of love is likely to have been addressed to a child, the detailed and devoted descriptions immediately change from passages with a certain beauty into objects of disgust. This can provoke moments of realisation in recipients that they have, despite clear indications that A is a paedophile, been led to overlook this fact.

While this realisation can become manifest in an initial rejection of the abuser A as well as in a kind of self-disgust for having become complicit in the act of looking away, a straightforward condemnation of A is not so easily accomplished because his devotion seems to be so sincere. We thus not only learn how easy it is to become complicit in the act of looking away (like M consistently does), but also how difficult it might be to acknowledge the severe damage that has been done to C, and how difficult it is to emotionally and cognitively 'deal' with the abuse once we acknowledge A's 'truth' to be sincere and different from ours (cf. V.ii Ambiguity).

4.48 Psychosis: "we are the abjects"

Kane's final play *4.48 Psychosis* was put on stage posthumously at the Jerwood Theatre Upstairs, London in 2000. *4.48 Psychosis* is Kane's most experimental play. In it we find an extremely *heterogeneous* assemblage of signifiers, which can be regarded as an aesthetic continuation and intensification of Kane's artistic endeavour in *Crave*. As Elzbieta Baraniecka notes in her analysis of the play, a synopsis of *4.48 Psychosis* is an impossible endeavour (207ff.; cf. also Pankratz 158f.). The play does not include any traditional framing structures such as indications of setting, *dramatis personae*, or any kind of plot structure. Orthographical signs such as spaces, dashes, hyphens, and slashes, however, offer some clues as to possible changes of space, speakers, or time.[38] The dominant theme of these "bewildered fragments" (210) is the speaker's trouble to find meaning in a world that s/he has come to find meaningless and her/his contemplation of suicide as a consequence. The loss of meaning and the resulting state of despair can also be described as a breakdown of the 'symbolical order', which is mirrored in the literary style of the piece, where the speaker's suffering is played out in a language of *abjection*.[39] In *4.48 Psychosis*, we thus find the most radical convergence of content and form which taps into and communicates humanity's most essential conflict of "death infecting life" (Kristeva 4; cf. III.ii) or coming to terms with the Silenian wisdom (cf. II.ii).

4.48 Psychosis has, despite reviewers' initial restraints regarding its artistic quality on the basis of it being a mere 'suicide note', gained much attention in academic

---

38 I read the different voices in *4.48 Psychosis* to all be the content of one speaker's consciousness. This consciousness, however, also contains memories of conversations with other speakers, especially doctors (indicated by dashes as well as changes in register). Since other than in *Crave*, there are no indications of a name, and some 'character' attributes are determinately ambiguous (e.g. gender; cf. Baraniecka 208ff.), I shall refer to the persona of this play as 'speaker' and use 's/he' to pay tribute to the deliberate ambiguity.

39 Cf. Carolina Sanchez-Ralencia Carazo's article on "*4.48 Psychosis*: Sarah Kane's 'bewildered fragments'", which takes Kristeva's notion of *abjection* to pursue a "biographical interpretation" (2).

discourse since its first staging in 2000.[40] Saunders notes that the term 'suicide note' was omnipresent in critical reviews of the play's first staging (cf. *About Kane* 35f., 150; *Love Me* 109ff.). He points to both the inevitability of a biographical reading due to the author's suicide in 1999 and to the limitations that can result from not regarding the play as an 'author-independent' piece of work (cf. *ibid.*). I would argue that in terms of a straight-forward dramatic analysis, the question of the author's suicide does not really arise as a relevant issue unless one is set on doing a determined autobiographical reading of the artist's work.[41] Since Kane had been working on the play for more than a year in constant communication with her literary agent before she handed it in as a piece of writing intended for theatrical staging, there is no indication that *4.48 Psychosis* could have been 'mistaken' for a personal note of the author (cf. Saunders, *Love Me* 111f.). The play undeniably deals with states of depression and contemplations on suicide and can in this regard in fact be perceived as a dramatic realisation of a 'suicide note' which, according to the *Merriam Webster Dictionary*, denotes "a note or letter explaining why one killed oneself" ("suicide note" n.p.). Yet if one is to evaluate the contemplation of suicide as the main theme, it seems nevertheless mandatory within the realm of a literary analysis to regard this thematic focal point first and foremost as the contemplation of the dramatic character/voice and not as that of the author (despite possible correlation between the two). The extent of the debate concerning the author's biographical background[42] is surprising since enquiries concerning authors' lives rarely arise in the context of contemporary literary studies.[43] It is, for example, hard to imagine a scholarly discussion where the aesthetic quality of a play written by a black author and openly addressing issues of ethnic identity would be questioned on the basis of it (possibly) reflecting the writer's personal experiences. The thematic focus on mental illness in *4.48 Psychosis* should thus be approached in the same way that other forms of 'otherness' (i.e. individuals or groups that defy hegemonic norms) are being addressed in literary studies. Aesthetic representation of 'otherness' in the form of mental illness has the same potential to give a voice to those that usually remain unheard in hegemonic discourse; it can raise awareness

---

40 The play's idiosyncratic dramatic style, its entire lack of marked characters or stage directions led to numerous academic discussions concerning the play's formal features, which range from biographical readings (cf. Singer 139-171; Sanchez-Palencia Carazo 1-9; Rabey 204ff.) to questions whether *4.48 Psychosis* can still be considered to be a piece of drama or falls into the category of what Lehmann calls 'postdramatic theatre' (cf. Lehmann ix, Barnett 14-23).
41 Rebellato also emphasises the danger inherent in looking at Kane's work from a primarily biographical perspective, stating that "it would be a second tragedy if her death were to become an easy way of not confronting the seriousness of her work" ("Appreciation" 281).
42 Cf. Saunders' detailed commentary on this discussion in *Love Me* (109ff.) and *About Kane* (34ff.).
43 Since Roland Barthes' seminal essay on "The Death of the Author" (1967) the integration of authors' intentions and biographical backgrounds in literary analyses has basically become a 'no-go-area' (cf. Compagno 38).

of reasons and causes for suffering, and point to shortcomings in societies' modes of dealing with "the abjects" (Kane 229) within institutions established to maintain the 'symbolical order' (cf. V.ii Social Critique).

Confronting *Abjection*: "the cockroaches comprise a truth which no one ever utters"

4.48 Psychosis opens with a fragment that most likely reflects a remembered dialogue between the speaker and her/his treating doctor who asks the speaker what s/he has to "offer [her/his] friends to make them so supportive" (205). This opening allows us to read the following text as the speaker's answer to the question, which contains an intricate act of self-exploration and repeated attempts to put into words the troubles that cause her/his current state of psychological despair. What the speaker 'offers' is, on the one hand, an explanation for her/his suffering, and on the other, a language that makes palpable the tragic core of human existence as it becomes manifest in the Silenian wisdom:

> 'Wretched, ephemeral race, children of chance and tribulation, why do you force me to tell you the very thing which it would be most profitable for you *not* to hear? The very best thing is utterly beyond your reach: not to have been born, not to *be*, to be *nothing*. However, the second best thing for you is: to die soon.' (Nietzsche, *The Birth of Tragedy* 23; original emphasis; cf. II.ii)

4.48 Psychosis can thus be argued to represent the existential struggle of a speaker who, having come to fully acknowledge the fact of humans' mortality and the futility of all endeavours to deny this fact, finds her/himself at the core of *abjection*, desperately trying to find meaning, sense, order, and, above all, help from within as well as from others (e.g. institutions and systems of belief). In the sequence following the opening dialogue with the doctor, the speaker encapsulates the moment of having gained the ultimate insight into humans' tragic core of existence in the following image:

> a consolidated consciousness resides in a darkened banqueting hall near the ceiling of a mind whose floor shifts as ten thousand cockroaches when a shaft of light enters as all thoughts unite in an instant of accord body no longer expellent as the cockroaches comprise a truth which no one ever utters
>
> I had a night in which everything was revealed to me. How can I speak again? (205)

That it is the knowledge inherent to the Silenian wisdom to which the speaker alludes through the image of 'truth-comprising cockroaches' in this passage is supported by a number of further statements. In a sequence that recapitulates another encounter between the speaker and her/his treating doctors, s/he explains:

"[I] have nothing to say about my 'illness' which anyway amounts only to knowing that there's no point in anything because I'm going to die" (209; cf. also 207, 210, 214, 220, etc.). Like the Dionysian man and Shakespeare's Hamlet, the speaker feels nothing but disgust at existence since s/he has come to acknowledge the superficiality of the 'symbolical order' (cf. II.ii; III.ii). S/he asks her/himself: "How can I return to form / now my formal thought has gone?" (213) and comes to the conclusion of having "reached the end of this dreary and repugnant tale of a sense interned in an alien carcass and lumpen by the malignant spirit of the moral majority" (214). The only form of communication that is left to the speaker once the superficiality of 'meaning' has been acknowledged is a Dionysian kind of semiotic rendering: "I have been dead for a long time / Back to my roots / I sing without hope on the boundary" (ibid.), which, as Nietzsche explained in *The Birth of Tragedy*, was initially borne out of the "spirit of music" (cf. I; II.ii).[44]

Psychosis: Breakdown of the Symbolical Order

The play's title, *4.48 Psychosis*, is noteworthy for several reasons regarding the dramatic content as well as the form. The speaker informs us that the number '4.48' refers to a time in the morning when s/he would usually wake up and experience "[a]n instant of clarity before eternal night" (206), "when sanity visits" (229). These moments, which according to the play's title indicate states of psychosis, are paradoxically those times when the speaker feels most sane and clear (cf. Sanchez-Palencia Carazo 1). The fact that these experiences are described in terms of psychosis should, however, not lead us to conclude that the play deals with psychopathological states of psychosis in general or that psychosis is in fact the condition which afflicts the speaker, as some have argued (e.g. Greig xvii; Sanchez-Palencia Carazo 5).[45] The symptoms of mental illness described by the speaker of *4.48 Psychosis* provide little evidence to suggest the 'diagnosis' of a psychotic disease since these are explicitly characterised by a complete loss of contact with 'reality' (and the construction of alternative worlds/realities), whereas the speaker struggles with a breakdown of the language and structures that give meaning to 'reality' as we know it (cf. Singer 166). The symptoms s/he describes, which alongside suicidal phantasies include self-harm, eating disorders, substance abuse, and occasional states of dissociation (216f., 224f., 231f., etc.), rather indicate

---

44 According to Baraniecka, it is precisely this ambiguity, the "almost simultaneous experience of life and death, or creation and destruction of meaning, that is visibly at work in the play's character [that] makes up the core of the experience of the sublime" (210; cf. V.ii Ambiguity; Sublime).

45 While it is certainly true that forms of psychosis may converge with states of depression or suicidal thoughts or actions, it does not follow logically that states of depression necessarily become manifest in psychosis (cf. "Psychosis" n.p.).

the condition of a so-called 'borderline personality disorder', which according to the Statistical Manual of Mental Disorders (DSM-5) includes all of the symptoms mentioned by the speaker (e.g. instability of interpersonal relationships, self-image, and affects, suicidal behaviour, chronic feeling of emptiness, dissociative symptoms, substance abuse, intense anger; cf. n.p.).

In my reading, we should not take Kane's title of the play too literally (as inviting as it seems), especially since it is connected to a specific and very limited time of the day and never used by the speaker as a generic 'diagnosis' of her/his affliction. In this regard I agree with Norbert Greiner who suggests we should rather focus on the metaphorical function of the psychological illness (cf. 80). The speaker suffers precisely not from a complete separation from 'reality', which in terms of psychosis would entail the establishment of an alternative reality, but from finding him/her self in a space in-between, an ambiguous Dionysian world and non-world determined by meaning and non-meaning, on a 'borderline' between life and death which causes a feeling of utmost repulsion at the – in Nietzsche's terms 'Apollonian' – "dreary and repugnant tale of a sense" (214; II.ii).

It is interesting to note that Kristeva, like the speaker of *4.48 Psychosis*, relates states of psychosis to the ultimate breakdown of the symbolic function of language. For Kristeva this is more than a rare psychopathological condition suffered by a few. In her point of view, contemporary society is collectively experiencing a state of crisis that is similar to states of psychosis because of the loss of set values and beliefs. She argues that "the crisis we are living through is deeper than anything since the beginning of our era, the beginning of Christianity" (in Morgan and Morris 27). She also sees similarities between this increasingly common phenomenon and symptoms "of borderline patients on an unstable frontier between the inside and the outside", where "[t]he frontiers between sign and body, inside and outside, self and other are threatened" (*ibid.*).[46] The speaker's statements offer clear evidence of such an unstable relationship to her/his sense of self:

> Body and soul can never be married
> I need to become who I already am and will bellow forever at this incongruity
> which has committed me to hell
> Insoluble hoping cannot uphold me
> I will drown in dysphoria
> in the cold black pond of my self
> the pit of my immaterial mind (212f.)

---

46 For further elaboration cf. Kristeva's *New Maladies of the Soul* (1995).

Moving Beyond Disgust towards Death

Like C in *Crave*, the speaker does not find any support from her/his surroundings (in her/his case the professional healthcare system s/he appears to have had her/himself committed to). Finding that the institution which is supposed to help her/him deal with her/his afflicted mind merely functions to enhance her/his disgust with the superficial functioning systems of the 'symbolical order' – "Please. Don't switch off my mind by attempting to straighten me out. Listen and understand" (220); "There's not a drug on earth can make life meaningful" (*ibid*.); "let's do the chemical lobotomy, let's shut down the higher functions of my brain and perhaps I'll be a bit more fucking capable of living" (221) – s/he, like C, comes to the conclusion that neither life, surroundings, nor language are able to relieve her/him from the insight into the Silenian wisdom: "[D]rowning in a sea of logic / this monstrous state of palsy / still ill" (223). The speaker, like C and the other characters in *Crave*, decides to cross the 'borderline' of "death infecting life" (Kristeva, *Powers of Horror* 4), leaving her/his feelings of unbearable existential disgust behind by letting her/himself fall into the Dionysian pit of *abjection* towards death. Where there is 'pure death', there is no space left for disgust. For example, a skull as a signifier of death is generally not found to be as appalling as a corpse or a wound infested by maggots. It is the in-between, the *abject*, the inconceivability of death as a fact of life and vice versa that is beyond our comprehension and is thus held at bay in human societies via the rules and restrictions of 'symbolical orders'. Whereas our engagement with disgust reaches its end once death wins over, the more complex notion of *abjection* offers the tools to move on to the realms that lie beyond disgust and to conceptually grasp the intrinsic relation between disgust and, in the case of Kane's ultimate play, states of depression (where disgust, i.e. the ambivalent fight for life in the face of death, tend to give way to the death wish), and death itself.

VI.iii   Summary

The analysis of Kane's *oeuvre* demonstrates how productive the category of dramatic disgust and the underlying notion of *abjection* are for the study of drama. By relating to the different forms, functions, and effects of dramatic disgust in a close reading of Kane's plays, we illustrated the suitability of categories of typical disgust-elicitation for approaching essential human conflicts as they become manifest in aesthetic representations in works of drama. Above all, this is our having to come to terms with the Silenian wisdom, the acceptance of human existence as being determined by "death infecting life" – *abjection* (Kristeva 4), but also the conflict of the needs and desires of the individual within and outside of the social and cultural rules and restrictions which form the 'symbolical orders' of societies.

VI. Case Study: Dramatic Disgust in the Works of Sarah Kane 169

The chapter was divided into two parts, with the first focusing on Kane's early, more physical plays and looking at manifestations of dramatic disgust primarily on the level of content, while the second part dealt more closely with *abject* language in Kane's later, increasingly *heterogeneous* and experimental plays. In the analysis of *Blasted* in the first sub-chapter the categories of food-loathing and pollution were used as focal points to show how dramatic disgust functions to set the scene and atmosphere, build characters, and work as a foreshadowing device. It also demonstrated how the idea of pollution, which still functions very similarly to the ancient notion of *miasma* (cf. I), can help us to understand the change of character and the progression of the plot through the 'infected' character Cate.

In *Skin*, the examination of food-loathing was extended to take a more detailed look at how disgust functions to establish social identities. In this play, food and modes of consumption are used as symbols to mark the difference between the main character Billy himself and his entourage of racist nationalists. Disgust as a form of negative evaluation of others and a means of establishing social identities drives the action of the play, with Billy, as a questioner of not only his friends' dogma of meat-consumption, constantly veering in-between not-so-simplistic binaries of black/white, perpetrator/victim, etc. The breakdown of the protagonist Billy's superficial 'skin-identity' at the end of the play as well as his possible redemption (*katharsis*) and resurrection through the fatherly figure Neville also illustrates the possibility of overcoming these kinds of pre-set modes of identification within particular social settings. The analysis of *Phaedra's Love* concentrated on the ambiguity inherent to states of *abjection*, the repulsion they cause as well as the pleasures the *abject* can provide via border transgression in the form of *jouissance*. Another emphasis was placed on the function of language in its ability to convey 'the truth' in Nietzsche's sense of differentiating between the Apollonian principle of presenting 'meaning' in a beautiful and comprehensible manner versus the Dionysian principle which enables insight into the more difficult and appalling, yet 'real' facts of life (i.e. *Schein* versus *Sein*; cf. II.ii). In *Phaedra's Love* we encountered a reversal of the evaluation of characters and their actions similar to the ones we discussed in the ancient tragedies of Euripides and Sophocles (cf. I), or to put it in Shakespeare's words, a turning from "fair" into "foul" and "foul" into "fair" (*Macbeth* I.i). A close reading of *Phaedra's Love* thus once again highlights the arbitrariness of the presuppositions that inform cultural and social conviction and ensuing world views. In *Cleansed*, which has been considered to be Kane's most brutal play, we focused on physical violence as conveyed through stage directions such as "[TINKER] *lets CARL finish what he is writing, then goes to him and reads it. He takes CARL by the arms and cuts off his hands*" (129). In this play, we witnessed Kane's language becoming increasingly multi-layered and thus even more than her previous plays confronting recipients with the ambiguity inherent to states of *abjection* and the *abject*'s force of destabilising meaning. The gruesome events that are predominantly presented in body metaphors, require a reading of not only the information disclosed in a strictly referential sense, but also of the poetic function of the multifaceted symbolical references included in stage directions and characters' speech. Through Kane's departure from a naturalistic style towards more surrealistic imagery in *Cleansed*, the traditional dramatic framing structures like the setting and the *dramatis personae* become abstract rather than particular entities, addressing universal structures of the conflicts individuals encounter in their navigation of personal needs within the framework of society's 'symbolical orders'.

In the second sub-chapter, the emphasis was placed on Kane's dramatic realisation of *abject* language in her late work. Her final two plays *Crave* and *4.48 Psychosis* present a radical shift away from the dramatic staging of repulsive and violent events towards a more poetic style, where all actions are played out exclusively in dramatic speech. In these plays, Kane employed a more symbolically and semiotically charged language to communicate states of *abjection*, such as the apprehension of life's futility in the Silenian wisdom, or instances of sexual abuse. For the analysis of *Crave* the focus lay on the theme of sexual child abuse, an instance of highest moral transgression in most societies which commonly functions as a particularly strong elicitor of moral disgust. We looked at the victim's struggles and failures to appropriate her past by articulating her experiences in 'plain' language and thus integrating them into a 'symbolical order' (i.e. making sense). We also took into account the token-abuser A's stance. As in all of Kane's plays, a straightforward condemnation of the abuser's character in *Crave* proved to be not as easily achievable as one might wish. Despite the fact that all of the gruesome consequences of A's paedophile inclinations were made tangible for recipients through the victim's blatant despair, the abuser was nevertheless able to evoke recipients' sympathies which stood in stark contrast to the negative evaluation of his character on the basis of his convictions. The constant oscillation of character evaluations between sympathy, anger, repulsion and pity had an overall nauseating effect as no 'easy' solution could be found. The way Kane managed to establish this effect on a predominantly structural and semiotic level proves her mastery of employing *abject* language to confront recipients with the instability of cultural and moral convictions that are rarely questioned, yet are an elementary part of how we define ourselves as individuals, our place within societies, and our world views.

Kane brought the depiction of the ambiguities of individual psychological suffering within social structures (in this case the health system) to a formal height in *4.48 Psychosis*. The play has no clearly marked characters. The dramatic content is rendered by an unspecified speaker who is suffering from severe suicidal depression. The speaker has gained insight into the Silenian wisdom and experiences the subsequent breakdown of a 'symbolical order' (i.e. language, sense, meaning). While s/he initially ardently tries to find alternative modes of articulation in semiotically-inflected *abject* forms of expression that mirror the way s/he experiences the world, the stark contrast to the highly 'functional' and superficial (in Nietzsche's terms 'Apollonian') discourse s/he finds herself surrounded by in the medical institution increasingly feeds her/his frustration and discourages her/his attempts to communicatively connect with others. Finding no way to overcome or integrate her/his nauseating feelings of inhabiting a space in-between meaning and non-meaning, hope and despair, life and death, s/he decides to cross the Dionysian borderline of 'death infecting life' in favour of the former and thus ultimately moves into a space beyond disgust.

Conclusion

In literary studies of drama, disgust has to this day led a rather 'closeted existence' compared to other more commonly discussed emotions like pity and fear. This study was aimed at shedding some light on the long-neglected sensation. It proposed that aesthetic disgust is a vital ingredient in works of drama that has animated the genre ever since its origin in Greek antiquity. The essential role of disgust in aesthetic practice and theory throughout history was demonstrated in the theoretical part of this study which delineated relevant stations in the history of dramatic disgust in aesthetic theory and practice from its origin in Greek antiquity (I. *miasma/dyschéreia*), through eighteenth- and nineteenth-century theoretical treaties by Kant and Nietzsche (II. *Ekel*), to early twentieth-century avantgarde artists' radical 'anti-aesthetic' approaches and psychoanalytical reflections on disgust and *abjection* (III. *Abjection*), and finally to the artistic and academic engagement with disgust that emerged around the new millennium (IV.).

The findings of this survey have a number of important implications. They demonstrated that since the dramatic genre's development from Dionysian rituals to post-industrial times, aesthetic manifestations of disgust have functioned to address universal conflicts that lie at the core of our existence as human beings, above all our having to come to terms with the incomprehensible yet ultimate fact of our own mortality (i.e. the Silenian wisdom, or "death infecting life" – *abjection*; cf. II.ii, III.ii). By extracting aesthetic disgust's properties and discussing in detail ancient manifestations of repulsive contents and forms in works of drama and philosophical reflections, we could furthermore demonstrate that the beginning of a 'history' of aesthetic disgust is not to be situated in eighteenth-century Europe, as Menninghaus maintains (cf. 10), but reaches well back into the fifth century BC. We were also able to show that the underlying structures and topics that are being addressed in works of drama through an engagement with typical disgust-elicitors have not changed significantly over time. Sophocles' detailed descriptions of Philoctetes' parasite-infested foot, or the *maenads* in Euripides' *Bacchae* playing ball with Pentheus' blood-dripping body parts (I) can be assumed to have had the same nauseating effect on ancient Greek audiences as they are likely to evoke in recipients today.

In order to develop the analytical tools that can help us to understand the disgust reactions elicited by these kinds of depictions, we combined recent scientific and psychological studies on disgust with Kristeva's psychoanalytical theory of *abjection*. A working definition of the three related notions of distaste, *abjection*, and disgust was advanced, which places the physiological instinct of food rejection (distaste), as a reflex mechanism to protect the body from harm, at the evolutionary origin of *abjection* and disgust. Both *abjection* and disgust constitute uniquely human adaptations that function above all to protect the soul from perceived harm (i.e. the human subject's sense of self-hood). *Abjection*, which in psychoanalytical theory is intrinsically linked to the development of the human subject's sense of selfhood at a pre-linguistic stage, was established as the broader category, with disgust (a learned emotion) presenting one possible psychosomatic reaction (aside others like *jouissance* or fear) that can result from encounters with *abjection*.

The most important contribution to current literature that this study established is the development of a unique model of aesthetic disgust's forms, functions, and effects for the analysis of drama. From the working definition of the relation between abjection and disgust, we deduced that the evocation of disgust in drama can be viewed as an aesthetic mode of representing the universal experience of *abjection*. Categories of dramatic disgust were established on three interrelated levels: (1) as a dramaturgical and stylistic device (*poiesis*: setting the scene, building characters, driving the plot, etc.), (2) as a mode of non-linguistic representation (*mimesis*: body metaphors, voice, etc.), and (3) as a facilitator of particular effects on recipients (*aisthesis*: shock, evocation of 'aesthetic ideas', *jouissance*, *sublime*, *katharsis*, etc.).

From the insights into aesthetic manifestations of disgust which were gained in the historical survey, we established a number of semantic fields of typical disgust-elicitation as they commonly prevail on the level of content in works of drama (*poiesis*, *mimesis*), namely animality, body boundaries, pollution, and moral transgression. Stylistically, dramatic disgust can become manifest particularly in: lists, onomatopoeia, interjections, and slang.

Several important aesthetic functions and effects (*aisthesis*) of dramatic disgust were compiled. The highly valuable dramatic potential of disgust became evident in the list of possible functions we compiled which, alongside the commonly associated ability to shock and provoke, featured: a confrontation with ambiguity and death (*abjection*), a mode of ordering or othering, and a form of voicing social critique as well as a number of effects which, taken together, account for the 'negative' aesthetic pleasure of the *sublime*. The positive elements which determine this aesthetic experience range from *jouissance* evoked by the transgression of social and cultural boundaries, to the pleasures of learning about crucial aspects of human existence, and admiration of the craftsmanship involved in presenting such complex issues in a form able to provoke an 'aesthetic idea', to a release of the negative feelings involved in confrontations with *abjection* in the form of a *katharsis*. Experiencing such a strong ratio-affective encounter with art can furthermore induce feelings of consolation and communion among recipients.

The suitability and applicability of these established forms, functions, and effects became evident in the exemplary analysis of the works of Kane, which not only illustrated how well the established categories of dramatic disgust serve as analytical tools in close readings of theatrical texts, but also indicated that the topics Kane addressed in her plays go far beyond merely representing a particular 1990s' *zeitgeist* or a "new aesthetic sensibility" (Sierz, "In-yer-face" n.p.). They rather, it was concluded, tap into patterns of universal human conflicts. The investigation of the multiple layers of disgust contained in Kane's poetic dramatic language furthermore validated the claim that aesthetic engagement with this complex sensation has much more potential than to solely function as a tool to shock the recipients. It not only offers to teach us a great amount about how we define ourselves and position ourselves in relation to others, but also directly connects us to our innermost conflict of having to come to terms with the fact that our existence is ultimately determined by 'death infecting life' – *abjection*. Kane was only too aware of this Silenian wisdom and experimented extensively with language in order to communicate this inherently *logos*-evading experience. The increasing recognition her dramatic work has been receiving in recent years gives testimony to the fact that she accomplished the task of artistically creating something of universal value, which places her work in a line with a number of the most important and canonical plays in history (exemplified here a.o. Sophocles' *Oedipus the King*, Seneca's *Thyestes*, Shakespeare's *King Lear*). The dramatist Edward Bond, whose 1965 play *Saved* could well be added to the line of plays listed above, was one of the first to immediately grasp the scope of Kane's artistic genius and her understanding of the dramatic genre's essential core when upon viewing *Blasted* he stated:

> *Blasted* [...] comes [...] from the centre of our humanity and our ancient need for theatre. That's what gives it its strange, almost hallucinatory authority. It does not show us the images we will live with if we do not remake our moral vision. We already live those images – in the world where the two hands of the clock are birth and death, the world that is always there but becomes our dehumanised reality only when we do not try to make our daily world more just. The images of *Blasted* are ancient. They are seen in all great ages of art – in Greek and Jacobean theatre, Noh and Kabuki. The play changes some of the images – but all artists do that to bring the ancient imagery, changed and unchanged, into the focus of their age. (n.p.)

Outlook

This study was an attempt to take a systematic look at different historical and contemporary schools of thought that have dealt with the complex sensation of disgust (and its various cognates) and its role in, and for, the dramatic genre, in order to develop a synthesised model of aesthetic disgust for the analysis of drama. Since this is the first book-length study to address the particular forms, functions, and effects of aesthetic disgust that are specific to the dramatic genre, it is far from making any claim to completeness. There are numerous aspects that deserve further investigation. Historically, there are many further eras, artistic movements and particular genres that would be interesting to assess and compare to the ones analysed in this study, such as Roman tragedy, the Middle Ages, Jacobean tragedy, or Gothic literature, to name just a few. In terms of disgust's cognates, an examination of the *grotesque* and Mikhail Bakhtin's theoretical reflections on the concept in *Rabelais and His World* (1968) would offer a valuable addition to the terms discussed in the theoretical part of this study. A closely related category recommended for further research is the comical effect that dramatic disgust may elicit. It is well conceivable that the kind of laughter which can be provoked through encounters with states of *abjection* presents a specific form of *jouissance*, of taking pleasure at the transgression of borders, which fulfils a similar function (of release, *katharsis*) as vomiting does (cf. Menninghaus 384; cf. also Ben-Zvi 681ff.). Finally, we have only taken the dramatic text into closer consideration here, and not looked at examples of its realisation in performance. In order to fully determine the potential of dramatic disgust, empirical research would need to be conducted to determine how aesthetic experiences of encountering appalling events in real-life theatrical productions differ or compare to these scenes being 'played out' in the reader's imagination only. The entire field of investigating audience/reader responses to dramatic disgust, with the integration of, for example, neuroscientific approaches, is one yet to be covered.

Bibliography

Ablett, Sarah. "The Repulsive Other in Tim Crouch's *I, Malvolio*". *Journal for Contemporary Drama in English*, 7.1 (2019): 46-57. Print. https://doi.org/10.1515/jcde-2019-0004
---. "Disgust in Samuel Beckett's *Molloy*". In: Heike Hartung (ed.), *Embodied Narration: Illness, Death and Dying in Modern Culture*. Bielefeld: transcript. Aging Studies Book Series, 2018. 85-102. Print. https://doi.org/10.14361/9783839443064-006
---. "Approaching Abjection in Sarah Kane's *Blasted*". *Performance Research* 19.1 (2014): 63-71. Print. https://doi.org/10.1080/13528165.2014.908085
---. "Sarah Kane's *Blasted* – Genesis of the Subject". *Journal for Contemporary Drama in English*, 1.2 (2013): 249-260. Print. https://doi.org/10.1515/jcde-2013-0020
Aldama, Frederick L., ed. *Toward a Cognitive Theory of Narrative Acts*. Austin: U of Texas P, 2010. Print.
Alexander, Jeffrey C. "The Fate of the Dramatic in Modern Society: Social Theory and the Theatrical Avant-Garde". *Theory, Culture & Society* 31.1 (2013): 3-24. Print. https://doi.org/10.1177/0263276413506019
Allison, David B. *Reading the New Nietzsche: The Birth of Tragedy, The Gay Science, Thus Spoke Zarathustra, and on the Genealogy of Morals*. Lanham: Rowman & Littlefield, 2001. Print.
Angel, Maria. "Brainfood: Rationality, Aesthetics and Economies of Affect". *Textual Practice* 19.2 (2005): 323-348. Print. http://dx.doi.org/10.1080/09502360500091477
Angel-Perez, Elisabeth and Alexandra Poulain. *Hunger on the Stage*. Newcastle: Cambridge Scholars Pub, 2008. Print.
Aristotle and Joe Sachs. *Poetics*. Newburyport: Focus Publishing, 2006. Print.
Artaud, Antonin. *On Theatre*. London: Methuen Drama, 2001. Print.
---. *The Theater and its Double*. New York: Grove P, 1958. Print.
Arya, Rina. *Abjection and Representation: An Exploration of Abjection in the Visual Arts, Film and Literature*. Basingstoke: Palgrave Macmillan, 2014. Print. https://doi.org/10.1057/9780230389342_5

Aston, Elaine. "Feeling the Loss of Feminism: Sarah Kane's *Blasted* and an Experiential Genealogy of Contemporary Women's Playwriting". *Theatre Journal* 62.4 (2010): 575-591. Print. https://doi.org/10.1353/tj.2010.0053

---. *Feminist Views on the English Stage: Women Playwrights, 1990-2000*. Cambridge: Cambridge UP, 2003. Print. https://doi.org/10.1017/S0040557405330092

---. "Sarah Kane Before *Blasted*: The Monologues". *Sarah Kane in Context*. Ed. Graham Saunders and Laurens de Vos. Manchester: Manchester UP, 2010. 28-44. Print.

Aston, Elaine and Geraldine Harris. *Feminist Futures? Theatre, Performance, Theory*. Basingstoke: Palgrave Macmillan, 2006. Print. https://doi.org/10.1057/9780230554948

Aston, Elaine and Janelle G. Reinelt. *The Cambridge Companion to Modern British Women Playwrights*. Cambridge: Cambridge UP, 2000. Print. https://doi.org/10.1017/CCOL9780521594226

Bacci, Francesca and David Melcher, eds. *Art and the Senses*. Oxford: Oxford UP, 2011. Print.

Bakhtin, Mikhail M. *Rabelais and His World*. Bloomington: Indiana UP, 1984. Print.

---. "The Grotesque Image of the Body and its Sources". *The Body: A Reader*. Ed. Mariam Fraser and Monica Greco. London: Routledge, 2004. 92-95. Print.

Balme, Christopher. *Einführung in Die Theaterwissenschaft*. 4th ed. Berlin: Schmidt, 2008. Print.

Baraniecka, Elżbieta. *Sublime Drama: British Theatre of the 1990s*. Berlin: De Gruyter, 2014. Print. https://doi.org/10.1515/9783110309935

Barker, Howard. *Arguments for a Theatre*. Manchester: Manchester UP, 1998. Print.

---. "Sarah Kane and Forced Entertainment". *Contemporary Theatre Review* 18.3 (2008): 328-340. Print. https://doi.org/10.1080/10486800802123617

Barnett, David. "When is a Play not a Drama? Two Examples of Postdramatic Theatre Texts". *New Theatre Quarterly* 24.1 (2008): 14-23. Print. https://doi.org/10.1017/S0266464X0800002X

Barrett, Estelle. *Kristeva Reframed: Interpreting Key Thinkers for the Arts*. London: I.B. Tauris, 2011. Print.

Bartfleet, Carina. "The Scene of Disgust: Realism and its Malcontents, the Audience and the Abject". *Theatres of Thought: Theatre, Performance and Philosophy*. Ed. Daniel Watt and Daniel Meyer-Dinkgräfe. Newcastle: Cambridge Scholars Pub, 2007. 13-30. Print.

Barthes, Roland. *A Lover's Discourse: Fragments*. New York: Hill and Wang, 1978. Print.

---. *Image, Music, Text*. New York: Hill and Wang, 1977. Print.

---. "The Death of the Author". *Image, Music, Text*. Ed. Roland Barthes. New York: Hill and Wang, 1977. 142-148. Print.

Bataille, Georges. "Attraction and Repulsion II". *The College of Sociology 1937-1939*. Ed. Dennis Hollier. Minneapolis: U of Minnesota P, 1988. Print.

---.*Death and Sensuality: A Study of Eroticism and the Taboo*. New York: Walker, 1962. Print.

---.*The Bataille Reader*. Oxford: Blackwell, 1997. Print.

---.*The History of Eroticism*. New York: Zone, 1991. Print.

---."The Use Value of D. A. F. de Sade". *Visions of Excess: Selected Writings, 1927-1939*. Ed. Allan Stoekl. Minneapolis: University of Minnesota P, 1985. 91-105. Print.

---.*Visions of Excess: Selected Writings, 1927-1939*. Minneapolis: Minnesota UP, 1985. Print.

Baudrillard, Jean. *Simulacra and Simulation*. Ann Arbor: U of Michigan P, 1994. Print. https://doi.org/10.3998/mpub.9904

Baumgarten, Alexander G. "Metaphysica". *Texte zur Grundlegung der Ästhetik*. Ed. Hans R. Schweizer. Hamburg: Felix Meiner, 1983. §§ 501-623. Print. https://doi.org/10.28937/978-3-7873-2574-0

---.*Texte zur Grundlegung der Ästhetik*. Hamburg: Felix Meiner, 1983. Print.

Beck, Martha C. *Interpreting Sophocles' Philoctetes through Aristotle's Theory of Tragedy. How Do We Educate People to Be Wise?* New York: Edwin Mellen P, 2008. Print.

Becker-Leckrone, Megan. *Julia Kristeva and Literary Theory*. Basingstoke: Palgrave Macmillan, 2005. Print. https://doi.org/10.1007/978-0-230-80195-0

Benjamin, Walter. *Gesammelte Schriften*. Frankfurt am Main: Suhrkamp, 1991.Print.

---.*The Origin of German Tragic Drama*. London: Verso, 1998. Print.

Bennett, Jill. *Empathetic Vision: Affect, Trauma, and Contemporary Art*. Stanford: Stanford UP, 2005. Print.

Ben-Zvi, Linda. "Beckett and Disgust: The Body as 'Laughing Matter'". *Modernism* 18.4 (2011): 681-698. Print. https://doi.org/10.1353/mod.2011.0092

Bexley, Erica. "Show or Tell? Seneca's and Sarah Kane's Phaedra Plays". *Trends in Classics* 3.2 (2011): 365-393. Print. https://doi.org/10.1515/tcs.2011.016

Billington, Michael. "How Do You Judge a 75-minute Suicide Note?" *The Guardian* (2000). Web.

Bloom, Harold, ed. *Sophocles' Oedipus Rex*. New York: Chelsea House, 2007. Print.

Bond, Edward. "A Blast at Our Smug Theatre." *The Guardian* (1995). Web.

---."Epilogue: 'The Mark of Kane'". *Sarah Kane in Context*. Ed. Graham Saunders and Laurens de Vos. Manchester: Manchester UP, 2010. 209-220. Print.

"Borderline". *Statistic Manual of Mental Disorders (DSM-5)* (2016). Web.

Borowski, Mateusz. "Under the Surface of Things: Sarah Kane's *Skin* and the Medium of Theatre". *Sarah Kane in Context*. Ed. Graham Saunders and Laurens de Vos. Manchester: Manchester UP, 2010. 184-194. Print.

Brockett, Oscar G. and Franklin J. Hildy. *The History of Theatre*. Boston: Pearson, 2008. Print.

Broich, Ulrich. "New Trends in British Theatre: The Theatre of Blood and Sperm". *European Studies* 16 (2001): 207-226. Print. https://doi.org/10.1163/9789004333970_012

Brown, Sarah A. and Catherine Silverstone, eds. *Tragedy in Transition*. Oxford: Blackwell, 2007. Print. https://doi.org/10.1002/9780470692028

Brusberg-Kiermeier, Stefani. "Cruelty, Violence, and Rituals in Sarah Kane's Plays". *Sarah Kane in Context*. Ed. Graham Saunders and Laurens de Vos. Manchester: Manchester UP, 2010. 80-87. Print.

Büchner, Georg. *Danton's Death, Leonce and Lena, Woyzeck*. Oxford: Oxford UP, 1988. Print.

---. *Dantons Tod*. Frankfurt am Main: Diesterweg, 1983. Print.

Burke, Edmund and Adam Phillips. *A Philosophical Enquiry into the Origin of Our Ideas of the Sublime and Beautiful*. Oxford: Oxford UP, 2008. Print.

Burnham, Douglas and Martin Jesinghausen. *Nietzsche's The Birth of Tragedy: A Reader's Guide*. London: Continuum, 2010. Print.

Bushnell, Rebecca, ed. *A Companion to Tragedy*. Oxford: Blackwell, 2005. Print. https://doi.org/10.1111/b.9781405107358.2005.00007.x

Butler, Judith. "The Body Politics of Julia Kristeva". *Hypatia* 3.3 (1989): 104-118. Print. https://doi.org/10.1111/j.1527-2001.1988.tb00191.x

Campbell, Peter A. "Sarah Kane's *Phaedra's Love*: Staging the Implacable". *Sarah Kane in Context*. Ed. Graham Saunders and Laurens de Vos. Manchester: Manchester UP, 2010. 173-183. Print.

Camus, Albert. *La Peste*. Paris: Gallimard, 1947. Print.

---. *The Plague*. New York: Vintage, 1991. Print.

Cancik, Hubert and August Friedrich von Pauly, eds. *Der neue Pauly: Enzyklopädie der Antike*. München: Metzler, 1997. Print.

Carlson, Marla. *Performing Bodies in Pain: Medieval and Post-modern Martyrs, Mystics, and Artists*. Basingstoke: Palgrave Macmillan, 2010. Print. https://doi.org/10.1057/9780230111486

Carney, Sean. "The Tragedy of History in Sarah Kane's *Blasted*". *Theatre Survey* 46.2 (2005): 275-296. Print.

Carroll, Noël. *The Philosophy of Horror or, Paradoxes of the Heart*. New York: Routledge, 1990. Print.

Céline, Louis-Ferdinand. *Journey to the End of the Night*. Richmond: Alma Classics, 2012. Print.

Chance, Jane. "Cognitive Alterities: From Cultural Studies to Neuroscience and Back Again". *Postmedieval: A Journal of Medieval Cultural Studies* 3.3 (2012): 247-261. Print. https://doi.org/10.1057/pmed.2012.19

Chanter, Tina. *The Picture of Abjection: Film, Fetish, and the Nature of Difference*. Bloomington: Indiana UP, 2008. Print. https://doi.org/10.2307/j.ctt20060tq

Chaouli, Michel. "A Surfeit in Thinking: Kant's Aesthetic Ideas". *The Yearbook of Comparative Literature* 57.1 (2011): 55-77. Print.

---."Human Voices and the Voice of Humanity in Kant's Third Critique". *Kultur-Schreiben als romantisches Projekt. Romantische Ethnographie im Spannungsfeld zwischen Imagination und Wissenschaft*. Ed. David Welbery. Würzburg: Königshausen & Neumann, 2012. 43-60. Print.

Chapman, Hanah A. and Adam K. Anderson. "Understanding Disgust". *Annals of the New York Academy of Sciences* 1 (2012): 62-76. Print. https://doi.org/10.1111/j.1749-6632.2011.06369.x

Chute, Hillary. "Victim. Perpetrator. Bystander: Critical Distance in Sarah Kane's Theatre of Cruelty". *Sarah Kane in Context*. Ed. Graham Saunders and Laurens de Vos. Manchester: Manchester UP, 2010. 161-172. Print.

Clapp, Susannah. "Blessed are the Bleak". *The Guardian* (2000). Web.

Cohen, William A. and Ryan Johnson. *Filth: Dirt, Disgust, and Modern Life*. Minneapolis: Minnesota UP, 2005. Print.

Cohn, Ruby. "Sarah Kane, an Architect of Drama". *Cynos* 18.1 (2008): 1-9. Web.

Collins, Margery and Christine Pierce. "Holes and Slime. Sexism in Sartre's Psychoanalysis". *Philosophical Forum* 5.5 (1973): 112-127. Print.

Compagno, Dario. "Theories of Authorship and Intention in the Twentieth Century". *Journal of Early Modern Studies* 1.1 (2012): 37-53. Print. https://doi.org/10.13128/JEMS-2279-7149-10633

Connelly, Frances S. *Modern Art and the Grotesque*. Cambridge: Cambridge UP, 2003. Print.

"Consumption". *Online Etymology Dictionary* (2017). Web.

Cotter, Holland. "Review/Art: At the Whitney, Provocation and Theory Meet Head-On". *The New York Times* (1993). Web.

Crandell, George. "Beyond Pity and Fear: Echoes of Nietzsche's *The Birth of Tragedy* in Tennessee William's *A Street Car Named Desire* and other Plays". *The Southern Quarterly* (2003): 91-107. Print.

Creed, Barbara. "Horror and the Monstrous Feminine: An Imaginary Abjection". *Cultural Studies*. Ed. Michael Ryan and Hanna Musiol. Malden: Blackwell, 2008. 243-265. Print.

---.*The Monstrous Feminine: Film, Feminism, Psychoanalysis*. London: Routledge, 1993. Print.

Critchley, Simon and Jamieson Webster. *Stay, Illusion! The Hamlet Doctrine*. New York: Pantheon, 2013. Print.

Csapo, Eric and William J. Slater, eds. *The Context of Ancient Drama*. Michigan: Michigan UP, 1995. Print. https://doi.org/10.3998/mpub.13922

Curtis, Valerie. "Why Disgust Matters". *Philosophical Transactions of the Royal Society of London. Biological Sciences* 366.1583 (2011): 3478-3490. Print. https://doi.org/10.1098/rstb.2011.0165

Cusack, Carmen M. "Two Films, One Law: An Analysis of Social Deviance in Gender, Family, or the Home." *Etudes* 7 (2011). Web.

Czarnecki, Kristin. "'Signs I don't understand': Language and Abjection in *Molloy*". *Journal of Beckett Studies* 17.1 (2007): 52-77. Print. https://doi.org/10.3366/E0309520709000089

Dalgleish, Tim and Mick J. Power, eds. *Handbook of Cognition and Emotion*. New York: John Wiley and Sons, 1999. Print.

Damasio, Antonio R. *The Feeling of What Happens: Body and Emotion in the Making of Consciousness*. New York: Harcourt, 2000. Print.

Daniels, Paul R. *Nietzsche and The Birth of Tragedy*. Durham: Acumen, 2013. Print.

Danto, Arthur C. "The Abuse of Beauty: Aesthetics and the Concept of Art". *Philosophy in Review* 25.1 (2005): 19-21. Print.

Darwin, Charles. *The Expression of the Emotions in Man and Animals*. New York: Appleton & Company, 1872. Print. https://doi.org/10.1037/10001-000

Defraeye, Piet. "In-Yer-Face Theatre? Reflections on Provocation and Provoked Audiences in Contemporary Theatre". *Extending the Code: New Forms of Dramatic and Theatrical Expression*. Ed. Hans-Ulrich Mohr and Kerstin Mächler. Trier: WVT, 2004. 79-97. Print.

Delgado-García, Cristina. "Subversion, Refusal, and Contingency: The Transgression of Liberal-Humanist Subjectivity and Characterization in Sarah Kane's *Cleansed*, *Crave*, and *4.48 Psychosis*". *Modern Drama* 55.2 (2012): 230-250. Print. https://doi.org/10.3138/md.55.2.230

Deubner, Paula. *"Into the light": Selbst und Transzendenz in den Dramen Sarah Kanes*. Trier: WVT, 2012. Print.

Diamond, Elin. *Unmaking Mimesis: Essays on Feminism and Theatre*. London: Routledge, 1997. Print. https://doi.org/10.4324/9780203358900

Dickson, Andrew. "'The strange thing is we howled with laughter': Sarah Kane's Enigmatic Last Play" *The Guardian* (2016). Web.

Diedrich, Antje. "'Last in a long line of literary kleptomaniacs': Intertextuality in Sarah Kane's *4.48 Psychosis*". *Modern Drama* 56.3 (2013): 374-398. Print. https://doi.org/10.3138/md.0356

D'Monté, Rebecca and Graham Saunders. *Cool Britannia? British Political Drama in the 1990s*. Basingstoke: Palgrave Macmillan, 2008. Print.

Dollimore, Jonathan. *Radical Tragedy: Religion, Ideology, and Power in the Drama of Shakespeare and his Contemporaries*. Chicago: Chicago UP, 1984. Print.

Dorney, Kate. *The Changing Language of Modern English Drama, 1945-2005*. Basingstoke: Palgrave Macmillan, 2009. Print. https://doi.org/10.1057/9780230245211

Douglas, Mary. *Purity and Danger: An Analysis of the Concepts of Pollution and Taboo*. London: Routledge, 2004. Print. https://doi.org/10.4324/9780203361832

Douglas-Fairhurst, Robert. "Tragedy and Disgust". *Tragedy in Transition*. Ed. Sarah A. Brown and Catherine Silverstone. Oxford: Blackwell, 2007. 58-77. Print.

Dromgoole, Dominic. *The Full Room: An A-Z of Contemporary Playwriting*. London: Methuen, 2000. Print.

Duggan, Patrick. *Trauma Tragedy: Symptoms of Contemporary Performance*. Manchester: Manchester UP, 2012. Print. https://doi.org/10.1097/TA.0b013e31826601e6

Eagleton, Terry. *Holy Terror*. Oxford: Oxford UP, 2005. Print.

– – –. *Sweet Violence: The Idea of the Tragic*. Oxford: Blackwell, 2003. Print.

Earnest, Steve. "Review: 4.48 Psychosis". *Theatre Journal* 57.2 (2005): 298-300. Print.

– – –. "Review: Cleansed". *Theatre Journal* 58.1 (2006): 110-112. Print.

Eden, Cathy. "Aristotle's Poetics. A Defense of Tragic Fiction". *A Companion to Tragedy*. Ed. Rebecca Bushnell. Malden: Blackwell, 2007. 41-50. Print. https://doi.org/10.1002/9780470996393.ch4

Egger, Mario, ed. *Philosophie nach Kant: Neue Wege zum Verständnis von Kants Transzendental- und Moralphilosophie*. Berlin: De Gruyter, 2014. Print. https://doi.org/10.1515/9783110344110

"Ekelfernsehen". *Wort des Jahres, Gesellschaft für deutsche Sprache* (2004). Web.

Ekman, Paul. "An Argument for Basic Emotions". *Cognition and Emotion* 6 (1992): 169-200. Print. https://doi.org/10.1080/02699939208411068

Eschenbaum, Natalie and Barbara Correll, eds. *Disgust in Early Modern English Literature*. London: Routledge, 2016. Print.

Ette, Wolfram. "Die Tragödie als Medium philosophischer Selbsterkenntnis". *Handbuch Literatur und Philosophie*. Ed. Hans Feger. München: Metzler, 2012. 87-122. Print. https://doi.org/10.1007/978-3-476-00336-2_6

Euripides and David Kovacs. *Bacchae*. Cambridge: Harvard UP, 2002. Print.

Faulkner, Joanna. "Disgust, Purity, and a Longing for Companionship: Dialectics of Affect in Nietzsche's Imagined Community". *The Journal of Nietzsche Studies* 44.1 (2013): 49-68. Print. https://doi.org/10.5325/jnietstud.44.1.0049

Feger, Hans, ed. *Handbuch Literatur und Philosophie*. München: Metzler, 2012. Print. https://doi.org/10.1007/978-3-476-00336-2

Feinstein, Eve L. *Sexual Pollution in the Hebrew Bible*. Oxford: Oxford UP, 2014. Print.

Felman, Shoshana and Dori Laub. *Testimony: Crises of Witnessing in Literature, Psychoanalysis, and History*. New York: Routledge, 1991. Print.

Feloj, Serena, et al. "Is there a Negative Judgment of Taste? Disgust as the Real Ugliness in Kant's *Aesthetics*". *Lebenswelt* 3 (2013): 175-185. Print.

Fernie, Ewan. "Hardcore Tragedy". *Tragedy in Transition*. Ed. Sarah A. Brown and Catherine Silverstone. Oxford: Blackwell, 2007. 34-57. Print.

Ferrini, Cinzia. "Illusions of Imagination and Adventures of Reason in Kant's First Critique". *Philosophie nach Kant: Neue Wege zum Verständnis von Kants*

Transzendental- und Moralphilosophie. Ed. Mario Egger. Berlin: De Gruyter, 2014. 141-188. Print.

"Five of the Best...Sarah Kane Plays". Blog National Theatre UK (2017). Web.

Fontaine, Johnny R. J., Klaus R. Scherer, and Cristina Soriano. *Components of Emotional Meaning: A Sourcebook*. Oxford: Oxford UP, 2013. Print. https://doi.org/10.1093/acprof:oso/9780199592746.001.0001

"Food for Thought: Paul Rozin's Research and Teaching at Penn". *Penn Arts & Sciences* (1997). Web.

Fordyce, Ehren. "The Voice of Kane". *Sarah Kane in Context*. Ed. Graham Saunders and Laurens de Vos. Manchester: Manchester UP, 2010. 103-110. Print.

Foster, Hal. "Obscene, Abject, Traumatic". *October* 78 (1996): 107-124. Print. https://doi.org/10.2307/778908

---. *The Return of the Real. Art and Theory at the End of the Century*. Cambridge: MIT P, 1996. Print.

Fraser, Mariam and Monica Greco, eds. *The Body: A Reader*. London: Routledge, 2004. Print.

Freedberg, David and Vittorio Gallese. "Motion, Emotion and Empathy in Esthetic Experience". *Trends in Cognitive Sciences* 11.5 (2007): 197-203. Print. https://doi.org/10.1016/j.tics.2007.02.003

Freud, Sigmund. *Beyond the Pleasure Principle*. London: International Psycho-Analytical P, 1922. Web. Projekt Gutenberg. https://doi.org/10.1037/11189-000

---. *Civilization and its Discontents*. New York: W. W. Norton, 1962. Print.

---. *Darstellungen der Psychoanalyse*. Frankfurt am Main: Fischer, 1969. Print.

---. *Das Unbehagen in der Kultur und andere kulturtheoretische Schriften*. Frankfurt am Main: Fischer, 1994. Print.

---. *Totem and Taboo: Some Points of Agreement between the Mental Lives of Savages and Neurotics*. London: Routledge, 2001. Print.

Frießnegg, Andreas. "Sarah Kane – die hoffnungslose Romantikerin: Das Wechselspiel von Liebe und Gewalt im Werk von Sarah Kane". Diplomarbeit, Universität Wien. 2012. Web.

Fuchs, Elinor. *The Death of Character: Perspectives on Theater after Modernism*. Bloomington: Indiana UP, 1996. Print. https://doi.org/10.2307/j.ctt2005s83

Fuchs, Thomas, et al., eds. *The Embodied Self: Dimensions, Coherence, and Disorders*. Stuttgart: Schattauer, 2010. Print.

Fuhrmann, Manfred. *Aristoteles Poetik*. Stuttgart: Reclam, 1987. Print.

---. "Die Funktion grausiger und ekelhafter Motive in der lateinischen Dichtung". *Die nicht mehr schönen Künste: Grenzphänomene des Ästhetischen*. Ed. Hans R. Jauß. München: Wilhelm Fink, 1986. 23-66. Print.

Gallagher, Shaun. *How the Body Shapes the Mind*. Oxford: Clarendon P, 2005. Print. https://doi.org/10.1093/0199271941.001.0001

Gallagher, Shaun and Dan Zahavi. *The Phenomenological Mind. An Introduction to Philosophy of Mind and Cognitive Science*. London: Routledge, 2008. Print. https://doi.org/10.4324/9780203086599

Gallese, Vittorio. "Mirror Neurons and Art". *Art and the Senses*. Ed. Francesca Bacci and David Melcher. Oxford: Oxford UP, 2011. Print.

---."The Embodied Simulation and its Role in Intersubjectivity". *The Embodied Self: Dimensions, Coherence, and Disorders*. Ed. Thomas Fuchs, et al. Stuttgart: Schattauer, 2010. 78-92. Print.

Garner, Stanton B. *Bodied Spaces: Phenomenology and Performance in Cotemporary Drama*. Ithaca: Cornell UP, 1994. Print.

Gaut, Berys N. and Dominic Lopes, eds. *The Routledge Companion to Aesthetics*. London: Routledge, 2001. Print.

Gergen, Kenneth J. *The Saturated Self: Dilemmas of Identity in Contemporary Life*. New York: Basic Books, 1991. Print.

Geuss, Raymond. "Introduction". *The Birth of Tragedy and Other Writings*. Ed. Raymond Geuss and Ronald Speirs. Cambridge: Cambridge UP, 2007. vii-xxx. Print.

Geuss, Raymond and Ronald Speirs, eds. *The Birth of Tragedy and Other Writings*. Cambridge: Cambridge UP, 2007. Print.

Giannopoulou, Zina. "Staging Power: The Politics of Sex and Death in Seneca's *Phaedra* and Kane's *Phaedra's Love*". *Sarah Kane in Context*. Ed. Graham Saunders and Laurens de Vos. Manchester: Manchester UP, 2010. 57-67. Print.

Goethe von, Johann Wolfgang. *The Sorrows of Young Werther*. Richmond: Oneworld Classics, 2010. Print.

Goldman, Alvin I. "Mirroring, Simulating and Mindreading". *Mind and Language* 24.2 (2009): 235-252. Print. https://doi.org/10.1111/j.1468-0017.2008.01361.x

Goodnough, Abby. "Giuliani Threatens to Evict Museum Over Art Exhibit". *The New York Times* (1999). Web.

Gordon, Paul. "Tragedy and Psychoanalysis: Beyond the Pleasure Principle". *Tragedy after Nietzsche. Rapturous Abundance*. Illinois: U of Illinois P, 2001. 55-71. Print.

Gore-Langton, Robert. "Review: *Cleansed*". *Daily Express* (1998). Web.

Goswami, Nina. "The Greater Your Weight the Lower Your IQ." *The Telegraph* (2006). Web.

Gould, Thomas. *The Ancient Quarrel between Poetry and Philosophy*. Princeton: Princeton UP, 1990. Print. https://doi.org/10.1515/9781400861866

---."The Innocence of Oedipus Rex: The Philosophers on *Oedipus the King*, Part III". *Sophocles' Oedipus Rex*. Ed. Harold Bloom. New York: Chelsea House, 2007. 31-70. Print.

Grauer, Victor. "Formless: A Review". *Other Voices. The (e)Journal of Cultural Criticism* 2.2 (2002). Web.

"Great Chain of Being". *Encyclopdia Britannica* (2017). Web.

Greig, David. "Introduction". *Sarah Kane: Complete Plays*. London: Methuen, 2001. ix-xviii. Print.

Greiner, Norbert. "Konfigurationen des Selbstverlustes: Sarah Kanes *4.48 Psychosis*". *Cool Britannia: Literarische Selbstvergewisserungen vor der Jahrtausendwende*. Ed. Norbert Greiner and Robert Weidle. Trier: WVT, 2006. 75-90. Print.

Greiner, Norbert and Robert Weidle, eds. *Cool Britannia: Literarische Selbstvergewisserungen vor der Jahrtausendwende*. Trier: WVT, 2006. Print.

Gritzner, Karoline, ed. *Eroticism and Death in Theatre and Performance*. Herfordshire: U of Herfordshire P, 2010. Print.

---."(Post)Modern Subjectivity and the New Expressionism". *Contemporary Theatre Review* 18 (2008): 328-340. Print. https://doi.org/10.1080/10486800802123617

---."The Fading of the Subject in Sarah Kane's Later Work". *Consciousness, Theatre, Literature, and the Arts*. Ed. Daniel Meyer-Dinkgräfe. Newcastle: Cambridge Scholars Pub, 2006. 249-257. Print.

Gritzner, Karoline and David I. Rabey. *Theatre of Catastrophe: New Essays on Howard Barker*. London: Oberon Books, 2006. Print.

Gross, John. "Review: *Blasted*". *Sunday Telegraph* (1995). Web.

Hadley, Louisa and Elizabeth Ho. *Thatcher and After: Margaret Thatcher and Her Afterlife in Contemporary Culture*. Basingstoke: Palgrave Macmillan, 2010. Print. https://doi.org/10.1057/9780230283169

Haidt, Jonathan, et al. "Body, Psyche, and Culture: The Relationship between Disgust and Morality". *Psychology & Developing Societies* 9.1 (1997): 107-131. Print. https://doi.org/10.1177/097133369700900105

Hall, Edith. "Trojan Suffering, Tragic Gods, and Transhistorical Metaphysics". *Tragedy in Transition*. Ed. Sarah A. Brown and Catherine Silverstone. Oxford: Blackwell, 2007. 16-33. Print.

Hegel, Georg Wilhelm Friedrich. *Ästhetik*. Frankfurt am Main: Europa Verlag, 1965. Print.

Heine, Matthias. "Die neue alte Lust am Ekelhaften". *Die Welt* (2008). Web.

Heinz, Sarah. "'The shite of Dublin': Body Metaphors, Biopolitics, and the Functions of Disgust in Sebastian Barry's *The Pride of Parnell Street* and Gianna Carbunarius's *Kebab*". *JCDE* 1.1 (2013): 80-91. Print. https://doi.org/10.1515/jcde-2013-0008

Henderson, Jeffrey. "Obscene Language". *The Encyclopedia of Greek Tragedy*. Ed. Hanna Roisman. Chichester: Wiley-Blackwell, 2014. Print.

---. *The Maculate Muse: Obscene Language in Attic Comedy*. Oxford: Oxford UP, 1975. Print.

Henley, Jon. "Paedophilia: Brining Dark Desires to Light". *The Guardian* (2013). Web.

Henry, Anne C. "Tragedy and the Sign of the Eclipse: Tragedy in Transition". *Tragedy in Transition*. Ed. Sarah A. Brown and Catherine Silverstone. Oxford: Blackwell, 2007. 78-102. Print.

Henry, Joseph. "The Suffering Body of 1993: Whatever Happened to the 'Abject'". *Momus* (2015). Web.

Herz, Rachel. *That's Disgusting: Unraveling the Mysteries of Repulsion*. New York: W. W. Norton, 2012. Print.

Hetzel, Andreas and Peter Wiechens. *Georges Bataille: Vorreden zur Überschreitung*. Würzburg: Königshausen & Neumann, 1999. Print.

Horace. *The Works of Horace 1832-1885*. Projekt Gutenberg. Web.

Houlahan, Mark. "Postmodern Tragedy? Returning to John Ford". *Tragedy in Transition*. Ed. Sarah A. Brown and Catherine Silverstone. Oxford: Blackwell, 2007. 249-259. Print.

Howe Kritzer, Amelia. *Political Theatre in Post-Thatcher Britain: New Writing: 1995-2005*. Basingstoke: Palgrave Macmillan, 2008. Print. https://doi.org/10.1057/9780230582224

Howes, David. *Empire of the Senses: The Sensual Culture Reader*. Oxford: Berg, 2005. Print.

Huitfeldt Midttun, Birgitte. "Crossing the Borders: An Interview with Julia Kristeva". *Hypatia* 21 (2006): 164-167. Print. https://doi.org/10.1111/j.1527-2001.2006.tb01133.x

Hurley, Kelly. "Abject and Grotesque". *The Routledge Companion to Gothic*. Ed. Catherine Spooner and Emma McEvoy. London: Routledge, 2007. 137-146. Print.

Iball, Helen. *Sarah Kane's Blasted*. London: Continuum, 2008. Print. https://doi.org/10.5040/9781623567842

Innes, Christopher, ed. *Modern British Drama: The Twentieth Century*. Cambridge: Cambridge UP, 2002. Print.

---."Sarah Kane (1971-1999): The Poetry of Madness in Violent Dreams". *Modern British Drama: The Twentieth Century*. Ed. Christopher Innes. Cambridge: Cambridge UP, 2002. 528-537. Print.

Jacob, Pierre. "What Do Mirror Neurons Contribute to Human Social Cognition?" *Mind and Language* 23 (2008): 190-223. Print. https://doi.org/10.1111/j.1468-0017.2007.00337.x

James, Paul and Szeman Imre, eds. *Globalization and Culture*. London: Sage, 2010. Print.

Jauß, Hans R., ed. *Die nicht mehr schönen Künste: Grenzphänomene des Ästhetischen*. München: Wilhem Fink, 1968. Print.

Jobling, David, Tina Pippin, and Ronald Schleifer. *The Postmodern Bible Reader*. Oxford: Blackwell, 2001. Print.

Johnson, Dominic. "Ron Athey's Visions of Excess: Performance after Georges Bataille". *Papers of Surealism* 8 (2010): 1-12. Web.

Jürs-Munby, Karen. "Of Textual Bodies and Actual Bodies: The Abjection of Performance in Lessing's Dramaturgy". *Theatre Research International* 30.1 (1999): 19-35. Print. https://doi.org/10.1017/S0307883304000847

Kane, Sarah. *Complete Plays: Blasted, Phaedra's Love, Cleansed, Crave, 4.48 Psychosis, Skin*. London: Methuen, 2001. Print.
---.*Sämtliche Stücke*. Reinbek: Rowohlt, 2002. Print.
Kant, Immanuel. *Critique of the Powers of Judgment*. Cambridge: Cambridge UP, 2002. Print.
---.*Kritik der reinen Vernunft*. Hamburg: Felix Meiner, 1965. Print.
---.*Observations on the Beautiful and the Sublime*. Cambridge: Cambridge UP, 2011. Print.
Kastely, James L. *Rethinking the Rhethorical Tradition. From Plato to Post-modernism*. New Haven: Yale UP, 1997. Print.
Kelly, Daniel R. *Yuck! The Nature and Moral Significance of Disgust*. Cambridge: MIT P, 2011. Print. https://doi.org/10.7551/mitpress/8303.001.0001
Keltner, Stacey K. *Kristeva*. Cambridge: Polity, 2011. Print.
Kendall, Tina. "Tarring with Disgust". *Film-Philosophy* 15.2 (2011): 1–10. Print. https://doi.org/10.3366/film.2011.0022
Keohane, Kieran, ed. *The Social Pathologies of Contemporary Civilization*. London: Routledge, 2013. Print.
Kim, Rina. *Cross-gendered Literary Voices: Appropriating, Resisting, Embracing*. Basingstoke: Palgrave Macmillan, 2012. Print. https://doi.org/10.1057/9781137020758
Knowles, Scott. *Dystopian Performatives: Negative Affect/Emotion in the Work of Sarah Kane*. Diss. University of Kansas, 2016. Web.
Kolnai, Aurel and Axel Honneth. *Ekel, Hochmut, Haß: Zur Phänomenologie feindlicher Gefühle*. Frankfurt am Main: Suhrkamp, 2007. Print.
Kolnai, Aurel, Carolyn Korsmeyer, and Barry Smith. *On Disgust*. Chicago: Open Court, 2004. Print.
Konstan, David. "The Tragic Emotions". *Comparative Drama* 33.1 (1999): 1-21. Print. https://doi.org/10.1353/cdr.1999.0005
Korsmeyer, Carolyn. *Savoring Disgust: The Foul and the Fair in Aesthetics*. New York: Oxford UP, 2011. Print. https://doi.org/10.1093/acprof:oso/9780199756940.001.0001
Krauss, Rosalind, et al. "The Politics of the Signifier II: A Conversation on the "Informe" and the Abject". *October* 67 (1994): 3-21. Print.
Krieger, Murray, ed. *The Aims of Representation: Subject, Text, History*. Stanford: Stanford UP, 1993. Print.
Kristeva, Julia. *Black Sun: Depression and Melancholia*. New York: Columbia UP, 1989. Print.
---.*Crisis of the European Subject*. New York: Other Press, 2000. Print.
---.*Die neuen Leiden der Seele*. Giessen: Psychosozial-Verlag, 2007. Print.
---.*In the Beginning was Love: Psychoanalysis and Faith*. New York: Columbia UP, 1987. Print.

---. *Polylogue*. Paris: Editions du Seuil, 1977. Print. Collection "Tel Quel".
---. *Powers of Horror: An Essay on Abjection*. New York: Columbia UP, 1982. Print.
---. *Revolution in Poetic Language*. New York: Columbia UP, 1984. Print.
---. *Strangers to Ourselves*. New York: Columbia UP, 1991. Print.
---. *The Sense and Non-sense of Revolt*. New York: Columbia UP, 2000. Print.
Kristeva, Julia and Ross M. Guberman, eds. *Julia Kristeva. Interviews*. New York: Columbia UP, 1996. Print.
Kristeva, Julia and Toril Moi. *The Kristeva Reader*. New York: Columbia UP, 1986. Print.
Kristeva, Julia and Kelly Oliver. *The Portable Kristeva*. New York: Columbia UP, 1997. Print.
Lacan, Jacques. *Seminar VII: The Ethics of Psychoanalysis*. London: Routledge, 1992. Print.
Lane, David. *Contemporary British Drama*. Edinburgh: Edinburgh UP, 2010. Print.
Lateiner, Donald and Dimos Spatharas, eds. *The Ancient Emotion of Disgust*. New York: Oxford UP, 2017. Print. https://doi.org/10.1093/acprof:oso/9780190604110.001.0001
Lear, Jonathan. "Katharsis". *Essays on Aristotle's Poetics*. Ed. Amélie Rorty. Princeton UP, 1992. 315-340. Print.
Lechte, John. *Key Contemporary Concepts: From Abjection to Zeno's Paradox*. London: Sage, 2003. Print.
Lechte, John and Maria Margaroni. *Julia Kristeva: Live Theory*. London: Continuum, 2004. Print.
Lechte, John and Mary Zournazi, eds. *The Kristeva Critical Reader*. Edinburgh: Edinburgh UP, 2003. Print.
Lee, Mireille M. "Maternity and Miasma". *Mothering and Motherhood in Ancient Greece and Rome*. Ed. Lauren Hackworth Petersen and Patricia Salzman- Mitchell. Austin: U of Texas P, 2012. 23-42. Print.
Lehmann, Hans-Thies. *Postdramatic Theatre*. London: Routledge, 2006. Print. https://doi.org/10.4324/9780203088104
Leonard, Miriam. *Tragic Modernities*. Cambridge: Harvard UP, 2015. Print. https://doi.org/10.4159/9780674286924
Levy, Aaron, ed. *Blood Orgies. Hermann Nitsch in America*. Philadelphia: Slought Books, 2008. Print.
Liebert, Rana S. "Pity and Disgust in Plato's *Republic*: The Case of Leontius". *Classical Philology* 108 (2013): 179-201. Print. https://doi.org/10.1086/672002
Lloyd-Bollard, Catrin. "The Powers of Horror in Sarah Kane's Theater of the Abject". Diss. Harvard University, 2008. Print.
Longinus. "On the Sublime". *Classical Literary Criticism*. Ed. Penelope Murray and Theodor S. Dorsch. London: Penguin, 2000. 113-166. Print.

Lotringer, Sylvére. "Mack Lecture: On Antonin Artaud" (2015). Web.
Lottmann, Joachim. "Hau ab, du Arsch!" *Der Spiegel* (2006). Web.
Lublin, Robert. "I love you now: Time and Desire in the Plays of Sarah Kane". *Sarah Kane in Context*. Ed. Graham Saunders and Laurens de Vos. Manchester: Manchester UP, 2010. 116. Print.
Luckhurst, Mary. "Infamy and Dying Young: Sarah Kane, 1971-1999". *Theatre and Celebrity in Britain, 1660-2000*. Ed. Mary Luckhurst and Jane Moody. Basingstoke: Palgrave Macmillan, 2005. 107-124. Print. https://doi.org/10.1057/9780230523845_7
---, ed. *Modern British and Irish Drama 1880-2005*. Malden: Blackwell, 2006. Print.
Luckhurst, Mary and Jane Moody, eds. *Theatre and Celebrity in Britain, 1660-2000*. Basingstoke: Palgrave Macmillan, 2005. Print. https://doi.org/10.1057/9780230523845
Lyne, Raphel. "Neoclassicism". *Tragedy in Transition*. Ed. Sarah A. Brown and Catherine Silverstone. Oxford: Blackwell, 2007. 123-140. Print.
Machon, Josephine. *Immersive Theatres: Intimacy and Immediacy in Contemporary Performance*. Basingstoke: Palgrave Macmillan, 2013. Print. https://doi.org/10.1007/978-1-137-01985-1
---. *(Syn)aesthetics: Redefining Visceral Performance*. Basingstoke: Palgrave Macmillan, 2009. Print.
Macintosh, Fiona. "Patricide versus Filicide: *Oedipus* and *Medea* on the Modern Stage". *Tragedy in Transition*. Ed. Sarah A. Brown and Catherine Silverstone. Oxford: Blackwell, 2007. 192-211. Print.
Manning, Robert T. "The Serial Sevens Test". *Archives of Internal Medicine* 142.6 (1982): 1192. Print. https://doi.org/10.1001/archinte.1982.00340190148022
Marshall, Hallie R. "Saxon Violence and Social Decay in Sarah Kane's *Phaedra's Love* and Tony Harrison's *Prometheus*". *Helios* 38.2 (2011): 165-179. Print. https://doi.org/10.1353/hel.2011.0009
McAfee, Noëlle. *Julia Kristeva*. New York: Routledge, 2004. Print. https://doi.org/10.4324/9780203634349
McConachie, Bruce. *Theatre and Mind*. Basingstoke: Palgrave Macmillan, 2012. Print. https://doi.org/10.1007/978-1-137-01561-7
McConachie, Bruce and Elizabeth Hart. *Performance and Cognition: Theatre Studies and the Cognitive Turn*. London: Routledge, 2006. Print. https://doi.org/10.4324/9780203966563
McCoy Berzins, Marina. *Wounded Heroes: Vulnerability as a Virtue in Ancient Greek Literature and Philosophy*. Oxford: Oxford UP, 2013. Print. https://doi.org/10.1093/acprof:oso/9780199672783.001.0001
McGinn, Colin. *The Meaning of Disgust: Life, Death, and Revulsion*. Oxford: Oxford UP, 2011. Print. https://doi.org/10.1093/acprof:oso/9780199829538.001.0001

McRobbie, Angela. *In the Culture Society. Art, Fashion and Popular Music*. London: Routledge, 2013. Print. https://doi.org/10.4324/9781315004808

Meinel, Fabian. *Pollution and Crisis in Greek Tragedy*. Cambridge: Cambridge UP, 2015. Print. https://doi.org/10.1017/CBO9781107360570

Meisel, Perry and Julia Kristeva. "Interview with Kristeva". *Parisian Review* 51.1 (1984). Print.

Mendik, Xavier and Steven J. Schneider. "A Tasteless Art: Waters, Kaufman and the Pursuit of 'Pure' Gross-Out". *Underground U.S.A. Filmmaking Beyond the Hollywood Canon*. Ed. Xavier Mendik and Steven J. Schneider. New York: Columbia UP, 2002. 204-220. Print.

---, eds. *Underground U.S.A. Filmmaking Beyond the Hollywood Canon*. New York: Columbia UP, 2002. Print.

Menke, Christoph. *Tragödie im Sittlichen: Gerechtigkeit und Freiheit nach Hegel*. Frankfurt am Main: Suhrkamp, 1996. Print.

Menninghaus, Winfried. *Disgust: Theory and History of a Strong Sensation*. Albany: State U of New York P, 2003. Print.

---. *Ekel: Theorie und Geschichte einer starken Empfindung*. Frankfurt am Main: Suhrkamp, 1999. Print.

Michalska, Julia. "Politics and Performance Take Centre Stage at Documenta 14 in Athens". *The Art Newspaper* (2017). Web.

Middeke, Martin, Peter P. Schnierer, and Aleks Sierz. *The Methuen Drama Guide to Contemporary British Playwrights*. London: Methuen Drama, 2011. Print. https://doi.org/10.5040/9781408183045

Miller, Susan B. *Disgust: The Gatekeeper Emotion*. Hillsdale: Analytic P, 2004. Print.

Miller, William I. *The Anatomy of Disgust*. Cambridge: Harvard UP, 1997. Print.

Mills, Liz. "When the Voice Itself Is Image". *Modern Drama* 52.4 (2010): 389-404. Print. https://doi.org/10.1353/mdr.0.0139

Mills, Sophie. *Euripides: Bacchae*. London: Duckworth, 2006. Print.

Mitchell-Boyask, Robin. *The Plague and the Athenian Imagination*. Cambridge: Cambridge UP, 2008. Print. https://doi.org/10.1017/CBO9780511482304

Mohr, Hans-Ulrich and Kerstin Mächler, eds. *Extending the Code: New Forms of Dramatic and Theatrical Expression*. Trier: WVT, 2004. Print.

Moreau, Elise. "What Does it Mean to Go Viral Online? Exploring How Content Goes Viral on the Web". *Lifewire* (2016). Web.

Morgan, Stuart and Frances Morris. *Rites of Passage: Art for the End of the Century*. London: Tate Gallery Publications, 1995. Print.

Morley, Sheridan. "Review: *Blasted*". *Spectator* (1995). Web.

Morsch, Thomas. "Der Körper des Zuschauers: Elemente einer somatischen Theorie des Kinos". *Medienwissenschaft* 3 (1997): 271-289. Print.

Morton, Timothy. *Cultures of Taste*. Basingstoke: Palgrave Macmillan, 2004. Print.

Murray, Penelope. "Introduction". *Classical Literary Criticism*. Ed. Penelope Murray and Theodor S. Dorsch. London: Penguin, 2000. vii-lviii. Print.

---. *Plato on Poetry*. Cambridge: Cambridge UP, 1996. Print.

Nägele, Rainer. *Der andere Schauplatz: Büchner, Brecht, Artaud, Heiner Müller*. Frankfurt am Main: Stroemfeld, 2013. Print.

Nally, Claire and Angela Smith. *Naked Exhibitionism: Gendered Performance and Public Exposure*. London: I.B. Tauris, 2013. Print.

Nancy, Jean-Luc. *Noli me tangere: On the Raising of the Body*. New York: Fordham UP, 2008. Print.

Ngai, Sianne. *Ugly Feelings*. Cambridge: Harvard UP, 2005. Print. https://doi.org/10.4159/9780674041523

Nietzsche, Friedrich Wilhelm. *Also Sprach Zarathrustra: Ein Buch für Alle und Keinen*. Chemnitz: Ernst Scmeitzer, 1883. Print.

---. *Dawn*. Stanford: Stanford UP, 2011. Print.

---. *Die Geburt der Tragödie: Oder Griechenthum und Pessimismus: Versuch einer Selbstkritik*. Leipzig: E.W. Fritsch, 1878. Print.

---. *The Birth of Tragedy And Other Writings*. Cambridge: Cambridge UP, 2007. Print. Cambridge Texts in the History of Philosophy.

---. *Thus Spoke Zarathustra. A Book for All and None*. Cambridge: Cambridge UP, 2006. Print.

Noys, Benjamin. *Georges Bataille: A Critical Introduction*. London: Pluto P, 2000. Print.

Nussbaum, Martha. *Hiding from Humanity: Disgust, Shame, and the Law*. Princeton: Princeton UP, 2004. Print.

---. "Narrative Emotions: Beckett's Genealogy of Love". *Ethics* 98.2 (1988): 225-254. Print. https://doi.org/10.1086/292939

"Obesity and Overweight, Fact Sheet No. 311." *World Health Orgnisation (WHO)* (2014). Web.

Olatunji, Bunmi O. and Craig N. Sawchuk. "Disgust: Characteristic Features, Social Manifestations, and Clinical Implications". *Journal of Social and Clinical Psychology* 24.7 (2005): 932-962. Print. https://doi.org/10.1521/jscp.2005.24.7.932

Oliver, Kelly and Stacey K. Keltner. *Psychoanalysis, Aesthetics, and Politics in the Work of Kristeva*. Albany: SUNY P, 2009. Print.

Paglia, Camille. *Sexual Personae*. New Haven: Yale UP, 1990. Print.

Pankratz, Annette. "Neither Here nor There: Theatrical Space in Kane's Work". *Sarah Kane in Context*. Ed. Graham Saunders and Laurens de Vos. Manchester: Manchester UP, 2010. 149. Print.

---. "Signifying Nothing and Everything: The Extension of the Code and Hyperreal Simulations". *Extending the Code: New Forms of Dramatic and Theatrical Expression*. Ed. Hans-Ulrich Mohr and Kerstin Mächler. Trier: WVT, 2004. Print.

Pappas, Nickolas. *The Routledge Guidebook to Plato's Republic*. London: Routledge, 2013. Print. https://doi.org/10.4324/9780203094204

Parker, Robert. *Miasma: Pollution and Purification in Early Greek Religion*.Oxford: Oxford UP, 1983. Print.
Peters, Julia. "A Theory of Tragic Experience According to Hegel". *European Journal of Philosophy* 19.1 (2011): 85-106. Print. https://doi.org/10.1111/j.1468-0378.2009.00373.x
Pfister, Manfred. *The Theory and Analysis of Drama*. Cambridge: Cambridge UP, 1988. Print. https://doi.org/10.1017/CBO9780511553998
Pilný, Ondřej. *The Grotesque in Contemporary Anglophone Drama*. London: Palgrave McMillan, 2016. https://doi.org/10.1057/978-1-137-51318-2
Pinter, Harold. "Beckett". *Beckett at 60: A Festschrift*. Ed. W. J. McCormack. London: Calder & Boyars, 1967. 86. Print.
Plato and Allan Bloom. *The Republic*. New York: Basic Books, 1991. Print.
Pollak, Anne. "Sinnliche Erkenntnis und Anthropologie". *Handbuch Literatur und Philosophie*. Ed. Hans Feger. München: Metzler, 2012. 21-46. Print. https://doi.org/10.1007/978-3-476-00336-2_3
Porter, James I. *The Invention of Dionysus: An Essay on The Birth of Tragedy*. Stanford: Stanford UP, 2000. Print.
Poulakos, John and Nathan Crick. "There is Beauty Here, too: Aristotle's Rhetoric for Science". *Philosophy and Rhetoric* 45.3 (2012): 295-311. Print. https://doi.org/10.5325/philrhet.45.3.0295
"Psychosis." *National Health Service (NHS)* (2015). Web.
Rabaté, Jean-Michel. *Think, Pig! Beckett at the Limit of the Human*. New York: Fordham UP, 2016. Print. https://doi.org/10.5422/fordham/9780823270859.001.0001
Rabey, David I. *English Drama since 1940*. Princeton: Longmann, 2003. Print.
---."Flirting with Disaster". *Eroticism and Death in Theatre and Performance*. Ed. Karoline Gritzner. Herfordshire: U of Herfordshire P, 2010. 123-143. Print.
Radden, Jennifer. "The Mourning of the Lost Mother and the Lost Self". *The Nature of Melancholy: From Aristotle to Kristeva*. Ed. Jennifer Radden. Oxford: Oxford UP, 2000. 335-344. Print. https://doi.org/10.1093/acprof:oso/9780195151657.003.0031
---, ed. *The Nature of Melancholy: From Aristotle to Kristeva*. Oxford: Oxford UP, 2000. Print.
Rebellato, Dan. *1956 and All That: The Making of Modern British Drama*. London: Routledge, 1999. Print.
---."Sarah Kane: An Appreciation". *New Theatre Quarterly* 15.3 (1999): 280-281. Print. https://doi.org/10.1017/S0266464X00013063
---.*Theatre & Globalization*. Basingstoke: Palgrave Macmillan, 2009. Print.
Reitz, Bernhard and Mark Berninger, eds. *British Drama of the 1990s*. Heidelberg: Winter, 2002. Print.
Reitz, Bernhard and Heiko Stahl, eds. *What Revels Are in Hand? Assessments of Contemporary Drama in English in Honour of Wolfgang Lippke*. Trier: WVT, 2001. Print.

Rice, Philip and Patricia Waugh, eds. *Modern Literary Theory*. London: Arnold, 2001. Print.
Richardson, Alan and Ellen Spolsky, eds. *The Work of Fiction: Cognition, Culture, and Complexity*. London: Routledge, 2004. Print.
Richter, Simon. "German Classical Tragedy". *A Companion to Tragedy*. Ed. Rebecca W. Bushnell. 2007. 435-451. Print.
Roger, Robert et al. "The Relationship between Childhood Obesity, Low Socioeconomic Status, and Race/Ethnicity." *Childhood Obsity* 11.6 (2015): 691-695. Print. https://doi.org/10.1089/chi.2015.0029
Roisman, Hanna, ed. *The Encyclopedia of Greek Tragedy*. Chichester: Wiley- Blackwell, 2014. Print. https://doi.org/10.1002/9781118351222
Rokotnitz, Naomi. "'Too far gone in disgust': Mirror Neurons and the Manipulation of Embodied Responses in *The Libertine*". *Configurations* 16.3 (2008): 399-426. Print. https://doi.org/10.1353/con.0.0060
Rorty, Amélie, ed. *Essays on Aristotle's Poetics*. Princeton: Princeton UP, 1992. Print.
"Rotten.com" (2017). Web.
Rozin, Paul and April Fallon. "A Perspective on Disgust". *Psychological Review* 94.1 (1987): 23-41. Print. https://doi.org/10.1037//0033-295X.94.1.23
Rozin, Paul and Jonathan Haidt. "The Domains of Disgust and their Origins: Contrasting Biological and Cultural Evolutionary Accounts". *Trends in Cognitive Sciences* 17.8 (2013): 367-368. Web. https://doi.org/10.1016/j.tics.2013.06.001
Rozin, Paul, Jonathan Haidt, and Clark R. McCauley. "Disgust". *Handbook of Emotions*. 2008. 757-776. Print.
---."The Body and Soul Emotion". *Handbook of Emotion and Cognition*. Ed. Tim Dalgleish and Mick J. Power. New York: John Wiley and Sons, 1999. Print.
Rozin, Paul, Laura Lowery, and Rhonda Ebert. "Varieties of Disgust Faces and the Structure of Disgust". *Journal of Personality and Social Psychology* 66.5 (1994): 870-881. Print. https://doi.org/10.1037//0022-3514.66.5.870
Rozin, Paul, Linda Miller, and Carol Nemeroff. "Operation of the Laws of Sympathetic Magic in Disgust and Other Domains." *Journal of Personality and Social Psychology* 4.50 (1986): 703-712. Print. https://doi.org/10.1037//0022-3514.50.4.703
Rozin, Paul, et al. "The Child's Conception of Food: Differentiation of Categories of Rejected Substances in the 1.4 to 5 Year Age Range". *Appetite* 7 (1986): 141-151. Print. https://doi.org/10.1016/S0195-6663(86)80014-9
Sachs, Joe. "Introduction". *Aristotle's Poetics*. Newburyport: Focus Publishing, 2006. 1-16. Print.
Sartre, Jean-Paul. *Das Sein und das Nichts: Versuch einer phänomenologischen Ontologie*. Hamburg: Rowohlt, 1974. Print.
---.*Der Ekel*. Hamburg: Rowohlt, 1981. Print.
---.*La Nausée*. Paris, 1982. Print. Collection Folio.

Sartre, Jean-Paul and Hazel E. Barnes. *Being and Nothingness: An Essay in Phenomenological Ontology*. New York: Citadel. Print.

Saunders, Graham. *About Kane: The Playwright and the Work*. London: Faber and Faber, 2009. Print.

---."'Just a Word on a Page and there is the Drama.' Sarah Kane's Theatrical Legacy". *Contemporary Theatre Review* 13.1 (2003): 97-110. Print. https://doi.org/10.1080/1048680031000077816

---.*'Love Me or Kill Me': Sarah Kane and the Theatre of Extremes*. Manchester: Manchester UP, 2002. Print.

---."The Apocalyptic Theatre of Sarah Kane". *British Drama of the 1990s*. Ed. Bernhard Reitz and Mark Berninger. Heidelberg: Winter, 2002. 123-135. Print.

Saunders, Graham and Laurens de Vos. "Introduction". *Sarah Kane in Context*. Ed. Graham Saunders and Laurens de Vos. Manchester: Manchester UP, 2010. 1-7. Print.

---, eds. *Sarah Kane in Context*. Manchester: Manchester UP, 2010. Print.

Schnall, Simone, et al. "Disgust as Embodied Moral Judgment". *Personality and Social Psychology Bulletin* 34.8 (2008): 1096-1109. Print. https://doi.org/10.1177/0146167208317771

Schneemann, Carolee. "The Obscene Body/Politic". *Art Journal* 50.4 (1991): 28-35. Print. https://doi.org/10.1080/00043249.1991.10791476

Schüller, Marco. "Immanuel Kants *Ästhetik*: Kritik der Urteilskraft". *Texte zur Ästhetik: Eine kommentierte Anthologie*. Ed. Marco Schüller. Darmstadt: WBG, 2013. 46-52. Print.

---."Nietzsches Ästhetik: *Die Geburt der Tragödie aus dem Geist der Musik*". *Texte zur Ästhetik: Eine kommentierte Anthologie*. Ed. Marco Schüller. Darmstadt: WBG, 2013. 144-150. Print.

---, ed. *Texte zur Ästhetik: Eine kommentierte Anthologie*. Darmstadt: WBG, 2013. Print.

Seaford, Richard. "Tragedy and Dionysus". *A Companion to Tragedy*. Ed. Rebecca Bushnell. Oxford: Blackwell, 2005. 25-38. Print.

Segal, Charles. *Dionysiac Poetics and Euripides' Bacchae*. Princeton: Princeton UP, 1997. Print.

---.*Tragedy and Civilization: An Interpretation of Sophocles*. Norman: U of Oklahoma P, 1999. Print.

"Sensational Hit for Royal Academy". *BBC News* (1997). Web.

Shakespeare, William. *The Complete Works of William Shakespeare*. Ed. William J. Craig. Oxford: Oxford UP, 1962. Print.

Shellard, Dominic. *British Theatre Since the War*. New Haven: Yale UP, 1999. Print.

Shepherd, Melanie. "Nietzsche's Tragic Performance: The Still-Living Mother and the Dionysian in *Ecce Homo*". *Philosophy and Literature* 37.1 (2013): 20-35. Print. https://doi.org/10.1353/phl.2013.0009

Sheppard, Darren. *Plato's Republic: An Edinburgh Philosophical Guide*. Edinburgh: Edinburgh UP, 2009. Print.

Shields, Christopher. "Aristotle." *The Stanford Encyclopedia of Philosophy* (2016). Web.

Shilling, Chris. *The Body and Social Theory*. London: Sage, 2012. Print. https://doi.org/10.4135/9781473914810

Sierz, Aleks. "Beyond Timidity? The State of British New Writing". *PAJ: A Journal of Performance and Art* 27.3 (2005): 55-61. Print. https://doi.org/10.1162/pajj.2005.27.3.55

---."In-Yer-Face Theatre" (2016). Web.

---.*In-yer-face Theatre: British Drama Today*. London: Faber and Faber, 2001.Print.

Singer, Anabelle. "Don't Want to Be This: The Elusive Sarah Kane". *Drama Review* 48 (2004): 139-171. Print. https://doi.org/10.1162/105420404323063445

Sobchack, Vivian C. *Carnal Thoughts: Embodiment and Moving Image Culture*. Berkeley: U of California P, 2004. Print.

Solga, Kim. "*Blasted*'s Hysteria: Rape, Realism, and the Thresholds of the Visible". *Modern Drama* 50.3 (2007): 346-374. Print. https://doi.org/10.1353/mdr.2007.0062

Sontag, Susan. *Under the Sign of Saturn*. New York: Picador, 1981. Print. https://doi.org/10.3817/0681048189

Sophocles and Oliver Taplin. *Sophocles: Four Tragedies. Oedipus the King, Aias, Philoctetes, Oedipus at Colonus*. Oxford: Oxford UP, 2015. Print. https://doi.org/10.1093/actrade/9780199286232.book.1

Sourvinou-Inwood, Christiane. "Greek Tragedy and Ritual". *A Companion to Tragedy*. Ed. Rebecca W. Bushnell. 2005. 7-24. Print. https://doi.org/10.1111/b.9781405107358.2005.00003.x

Spambalg-Berend, Eva. *Dramen der Abjektion: Der Umgang mit den "Mächten des Grauens" in den Theaterstücken Sarah Kanes*. Trier: WVT, 2017. Print.

Spencer, Charles. "Review: *Cleansed*". *Daily Telegraph* (1998). Web

Spooner, Catherine and Emma McEvoy, eds. *The Routledge Companion to Gothic*. London: Routledge, 2007. Print. https://doi.org/10.4324/9780203935170

Stephens, Simon. "Sarah Kane's Debut Play *Blasted* Returns". *The Guardian* (2010). Web.

Stephenson, Heidi and Natasha Langridge. *Rage and Reason: Women Playwrights on Playwriting*. London: Methuen Drama, 1997. Print. https://doi.org/10.5040/9781408162804

Strindberg, August. *The Father, Miss Julie and The Ghost Sonata*. London: Methuen, 1976. Print.

Strohminger, Nina. "The Meaning of Disgust: A Refutation". *Emotion Review* 6.3 (2014): 214-216. Print. https://doi.org/10.1177/1754073914523072

"Suicide Note." *Merriam Webster Dictionary* (2017). Web.

Szakolczai, Arpad. "The Social Pathologogies of Contemporary Civilization: Meaning-giving Experiences and Pathological Expectations Concerning Health and Suffering". *The Social Pathologies of Contemporary Civilization*. Ed. Kieran Keohane. London: Routledge, 2013. 25-42. Print. https://doi.org/10.4324/9781315552774-3

Szalwinska, Maxie. "Don't Blame Sarah Kane for New Brutalism's Easy Ride". *The Guardian* (2006). Web.

Tabert, Nils. *Playspotting*. Reinbek: Rowohlt, 1998. Print.

Taylor, Paul. "Review: Blasted". *The Independent* (2010). Web.

The Holy Bible. King James Version. Iowa Falls: World Bible Publishers, 2001. Print.

Thein, Karel. "Aristotle on Why Study Lower Animals". *Eirene — Studia Graeca et Latina* (2014): 208-229. Print.

Theophrastus. *Characters*. Ed. James Diggle. Cambridge: Campbridge UP, 2003. Print.

Thielemans, Joan. "Conversation with Sarah Kane and Vicky Featherstone". *European Theatre Review* 15 (1999): 50-52. Print.

Thomas, Calvin. *Masculinity, Psychoanalysis, Straight Queer Theory: Essays on Abjection in Literature, Mass Culture, and Film*. Basingstoke: Palgrave Macmillan, 2008. Print. https://doi.org/10.1057/9780230611856

Tinker, Jack. "This Disgusting Feast of Filth". *The Daily Mail* (1995). Web.

Tycer, Alicia. "'Victim. Perpetrator. Bystander': Melancholic Witnessing of Sarah Kane's *4.48 Psychosis*". *Theatre Journal* 60.1 (2008): 23-36. Print. https://doi.org/10.1353/tj.2008.0069

Urban, Ken. "An Ethics of Catastrophe: The Theatre of Sarah Kane". *PAJ: A Journal of Performance and Art* 23 (2001): 36-46. Print. https://doi.org/10.2307/3246332

---."Review: Crave". *Theatre Journal* 53.3 (2001): 496-498. Print.

---."Towards a Theory of Cruel Britannia: Coolness, Cruelty, and the Nineties". *New Theatre Quarterly* 20 (2004): 354-372. Print.

Vaitl, Dieter. "Neurobiology of Fear and Disgust". *International Journal of Psychophysiology* 57.1 (2005): 1-14. Print. https://doi.org/10.1016/j.ijpsycho.2005.01.005

"Viral". *Oxford Living Dictionaries* (2017). Web.

Voigt, Claudia. "Alpträume aus Essex". *Der Spiegel* 96.9 (1996): 13-15. Web.

Voigts-Virchow, Eckart. "Sarah Kane, a Late Modernist: Intertextuality and Montage in the Broken Images of *Crave*". *What Revels Are in Hand?* Ed. Bernhard Reitz and Heiko Stahl. Trier: WVT, 2001. 205-220. Print.

---."We are Anathema: Sarah Kane's Plays as Postdramatic Theatre versus the Dreary and Repugnant Tale of Sense". *Sarah Kane in Context*. Ed. Graham Saunders and Laurens de Vos. Manchester: Manchester UP, 2010. Print.

Vos de, Laurens. *Cruelty and Desire in the Modern Theater: Antonin Artaud, Sarah Kane, and Samuel Beckett*. Madison: Fairleigh Dickinson UP, 2011. Print.

---."Sarah Kane and Antonin Artaud: Cruelty towards the Subjectile". *Sarah Kane in Context*. Ed. Graham Saunders and Laurens de Vos. Manchester: Manchester UP, 2010. 129-135. Print.

Wald, Christina. "Genuine Violence on Stage: Jürgen Gosch's Macbeth". Wissenschaftliches Seminar Online (2006). Web.

Wallace, Claire. "Sarah Kane, Experiential Theatre and the Revenant Avantgarde". *Sarah Kane in Context*. Ed. Graham Saunders and Laurens de Vos. Manchester: Manchester UP, 2010. 374-398. Print.

Wallace, Jennifer. "Tragedy and Exile". *Tragedy in Transition*. Ed. Sarah A. Brown and Catherine Silverstone. Oxford: Blackwell, 2007. 141-156. Print.

Walsh, Fintan. *Male Trouble: Masculinity and the Performance of Crisis*. Basingstoke: Palgrave Macmillan, 2010. Print. https://doi.org/10.1057/9780230281752

Wandor, Michelene. *Post-war British Drama: Looking Back in Gender*. London: Routledge, 2001. Print.

Ward, Anne, ed. *Socrates and Dionysus*. Newcastle: Cambridge Scholars Pub, 2013. Print.

Ward, Ian. "Rape and Rape Mythology in the Plays of Sarah Kane". *Comparative Drama* 47.2 (2013): 225-248. Print. https://doi.org/10.1353/cdr.2013.0026

Waters, Steve. "Sarah Kane: From Terror to Trauma". *Modern British and Irish Drama 1880-2005*. Ed. Mary Luckhurst. Malden: Blackwell, 2006. 371-382. Print. https://doi.org/10.1002/9780470751480.ch31

Watson, Ariel. "Cries of Fire: Psychotherapy in Contemporary British and Irish Drama". *Modern Drama* 51.2 (2008): 188-210. Print.

Watt, Daniel and Daniel Meyer-Dinkgräfe, eds. *Theatres of Thought: Theatre, Performance and Philosophy*. Newcastle: Cambridge Scholars Pub, 2007. Print.

Weber, Julia. "'My mind is the subject of these bewildered fragments'". *Arcadia. International Journal for Literary Studies* 45.1 (2010): 120-149. Print. https://doi.org/10.1515/arca.2010.007

Wicker, Bruno, et al. "Both of Us Disgusted in My Insula: The Common Neural Basis of Seeing and Feeling Disgust". *Neuron* 40.3 (2003): 655-664. Print. https://doi.org/10.1016/S0896-6273(03)00679-2

Williams, Linda. "Film Bodies: Gender, Genre and Excess". *Film Quarterly* 44.4 (1991): 2-13. Print. https://doi.org/10.1525/fq.1991.44.4.04a00020

Williams, Raymond. *Modern Tragedy*. London: Chatto and Windus, 1996. Print.

Wilson, Rawdon. *The Hydra's Tale: Imagining Disgust*. Edmonton: U of Alberta P, 2002. Print.

Winkler, John J. and Froma Zeitlin, eds. *Nothing to Do with Dionysos? Athenean Drama in its Social Context*. Princeton: Princeton UP, 1990. Print.

Wixson, Christopher. "'In Better Places': Space, Identity, and Alienation in Sarah Kane's Blasted". *Comparative Drama* 39.1 (2005): 75-91. Print. https://doi.org/10.1353/cdr.2005.0003

Woodworth, Christine. "'Summon up the Blood': The Stylized (or Sticky) Stuff of Violence in Three Plays by Sarah Kane". *Theatre Symposium* 18.1 (2010): 11-22. Print. https://doi.org/10.1353/tsy.2010.0003

Zahavi, Dan. "Beyond Empathy: Phenomenological Approaches to Intersubjectivity". *Journal of Consciousness Studies* 8 (2004): 151-167. Print.

Zajko, Vanda. "Narratives of Tragic Empathy: Prometheus Bound and Frankenstein". *Tragedy in Transition*. Ed. Sarah A. Brown and Catherine Silverstone. Oxford: Blackwell, 2007. 157-173. Print.

Zimmermann, Anja. *Skandalöse Bilder – Skandalöse Körper: Abject Art vom Surrealismus bis zu den Culture Wars*. Berlin: Reimer, 2001. Print.

Žižek, Slavoj. *Grimassen des Realen: Jacques Lacan oder die Monstrosität des Aktes*. Köln: Kiepenheuer und Witsch, 1993. Print.

– – –. *Violence*. London: Profile, 2008. Print.

Zunshine, Lisa, ed. *Introduction to Cognitive Cultural Studies*. Baltimore: Johns Hopkins UP, 2010. Print.

– – –, ed. *The Oxford Handbook of Cognitive Literary Studies*. Oxford: Oxford UP, 2015. Print.

Acknowledgements

I would like to express my deep gratitude to Eckart Voigts for head, heart, and ear. Albert Lang for expertise, spontaneous support, and encouragement. Johan Karlsson for love, patience, and format. Mirren Augustin, Unica Peters, and Marlene Martins Fernandes for relentless loyal proofs, friendly management, and commas. Corinna and Aleida Assmann, Andreas Witte, Stefan Schenk-Haupt, Anja Schwarz, Torben Vormweg, Yana Lemberska, Jan Rupp, Martin Middeke, Clare Wallace, and the CDE companions Cyrielle de Sade, Ariane de Waal, Maria Elena Capitani and Daniel Schulze for clever remarks and companionship. The Braunschweig team: Nora Plesske, Maria Marcsek-Fuchs, Monika Pietrzak-Franger, Stefanie John, Anja Kaminsky, Antonie Huff, Rüdiger Heinze, Kenton Barnes for assistance in all areas of academia and life. Niklas Bardeli, Nora Linnemann, Friedrich Lenz, Katherine Bennett, Janet McLaughlin, Gerald Kreissl and Rolf Schöneborn for running support and creative genius. Stefani Brusberg-Kiermeier, Graham Saunders, Dan Rebellato, Patrick Duggan, Guido Graf, Stephan Porombka, Vera Nünning, and Peter Paul Schnierer for their encouragement and advice when things got started. Anne Lehmann, Mathias Bach, Wolfgang Bruhnke, Jörg Stamm, Sina Rosenkrantz, Marisa Lange, Juli Fiebig, Sebastian Vogel, and Lisa Quaeschning for having made sure that I got to that start. Finally, I want to thank inspiring teachers and magnanimous family members, namely Sandra Hapke, Ian Pople, Wilma Topel, Anni Richter, Kath and Keith Curwen, my sisters Kirstin and Susan, and finally my parents Brigitte and Michael William Ablett who kindly kindled my love for reading.